Andrew Martin Fairbairn

The city of God : a series of discussions in religion

Sixth Edition

Andrew Martin Fairbairn

The city of God : a series of discussions in religion
Sixth Edition

ISBN/EAN: 9783337264024

Printed in Europe, USA, Canada, Australia, Japan

Cover: Foto ©Lupo / pixelio.de

More available books at **www.hansebooks.com**

THE CITY OF GOD

"οὐκ ἐπαισχύνεται αὐτοὺς ὁ Θεὸς, Θεὸς ἐπικαλεῖσθαι αὐτῶν· ἡτοίμασε γὰρ αὐτοῖς πόλιν."—*Heb.* xi. 16.

"ἐν ᾗ νῦν δὴ διήλθομεν οἰκίζοντες πόλει λέγεις, τῇ ἐν λόγοις κειμένῃ ἐπεὶ γῆς γε οὐδαμοῦ οἶμαι αὐτὴν εἶναι. Ἀλλ', ἦν δ' ἐγώ, ἐν οὐρανῷ ἴσως παράδειγμα ἀνάκειται τῷ βουλομένῳ ὁρᾶν καὶ ὁρῶντι ἑαυτὸν κατοικίζειν."
—*Plato: Repub.*, Book IX. ii. 592.

THE CITY OF GOD

A SERIES OF DISCUSSIONS
IN RELIGION

BY

A. M. FAIRBAIRN DD

PRINCIPAL OF MANSFIELD COLLEGE OXFORD
AUTHOR OF "STUDIES IN THE LIFE OF
CHRIST" "RELIGION IN HISTORY
AND IN THE LIFE OF
TO-DAY" ETC

SIXTH EDITION

LONDON
HODDER AND STOUGHTON
27 PATERNOSTER ROW
1897

BUTLER & TANNER,
THE SELWOOD PRINTING WORKS,
FROME, AND LONDON.

TABLE OF CONTENTS.

	PAGE
INTRODUCTORY: FAITH AND MODERN THOUGHT	1-32

 i. Statement of the problem; conditions of the conflict   3

 ii. Review of the cycle of modern thought; the eighteenth and nineteenth centuries; tendencies philosophic and social; Positivism; scientific speculation; Darwin's Theory; Mr. Herbert Spencer's philosophy of nescience   11

 iii. Characteristics of modern thought; Panphysicism; its positive and constructive, religious and reverent, and ethical spirit   19

 iv. Right attitude of Faith; thought—constructive, reverent, ethical—required; the right kind of teachers   23

PART FIRST.

I. THEISM AND SCIENCE   33-74

 i. Question of the possibility of reconciling theistic and scientific notions; mutual relations of theology and science; distinction of the scientific and metaphysical questions   35

 ii. Theism and theories of creation and design   45
  (1) Historical relation   46
  (2) Philosophical relation   51

 iii. New scientific doctrine of creation   57
  (1) As to method; Evolution theory; distinction between mode and cause   58
  (2) As to cause; Materialism; definitions of matter; Agnosticism . .   62

 iv. Need of constructive theistic argument adapted to the new conception of Nature   66
  (1) Idealism of Nature and Man   66
  (2) Interpretation of the process through the result; of Nature through man   70

II. MAN AND RELIGION   75-104

 i. Paul on Mars' Hill; his doctrine of Religion   75
 ii. Religion native to Man   79
  (1) Theories of the origin of Religion; "superstitious Atheism"—arguments against   80
  (2) Necessary to national welfare and progress   85
  (3) The higher the more the Religion civilizes   88

 iii. Comparison of Religions   90
  (1) Fictitious Religions;—"the Religion of Nature;"—Strauss' "reverence for the Universe"—the Apotheosis of Nature; the Religion of Humanity—the Apotheosis of Man   90

			PAGE
(2) Real Religions:—(1) Living; Confucianism and Brahmanism; (2) Universal: Buddhism, Islam; (3) Judaism			94
iv. The Religion of Christ			98
(1) Ideal, and			99
(2) Actual			101

PART SECOND.

I. GOD AND ISRAEL 105–142

  i. Moses; his training in Egypt and the wilderness; his call 110
  ii. The work of Moses; the making of Israel, his mission and personalities . 117
  iii. The new Name and the Religion; meaning of Iahveh 123
  iv. The "Ten Words;" the proem, first table, second table 128
  v. Issues involved 134
    (1) New notion of God; relation of the Name and the "Ten Words" 135
    (2) New notion of Religion 140
    (3) Consequent mission of Israel 141

II. THE PROBLEM OF JOB 143–189

  i. The Book of Job a Theodicy in poetry.
    (1) The outer, historical conditions of the rise of the problem; contradiction of faith and experience. 145
    (2) Its inner, logical necessity; the problem peculiar to Israel . . . 150
  ii. The Book itself; its poetry; its persons 154
    1. The prologue.
      (1) Portrait of the Hero 158
      (2) Of the Enemy 159
      (3) The problem in the prologue; doctrine of God and of Satan . 161
    2. The Drama 165
      (1) The speeches of the friends 167
      (2) The speeches of Job.
        a. The man in his sorrow.
        b. The man in the hands of his friends.
        c. The man in the hands of God 169
      (3) The speeches of God 176
      (4) Bearing of the speeches on the problem 179
  iii. Significance of the solution 181
    (1) Comparison with Greek and Buddhistic attempts at solution . . 182
    (2) A new stage in Israel's development; the "Servant of Jehovah;" Christ 186

III. MAN AND GOD 190–212

  i. Import of faith.
    (1) In a God; Scholastic substitutes for God discussed . . . 193
    (2) In a personal God 196
    (3) In an ethical God 199
  ii. Value of this faith in regard to
    (1) Man's needs 201
    (2) Man's spiritual condition 203
    (3) In (*a*) time and (*b*) eternity 206

PART THIRD.

I. THE JESUS OF HISTORY AND THE CHRIST OF FAITH . . . 213–252

    Meaning of Christ for criticism; comparison with Buddha; relation of the Person of Jesus to His Religion 215

    i. The problem stated; the Jesus of History; the Christ of Faith; how the one became the other; presuppositions of inquiry; Strauss; Tübingen School; Renan 219

    ii. The Jesus of History; the Person and His conditions 225

        (1) The situation, educational, national, religious, into which Jesus was born; its narrow particularism; His moral and ideal universalism 225

        (2) The sphere of His ministry; the out-caste classes; His sinlessness creates in others a consciousness of sin 231

        (3) The brevity of His ministry; unequalled influence of His teaching; comparison with Plato 235

        (4) The obscurity of His ministry; His creation of the ideal society of man 240

        (5) The position He claimed in the realization of His own ideals; the argument therefrom 244

    iii. The Christ of Faith; exists in the earliest literary presentation of the person; the Pauline Epistles; the Apocalypse; the Epistle to the Hebrews 245

    Reasonableness of the Apostles' belief; Christ to them a philosophy of God, of Nature, and of Man; argument from there having been only one Christ 248

II. CHRIST IN HISTORY 253–287

    Christ in prior Hebrew and in later Christian history.

    i. Christ's ideal; faced with the actual in Christianity; the ideal at once individual and universal 256

    ii. The Religion and the Person of Christ.

        (1) The greatest person in history 261
        (2) Relation to the realization of His ideal as regards God . . 264
        (3) His idea of God an absolute gift to the race 268

    iii. The relation of His person to the realization of His ideal of man . 270

        (1) His perfect humanity; in relation to law, man, God . . . 270
        (2) Its influence on the thought and life of the race; source of the humanest morality 272
        (3) Christ's realization of the human ideal; His second absolute gift to the race; *le grand Être* of Positivism 274

    iv. Christ's method of realizing His ideal 275

        (1) A society spiritually constituted; working from the unit to the mass; its consequent universalism; its adaptability to various forms of polity 275
        (2) A society universal, existing only for and by the truth; individuals made heroes through Christ 278
        (3) The moral power of the love of Christ; on the individual and on the race 281
        (4) This power in history; creative of the personalities that have made history; the inspiration of our service of man 284

	PAGE
III. THE RICHES OF CHRIST'S POVERTY	283–314

 Sacrifice the central truth of Christianity; Paul in Greece, in Corinth; his preaching, resistance, persistence; results 288
 i. The grace of Christ; meaning of "grace." The grace given to Paul; his place in history 294
 ii. The riches of Christ; the fulness of the universe and of the Godhead . 298
 iii. The poverty of Christ; in His poverty only the more enriched and enriching the world 301
 iv. The purpose of Christ in His poverty; our riches. Meaning of "wealth." Christ the Source of wealth; to the community; to the individual spirit; wealth unsearchable. Testimony of experience . . . 305

PART FOURTH.

I. THE QUEST OF THE CHIEF GOOD 317–334

 Right relation of holiness and happiness; Christ the illustration of his own principle 317
 i. The first quest of the individual; in a world of conflict and sin . . 324
 ii. Of man in the family; fatherhood; heredity; providence . . . 328
 iii. Of man in the State; influence of personal character on the community . 332

II. LOVE OF CHRIST 335–348

 i. Quality of love and quality of object. Love instinctive and natural; love rational and spiritual. Love for Christ spiritual; like love for the dead 335
 ii. Love of the visible and invisible Saviour. The disciples before and after the Ascension. Idealizing the invisible; help of the imagination; purifying influence of love of the unseen 340
 iii. Elements necessary to love; how affect relation to Christ. No portraiture given of Christ's physical appearance; no artist's skill equal to the representation of the spiritual ideal 344

III. THE CITY OF GOD 349–370

 i. The ideas of—
  (1) Augustine; the *Civitas Dei* 349
  (2) Abraham; "the city which hath the foundations" . . . 352
  (3) John in Patmos; the New Jerusalem 354
 ii. The Divine City an eternal ideal.
  (1) Eternally progressive and inexhaustible. Notions of sensuous heaven; of ecclesiastical organization. Modern *city;* Roman *civitas;* Greek πόλις; Jewish kingdom; God's ideal 355
  (2) Able to realize itself by its own means and agencies. Relation of this to foregoing discussions 358
 iii. Practical end.
  (1) Elevation of ordinary mortal life by faith in the city . . . 360
  (2) Object of hope; an immortality progressively obedient, social, and active; a state 366
  (3) Of God and as eternal as God 369

INTRODUCTORY.

FAITH AND MODERN THOUGHT.

"It is a work that requires our choicest thoughts, the exactest discussion that can be, a thing very material and desirable, to give unto reason the things that are reason's, and unto faith the things that are faith's; to give faith her full scope and latitude, and to give reason also her just bounds and limits; this is the first-born but the other has the blessing."—Nathanael Culverwel: "Light of Nature," p. 1 (ed. 1652).

"It was the speech of a good husbandman, 'It is but a folly to possess a piece of ground, except you till it.' And how then can it stand with reason, that a man should be possessed of so goodly a piece of the Lord's pasture as is this light of understanding and reason, which He hath endowed us with in the day of our creation, if he suffer it to lie untilled or sow not in it the Lord's seed."—John Hales' Works, vol. iii. p. 153.

"The proof of a system, the guarantee of its truth, lies not in its beginning, but in its end; not in its foundation-stone, but in its key-stone."—Rothe: "Stille Stunden," p. 37.

FAITH AND MODERN THOUGHT.[1]

I.

THE spirit of to-day is a spirit of restless inquiry, of ceaseless search, and of a search that is not always the parent of faith. The men who do our thinking, who lead the march of living mind, are essentially seekers, and they pursue their quest after truth often not very certain what it is or where it may be—only certain that it is somewhere, and can be found. We are all the children of our time, incarnate, in spite of ourselves, its spirit. That spirit floats in the air, penetrates every region of thought, steals subtly, unsuspected, into every mind, pierces the thickest and most seclusive walls authority or tradition can build round the intellect. The present is a universal presence, the daughter of the past, the mother of the future, rich with the wealth of ages that have been, fruitful with the germs of ages that are to be. And in it we live, its common life within, its common atmosphere around, feeling on us those plastic hands of its that are almost as powerful in shaping the resistent as the submissive.

1. The thought of living men is living thought, gifted with the potencies of a living thing. The

[1] A Lecture delivered in Airedale College, at the opening of the Session of 1878.

doubts of the past are for the most part dead doubts. They have been vanquished by time, if by nothing else; and have ceased to trouble any but the historians of thought. It is only by a strong effort of the imagination that we can appreciate the issues discussed by the early apologists, or realize the dismay with which the religious mind first heard of the new astronomy, or watched the birth of geology. But we grow fearful of our faith in the presence of certain modern doctrines and discoveries in science, or certain speculations in philosophy. The scientific doctrines may be but provisional, the dominant philosophy may only represent a transient phase of speculation, but, all the same, they disquiet, disturb almost as much as if they had been proved to be eternal and immutable truths. We have no right, even if we had the power, to comfort ourselves with the thought that our sons will feel in regard to our doubts much as we feel in regard to those of our fathers. Our duty is to make our faith credible to living minds, reasonable first to our own reason, and then to the reasons we seek to persuade. No man or Church has any right to ask men to believe what they cannot rationally conceive, or what contradicts ascertained and certain truths. If the truths of religion are eternal, they must be in harmony with the no less eternal truths of nature and mind; and this harmony it is the business of the religious teacher to prove. Faith could not have lived so long as it has done had its fundamental truths stood in manifest contradiction with reason. It has lived because it has been necessary to reason, its complement, not its contradiction. The foremost religious teachers of the past showed their respect for reason by doing their best to answer the doubts it started; that is, to make their faith seem rational to reason. Had they not done so, their faith had died. Authority cannot keep alive what the intellect dooms to death. To be authoritative authority must be rational, and an age of faith simply means an age when faith satisfies reason. And what has ever been necessary to religion is the pre-eminent religious necessity of to-day. If religion is to live it must live in harmony with living thought, and win over it a rational authority. Only as its teachers speak to the new spirit in language it cannot choose but hear, shall they preserve for posterity the old faith, transmitting it not only unimpoverished, but improved and enriched.

What has just been said must not be understood to mean, that Christian teachers ought to be great apologists, men always engaged in defending their own system and assailing its rivals or opponents. The men who would teach man must respect him, speak to him as to a rational being who, whether he questions or accepts the Faith, but exercises the inalienable rights of his reason. Ours is in a high degree a reverent age, and much of its doubt has come not from dislike but from love of Truth. It is not always the men that love her best that find her most easily. Our foremost thinkers are men of most noble spirit, honest alike in intellect and conscience, anxious to find and follow the truth. If they doubt what is to many as sure as it is holy, they do it through loyalty to what is held to be the true. It ought to be remembered that, if faith has its rights, so has the intellect, and those who require man to believe, ought to present their truths in forms that shall command his belief. A living religion can never repose on the past, be satisfied with its actual and achieved history; it must be ambitious to live a vigorous and progressive life. It is not enough that the Christian faith has done well, it ought to show that it is doing and can do still better. The old and feeble live by retrospect, the strong and active live in deed and endeavour. A living may be thought better than a reasoning Christianity; but in these days the life is impossible without the reason. We have no right to ask men to spare our faith for its past services; but the best right to require their belief if it can be proved to be the highest truth for the intellect, the surest light for the conscience, the purest life and love for the heart.

A religion always on the defensive is weak; an aggressive religion alone is strong. A science is best vindicated by its discoveries, proves by them at once the reality of its being and its right to be; and a religion that can show itself to be real, is certain to be able to prove itself right. Last century faith was throughout apologetic. Apologies for the Bible, analogies of religion, arguments *à priori* and *à posteriori* for the being and attributes of God, evidences of Christianity constituted the then religious literature. Yet in that pre-eminently apologetic age, the mightiest apologist of them all could write,[1] " It is come, I know not how, to be taken for granted by many persons that Christianity is not so much as a subject of inquiry, but that it is now at length discovered to be fictitious." The sixteenth century, again, was pre-eminently aggressive alike in its constructive and destructive work. It showed scant courtesy to the antique—thought that

[1] Butler's Analogy.—Advertisement.

old institutions were like certain old men, when foolish incorrigible in their follies; and it dealt with them in an altogether merciless way. That "elegant Pagan Pope," Leo X., might attempt to restore the vanished glories of the Augustan age, with so fine a gentleman as himself for its Augustus, but the age was too earnest to worship painted Virgins or sculptured Venuses, though the first might spring from the pencil of a Raphael, the second from the chisel of an Angelo. Its cry was for the spiritual realities that could alone satisfy soul and conscience. Luther was only its voice, uttering a faith in God and eternity, self and devil, that disdained apologies and laughed at opponents as Leviathan laughs at the shaking of a spear. Men like Leo the Virtuoso need apologists, men like Luther the Reformer trust God, do what He sent them to do, and are justified by their works. And as then so now, the best apologist of the Faith is the man who can best make it a living, reasonable, and therefore victorious belief.

The conflict of Faith in our day is most arduous and fell. It lives surrounded by real or potential enemies. Science cannot publish her discoveries without letting us hear the shock of their collision with the ancient Faith. The political philosopher seeks to show how the State can live and prosper without religion; the ethical thinker how right can exist and law govern without God. A philosophy that denies the surest and most necessary religious truths works in harmony with a criticism that resolves into mythologies the holiest religious histories. A large section of our literature, including some of the finest creations of living imagination, interpret Nature and man, exhibit life and destiny from the standpoint of those who have consciously renounced belief in God and can find on earth nothing divine but humanity. Our working men listen to theories of life that leave around them only blank material walls, within them no spiritual reality, before them no higher and larger hope. With so many forces inimical to faith at work in our midst, men find it easiest to assume an attitude of absolute antagonism either, on the one hand, to Faith, or, on the other to Knowledge. There is a so fine simplicity in such an attitude that the simplest person can hold it and feel himself both strong and safe. Yet that position alone is secure and permanent where the man can say, "Faith and reason are alike sons of God, and have alike the right to be and to be honoured. The realities of the world are truths of God; the truths of God are realities of the spirit; and all that has its being in Him must be perfect and harmonious as Himself."

2. What do we mean by the terms "Faith and Modern Thought"? Faith is here used as the comprehensive name for the beliefs that form the heart, as it were, of the Christian religion. It denotes the intellectual content or substance of Christianity as presented in its sacred literature—its spiritual essence as distinguished from its political institutions, its creative as opposed to its created facts. The Christian Faith is not the synonyme of the Christian Churches. These Churches exist for the faith; the faith does not exist for the Churches. They are institutions, and Christianity is not an institution. They are composed, constituted, and administered, by men more or less penetrated and possessed by the

Spirit of Christ, but men still, with natures built of gold perhaps, but also of iron and miry clay. Nor is Christian Faith the equivalent of Christian theology—the thought of the Churches formulated, affirmed, and made historical. Theology is an attempt to interpret the Faith—to translate it into language intelligible to the reason. There are many theologies, but only one Faith, just as there are many sciences of nature—though nature has ever remained the same. The truths and facts that theology seeks to interpret constitute the Christian Faith—the truths that God is, that He made the world and man; the facts that Christ lived, taught, suffered, died, rose, reigns. The Thought that claims to be by pre-eminence Modern and is here opposed to Faith, is thought that would either deny its truths and facts or so explain them as to destroy their meaning. This thought is not the synonyme of modern knowledge. Knowledge is our science or consciousness, but thought our theory of what is. When we know we perceive, when we think we reason; and so what is here termed Modern Thought is not modern knowledge of man and nature, but reasonings based on it, interpretations of phenomena, scientific and philosophical speculations as to what is and how what is has come to be. There are many schools of Modern Thought, but their tendency is one, and so allows us to speak of it as a unity standing over against the unity of the Faith.

Knowledge and belief, or thought and faith do not form a necessary antithesis, and we must carefully distinguish between an essential and accidental antagonism. Reason may oppose forms or accidents that have been made necessary to faith, and in doing so may be held an enemy while indeed a most noble friend. Faith as the comprehensive name for the higher ideal truths that have ever awakened the reverence and governed the religious development of man, requires ever and again to be cleared from the accessories that tend to surround and obscure it, the parasites that tend to grow on its surface and live on its life. Men easily come to identify the accessories with the substance, the parasites with the organism, and to regard an assault on the injurious accident as directed against the vital essence, even though it may have been due to a loyalty to the essence too great to spare the accident that injured it. And so what has seemed doubt or even denial doing battle against Faith, has often been in reality Faith doing battle against denial in its worst and most malignant form, a religion become so unreal as to be a negation of religion, a hypocrisy, an offence to the conscience, and an oppression to the life. Nothing so needs abolition as a religion or a church which has become a corrupt and tyrannical sacerdotal agency, perverted from the holy and beneficent ends of God to the evil purposes of man. Sokrates was by the official and political religion of his day declared an enemy of the gods, and sentenced to drink the deadly hemlock; but he was in truth the most religious man of his age, and has powerfully influenced for good the religion of other times and lands. Luther contending against a church with claims so extravagant as those of Rome in order that he might bring man into direct and personal relation with God, seemed to the men he opposed as an enemy of Faith, while to those of clearer eye and freer soul he appeared as one who denied old and venerable falsehoods that he might establish eternal verities. The French Revolution in fighting against the wicked and pitiless and time-serving church of France, fought, in a sense, the battle of Faith. That church had become the ally of Louis XIV. and his infamous successor, and had left the wrongs of the poor unrighted, their poverty unrelieved, their ignorance untouched. The men who rose up and in the sacred, though not always respected, names of liberty, equality, and fraternity, swept away that unrighteous institution, accomplished what was essentially a divine revenge. And so the mere opposition of what claims to be thought to what claims to be faith is not necessarily irreligious. The thought may represent a higher faith, a purer religion, may be the struggle of the spirit towards a diviner ideal, a nobler and more august conception of the universe and man. Are we in presence of such a struggle? And does the conflict of Faith and Modern Thought but mean the endeavour of the human spirit to free itself from an old and exhausted religion and win one fresher, higher, purer?

II.

1. These are questions which can best be answered by an exposition of the nature, spirit, and tendency of Modern Thought. But to understand it we must look beyond our own day, which is but a section of a cycle still far from completed. The eighteenth and nineteenth centuries stand in strong contrast to each other—are, indeed, almost intellectual opposites. The eighteenth was essentially the century of revolt, marked

throughout its whole course by the attempt to escape from the beliefs, the authorities, religious and intellectual of the past. Its first years were agitated by the Deist controversy; its last saw the French Revolution. Its tone was polemical—its aims destructive rather than constructive. Its real achievements were negative; when it attempted to be positive it was simply artificial. The most that the Deists dreamed of doing was to disprove the claims of Christianity; they never imagined that it was a higher task to explain than to refute, and nothing was more characteristic of the men than the reckless way in which they threw about charges of falsehood, invention, and deceit. Hume was simply a sceptic, the author of a philosophy that explained nothing, that reduced the universe to an unsolved and insoluble riddle. Voltaire, though a Deist, is not remembered as the apologist of God and immortality, but as the fierce assailant of historical Christianity, and the church that so 'ill represented the spirit of Christ. Rousseau's invectives against society were more potent than the colourless and impotent confession of his vicar, and his state of nature as little natural as any state could well be. The Encyclopædists crowned the edifice of religious negation, and the sensuous philosophers added to a universe without God, man without mind. But once the Revolution had come and gone, once Europe had tasted the misery of war, the folly of vain dreams, the agonies of evil anarchy and worse tyranny, the reaction came. In France Catholicism revived. De Maistre glorified authority. Chateaubriand discovered the romance, the poetry, and the art, in Christianity; Lamennais, its political ideas, its freedom and brotherhood; Lacordaire its spiritual and intellectual sublimity. Cousin strove to formulate and found a higher than the sensuous philosophy—to dignify man by making him awake to his true nature and destiny. Germany had been purified by disaster, regenerated by defeat. In the great war of liberation her spirit was emancipated, set free to accomplish the noblest intellectual tasks of any people in the century. The greatest series of modern thinkers rose and succeeded each other with an almost bewildering rapidity, and lifted the thought of Europe to points whence wondrous views were obtained into the Spirit of God and man. England, relieved from foreign fears, checked and guided by her own great thinkers and politicians, turned to the paths of political progress, and, in her own bloodless yet steadfast way, accomplished a revolution that gave her a fuller and more prosperous life, more of the freedom and the wealth she so strongly loves and strenuously pursues. And so everywhere, with the new century, man seemed to enter on a happier and more creative career.

The early part of this century was thus marked by a return to faith, and desertion of denial, by a spirit intenser, deeper, broader, and more reverent than had been known in Europe since the middle of the seventeenth century, the great Puritan age. The deistic and sceptic systems had failed in practice even more than in theory, in works more than dialectic. The reaction showed itself everywhere, in everything; the human spirit hastened to protest against the attempt to abolish either it or its Father. Hence poets like Wordsworth rose, who saw in nature the dwelling-place and garment of spirit, the translucent temple of the inly-present God; in the light that fell on sea and shore, in the silence that lived among the hills, in the round ocean and the living air, a Spirit that touched and moved ours; in man intimations of his immortality, reminiscences of the God who had been, anticipations of the God who was to be, his home. Hence, too, philosophers like Coleridge appeared — who though in things philosophical but a borrower, was yet a borrower of so splendid a kind, that he glorified what he appropriated, giving it back with a grace that compels us to condone the deed—searching out the root principles of mind, finding there, given in the very terms of our nature, the thought of the Infinite, proving man's power to think that thought, to create religious ideas and institutions; asserting as the pre-eminent and distinctive attribute of his manhood his right and therefore his duty to be religious. Hence, too, divines who had married the broadest culture to the intensest piety, like Schleiermacher in Germany, Arnold in England, Chalmers in Scotland, came forward to show in themselves how religion and science could dwell together in unity, in their countrymen how an honest and earnest voice, speaking what it believes to be God's truth, will never speak unheard. And so a deeper and more spiritual thought forced into the background the shallow Materialism and arid Rationalism that had in the previous century been threatening Europe with utter religious death.

2. But a reaction was inevitable. Philosophy became too transcendental, and, like vaulting ambition overleaping itself, fell on the other side. In building into heaven it forgot to lay its foundations deep and broad enough in the earth, and it suffered the necessary fate of a great structure without an adequate base. The

reaction was led by a small band of singularly able men, the brilliant circle whose centre was James Mill. He had been a student of theology, and had been ordained a preacher in connection with the Scotch Church, had even preached, but had, for reasons not yet fully known, gone with a strong recoil from Calvinistic theology into sensuous philosophy. He maintained in the transcendental period the tradition, as it were, of the Scotch, English, and French empirical philosophy, and resolved mind into the senses, left man, indeed, with senses but without mind. As the ally of Bentham he found for his Utility a psychological basis, and together they applied it to conduct, on the one hand, and to politics and political economy on the other. The movement in England was helped by a corresponding movement in France, led first by the earlier Socialists, soon after by Comte. In England, too, social wealth, commercial prosperity, successful industrial enterprises, came upon the people too fast. Sudden wealth may be to a people utmost calamity. It is not good for a nation to acquire means faster than its power to use and spend them wisely. Luxury may enervate, may weaken the nobler qualities of a people; may induce men to listen to a voice other than the highest—the voice that teaches them to enjoy in ease and peace their great possessions, and find in things material a better measure of conduct and character than in things spiritual. And the voice men were but waiting for soon made itself heard. The time was ripe enough for the sensuous philosophy to attempt to become something more than a mere psychology. And the attempt was made. In the hands of Comte it aspired to be a philosophy of nature and man. He proclaimed that man could know nothing of causes, could know only antecedence and sequence, and he urged men to cease from inquiry after the primal cause. But his ignorance was used, however illogically, to exclude spirit from man and nature, and to make the observed the synonyme of the known. This negation of spirit was to Comte highest affirmation. He explained human history as the growth of man out of the lowest stage—that of Fetishism and Polytheism—through Monotheism into Positivism, where man gave up belief in the spiritual and was satisfied with what his senses recorded. And out of his philosophy he developed a religion, the religion of Humanity, which has rallied to it an enthusiastic band of disciples both here and in France, though it does seem strange how a faith—for faith it is—which denies spirit and affirms that the sensuously perceived is alone real, should be able to create enthusiasm in any human breast.

This philosophic movement was greatly strengthened by the scientific. Science has in this century, and especially in the present generation, advanced with immense strides. Perhaps it has been more distinguished for the number and brilliance of its scientific doctrines than even for the greatness of its scientific discoveries. There have been times, perhaps, marked by grander discoveries, but there has been no time so rich in hypotheses, guesses as to how what is came to be. Science, in repudiating metaphysics, has become metaphysical, and we have often now physical terms used to express the notions and to solve the problems that of old troubled the metaphysician. Many things favoured this development of scientific speculation.

Geology revealed how long and slow the creative process had been, how it had risen by slow gradation from lower to higher types. Charles Darwin, combining a wonderful knowledge of nature with a wonderful eye for the similarities and differences of natural objects, struck out his theory of the origin of species by natural selection. It fell like a living spark upon dry tinder, and while the naturalist used it to explain the genesis of species, it suggested to the physicist a still more comprehensive theory of evolution explanatory of the genesis of things. Men like Haeckel, far more daring than Darwin, have striven to show how, by mechanical or physical law, the primordial material or mass had become a well-ordered and rational world. The development hypotheses of Kant and Lamarck have been made to descend from the philosophical dreamland which had been thought to be their proper and congenial home, and changed into wonderful prophecies of scientific truth, foregleams of the dawn that had come to the men on the mountain top, while as yet men down in the valley walked in darkness. And so science ceased to be simply the interpretation of nature, and became a great inquiry after the being and working of its Cause.

But evolution needed a philosopher to elaborate it into a complete and consistent theory of things. In Mr. Darwin's hands it is a modal as distinguished from a causal theory of creation, shows how the creative force works, not what the creative cause is. Within its proper limits as a scientific theory it can never do more, and hence could but leave the Theistic question where it found it. Yet the idea was too fruitful to remain simply in its scientific form. It was capable of being worked by philosophy into a causal theory of creation. This was rather more than the dominant empiricism could consistently accomplish. That empiricism had declared that only phenomena could be known, that causes were radically inaccessible to the human intellect. And in saying so it was perfectly consistent with itself. A sensuous must be either an agnostic or a sceptical philosophy, must affirm either the reality of ignorance or the impossibility of knowledge. It can but know sensation, can never know its cause. But Mr. Herbert Spencer conceived the heroic and brilliant project of building on a philosophy of nescience a science of nature, man, and society. "Evolution" was the mystic word that was to accomplish the hitherto impossible, make a constructive theory of the universe spring from so unpromising a root as a sensuous, and therefore agnostic philosophy. Mr. Spencer's first Cause was the Unknown and Unknowable, which, as we can neither describe, nor define, nor conceive it, is to the intellect as good as the non-existent. But the unknown was boldly translated into what was believed to be the known, the terms of matter, motion, and force. On the principles of Mr. Spencer's philosophy our knowledge is here delusive, and persistence of force and the forces are terms that denote an unknown, not a known entity. Where all knowledge is knowledge of symbols, the realities they symbolize must continue inaccessible to us, objects of which nothing can be predicated because nothing can be known. Mr. Spencer's system is more wonderful than the Indian legend which rested the earth on an elephant and the elephant on a tortoise, for the elephant and tortoise were at least realities, which is a great deal more than either "the Unknown" or the "matter, motion, and force," of our English philosopher can claim to be.

III.

We are now in a position to indicate those characteristic qualities and tendencies in Modern Thought that have most significance for Faith.

1. Its most comprehensive and distinctive quality may be termed Pan-Physicism, or the attempt to explain nature through nature, without any appeal to any Power or Person above it. Here it stands in radical antithesis to Theism. Theism may conceive God as immanent in nature, may refuse to regard His action as either "supernatural," or an "interference" with natural order or law, but it can never identify Him with nature or nature with Him. The antitheses are here most direct, could not be sharper or more vital. In the first half of last century Christianity and Deism were in their fundamental conceptions alike. There was superficial difference but essential agreement. Their notions of God, nature, and man were alike, though they did not think alike as to their inter-relations and what these involved. It was this agreement in fundamentals which enabled Butler to construct in his Analogy an apology which the Deists could not answer—could not, simply because with their premisses his conclusions were inevitable. His work presented the dilemma, well illustrated in cases like that of James Mill—embrace Christianity or abandon Theism. But in these days Butler has lost his standing-point. The assumptions that gave force to

his argument are no longer possible, common beliefs have ceased to exist, and are replaced by radical contradictions. Modern Thought conceives the system within which we live, and which we help to constitute, as the result or product of physical forces, material in nature, mechanical in action, though ultimately conditioned and qualified by the behaviour of the organisms they have produced. Such a theory can only be regarded as the antithesis of Theism, of every truth essential to an ethical and religious faith.

2. But, again, Modern Thought is in its essential character positive, and in its general aims and endeavours constructive. Its negative attitude to Faith is, in a sense, an accident, not the result of intention, dislike to belief or love of denial, but simply the consequence of loyalty alike to its own principles and ends. The older sensuous philosophy was critical and sceptical, but the modern is dogmatic and affirmative. The older was more consistent, acted with a more thorough knowledge of its own position, principles, and possibilities; but the latter is the more courageous; as we have seen builds up its theory of being in disdainful defiance of its theory of knowing. Its constructive aims are of the most comprehensive sort, and its endeavours have been the same. It has attempted to determine the nature and character of the primal cause, to describe the becoming of the inorganic world, the origin and evolution of life, the formation and behaviour of mind, the rise and growth of religion, society, and the state, with all they represent and imply. Modern Thought aims at producing an exhaustive science of the universe and a complete philosophy of man; and the science and the philoso-

phy alike deny and exclude the ancient truths of Faith. Of two contradictories, both cannot be true. Panphysicism, in affirming its own doctrines, denies those of religion; but the affirmation is the essential thing, the denial the accidental. What has so positive a purpose deserves the respect of those who seek the truth, and labour to establish it. A constructive is ever nobler than a critical spirit—the one but wishes to expose error, the other to find and reveal reality. And the nobility of its spirit is manifest in the most distinctive creations of Modern Thought. Faith never had a worthier antagonist, and must become and attempt its best to be equal to its foe.

3. Again, Modern Thought must be characterized as most religious and reverent. It is too positive to be profane—too conscious of the mystery of the being it seeks to explain to be impious. The men who now stand not so much opposed to Christianity as without it, are not coarse infidels who denounce religion as priestcraft, worship as the unveracious flattery of the strong by the weak. They are men who recognise the value and permanence of the religious element in man, and proclaim the necessity of religion and worship to his highest moral and intellectual development. The Positivism which is to many in its relation to religious truth simply a comprehensive and coherent system of negations, has instituted the worship of Humanity; and he must be blind indeed who fails to see how it has quickened some of our noblest spirits to noble enthusiasm in the cause of the ignorant, the suffering, and the oppressed. Certain of our best known and most bellicose physicists delight in their more eloquent moods to express their awe and

exaltation in the presence of the mysterious Power which weaves in the roaring loom of time the many-hued garment nature presents to sense. The later Strauss thought that the old reverence for the Eternal might live in the new feeling for the universe, with its invariable order, its immensities of space and duration, its silence, its progress, its severe yet holy beneficence. And the new thought is as wishful to preserve old forms of belief as the ancient spirit of reverence. One of the most brilliant apologists of the Positivism that knows neither God nor Spirit has amazed the physicists and delighted the transcendentalists by his splendid invective against Materialism. The old faith in immortality has been transfigured, and in its new form glorified by one who was by right of rare culture and imagination a pre-eminent teacher of the age.

> "O may I join the choir invisible
> Of those immortal dead who live again
> In minds made better by their presence: live
> In pulses stirred to generosity,
> In deeds of daring rectitude, in scorn
> For miserable aims that end in self,
> In thoughts sublime that pierce the night like stars,
> And with their mild persistence urge men's search
> To vaster issues   .   .   .   .   .
>   This is life to come,
> Which martyred men have made more glorious
> For us who strive to follow."

And so we may say that Modern Thought, even when it stands in sharpest antithesis to the ancient faith, is grave, earnest, religious; and can neither be rightly understood nor wisely criticised unless by spirits as grave, as earnest, and as religious.

4. The Thought that now concerns us may still

further be described as eminently ethical in spirit and in aims. Many of our modern thinkers are men possessed with the enthusiasm of humanity, men who are anxious to lift man to a higher level, to purify and improve society, to dispel ignorance and create knowledge, to enlighten, if not organize, beneficence, and make our individual, commercial, social, political life wiser, nobler, and more humane. Their ethical theory may be inadequate; but the duties it involves can be, if not authoritatively enjoined, forcibly inculcated. It has been the moral creed of men who have been among the most unwearied workers in the cause of human progress and enlightenment, who have without ceasing laboured to create our liberties, to reform our laws, to extend and improve our education, to cure our miseries, lessen our vices, increase and ennoble our virtues. Some of the most powerful and persuasive appeals to England to be commercially honest and politically honourable in her dealings with lower races have come from disciples of Comte. And it is simply right that the humane and ethical spirit of men who belong to no church should be recognised by every church. The churches have no longer a monopoly of humanity—it exists without them as well as within; and till they know what this signifies they can never do their duty either by Modern Thought or the modern world.

IV.

But this discussion of the most characteristic qualities and aims of Modern Thought raises the question, How ought the representatives of faith to behave in its presence? How can they best be faithful to the trust they have received from the past and hold for the future? How vindicate their principles and positions against so formidable an antagonist? These questions concern not simply the continuance of the Christian Churches, but the very being of the Christian faith. For a religious society to be blind to their importance is but to prove itself effete and moribund.

1. One thing is evident, thought must be met by thought, reason alone can encounter and conquer reason. The days when authority was stronger than argument have passed, and knowledge can now be as merciless to it as it was once to knowledge. Faith is confronted by tendencies that have the spirit, the methods, and the consciousness of science, and it must be as they are if it is to prevail. Where an antagonist is neither simply sentimental, nor æsthetic, nor moral, but in the higher degree rational, he must be met by reason if he is to be met at all. And the reason that meets him must be the spokesman of a system as comprehensive as his own, must espouse principles higher, more evident and rational than their antitheses. The thinker when he needs to be answered must be answered by thought, not by being prayed at or preached at, not by a command to believe, or an exhortation to repentance, or an admonition that broadly hints that a place too hot to be comfortable is prepared for him, but, to use Cudworth's fine phrase, by "an intellectual system of the universe," a system that shall show not only that the religious idea can be expounded into an intellectual theory of things, but that it is the theory that can give the best reason for the existence alike of itself

and the universe. In short, if Religious is to conquer Modern Thought, it must not fear to face and attempt its problems, must, without shrinking, challenge a comparison of their respective solutions, and do so in the spirit that appeals to reason prepared to abide by its decision. In essaying this task Faith is doing no new thing. It has done it before, and can do it again, certain that its continuing to do so is a necessary condition of its continued life. Yet the new work is not a repetition of the old. Human thought as ever progressive is ever changing, widens with the process of the suns. Our religious beliefs can never be dissociated from our conceptions of the universe; and as the latter grow larger and truer, the former must be transfigured that they may live and shine in the new light. Hence it is not by affirming the faith in the forms fixed by the past that living thought is to be penetrated and possessed by religion, but by carrying the religious idea into the regions that thought explores, proving its right to live there, its claim to be the only rational interpreter of the universe. To do so, it must work along the lines and possess the characteristics of Modern Thought, in a degree, too, that will compel the confession that while ancient as Faith, it is as thought as modern as living mind.

Our religious thinkers, then, if they would be equal to the needs of the day, must not fear to formulate anew the truths of faith, to deepen and broaden the basis of religion, and to build from the rock sheer upwards. Conservative religious thought is as to its own claims too simply assertive, and in its attitude to the men and systems it opposes too purely critical;

progressive religious thought is too fluid, too much penetrated by sentiment, too little possessed by reason, more receptive than creative in its spirit. Neither is quite satisfactory either in character or conduct. To defend our own position by criticism of our assailants, is certainly neither a brave nor a sure method of achieving a victory. Criticism may be a greater service than disservice to an enemy, may help him to improve his position, while it does nothing to mend our own. His weak places ought to be confronted by our strong, and the thought spent in discovering where he can be assailed might be still better spent in making ourselves proof against his assaults. And an attitude too receptive is as bad as an attitude too critical. The religious ought to be a creative thinker, not allowing his idea to be modified from without, but causing it to develop from within, using it to interpret nature and man, not meekly permitting it to be interpreted by aliens in heart and speech. The so-called Broad Church is becoming more and more a Church without breadth —is losing the large and positive and constructive spirit of its earlier masters, and becoming too much a creature of the present to be a creator of the future, too much a thing of sentiment and aspirations, too little a system coherent and comprehensive, a nearer approximation to a true interpretation of God and man than the systems it wishes rather than seeks to supersede. The thought that is to live must be thought in earnest about the roots and realities of things, resolved to get face to face with them, to see them clearly, and to speak plainly and strongly what it has seen.

2. Again, religious thought must be constructive, must not be satisfied with developing doctrines and defending Churches, but courageously attempt the interpretation of the universe from the standpoint of religion. Apologies defensive of details are often more injurious to faith than to doubt; aggressive is ever stronger than apologetic thought. There is no theory of the universe so rational as Theism, and there is none that so little need fear an appeal to reason. The great constructive systems have ever been the most powerfully promotive alike of theological progress and religious life. The creative thinkers of the Eastern Church were the best apologists of ancient Christianity; the completest answer to Neoplatonic criticism was the conception of God—and therefore of the world—formulated by Athanasius and the Alexandrian theologians. That conception can never be intelligently or even sanely criticised unless as the antithesis of the philosophy that lived in the city and at the time of its birth. In modern times no system has had a more potent practical influence than Calvinism. It is a system of splendid daring, of courageous consistency in all its parts, in premiss, process, and conclusion. It was a reasoned system, reason could understand it, and the reason that understood it, it could control. It was the universe in its making, in its rule, purpose and destiny, explained by a given conception of God; and, though the conception might not be the most generous, the men who held it felt as if they had their feet upon the last and highest reality, as if they had, not simply a way of salvation, or a path to peace in death, but a system of absolute truth, that helped a man to look

at all things as if it were from the standpoint of their Maker. And a faith so strong and comprehensive made strong and commanding men. It entered like iron into the blood of nascent and incoherent Protestantism, and braced it to the most heroic endurances and endeavours. It made the men who in France fought the noble battles of the Huguenots; the soldiers and citizens who in the swamps of Holland resisted and broke the cruel and tyrannical power of Spain; the Puritans who in England and the forests of the Far West formed all that was and is bravest, brawniest, manliest in our religious life; the Covenanters who in Scotland, through years of persecution, held aloft and nobly followed the blue banner that proclaimed the sovereign rights of Christ. And what we need is a system as constructive, comprehensive, and sublime as Calvinism, but more generous—an interpretation of the universe through our higher idea of God. Men cannot live in these days by a faith which touches them only at one or a few points; they need a faith that embraces, penetrates, and possesses their spirits, and enables them to feel in harmony with ultimate and universal truth. Only as Theism is proved to give the best reason for the becoming of the world, the best explanation of its history, and the surest ground for all rational hopes as to its future, can its right to be be fully justified.

3. But there is need also to develop the elements in religion that can satisfy the nobler aspirations and more reverential feelings of man. It can lift the heart above the littleness and worry of life, fill man with emotions that exalt while they humble. No reverence he may feel for nature—for the infinities that embosom

our finite, for the order that, without break or pause, rules in the physical universe, can equal, or in any way be compared with, the reverence that can be evoked by our faith in the Eternal Father, the unsleeping, inexhaustible, personal love that made our being and is making our blessedness. The power of humanity to awaken our adoration is but impotence compared with the power that lives in the Christ, who stands before us idealizing the human, realizing the divine, showing how their natures are akin, how through man God can reach men, and men reach God. Christianity, too, can make us conscious of much in ourselves that deserves reverence, of a nature full of divine affinities, of a being capable of immortal progress along all the sublimest paths of knowledge, feeling, and action. Were all these elements lifted into their rightful prominence, Christianity would stand forward the peerless religion of reverence. It ought to scorn an appeal to the sensuous, which is ever the mark of a decayed and declining faith ; and live by its power to evoke and satisfy the highest aspirations of the spirit, the noblest admiration of the reason.

4. But another necessity deserves to be noticed : the ethical element in religion ought to be lifted into its proper place and made to do its proper work in relation to life, individual, industrial, commercial, social, and political. Christian teachers have never done even common justice to Christian ethics. Our age has a peculiar reverence for moral teaching, due, perhaps, to a sense of its peculiar needs. There is no teacher that has exercised on our age so immense and so righteous an influence as Thomas Carlyle, simply because he has more than any living man enforced

hatred of shams, love of reality, worship of the true and heroic, loyalty to duty, however commonplace, admiration of the manhood that strives after being and doing right. Matthew Arnold's "Stream of Tendency," inadequate as it is through its illogical impersonation to fill the throne of a conscious and active Deity, has yet been commended to many minds by the way in which he has declared that it "makes for righteousness." The Churches of to-day owe him much for the persistency with which he has attempted to interpret the old Hebrew idea of righteousness and to translate it into our living English speech. We need to go back to the old prophets to learn what they have to teach our age. We have been too anxious to find them seers of the future, to prove their words predictions; and too indifferent to what they were and said as preachers, speakers for the living God to living men. They knew that a righteous man could alone worship a righteous God, and so insisted on a service expressed not by rites but by righteousness. Where they were right, a living teacher cannot be wrong. Christianity is full of untouched ethical riches; its mines of moral teaching are almost unwrought. In the person, words, work of Christ, in His ideas of God's Fatherhood and man's brotherhood, in His Spirit, in the spirit He created in His disciples, in the words and deeds of His apostles, there lie seams of the finest moral wealth. To neglect these is to neglect Christian truth in its fairest and most fragrant flower. The Churches have been more concerned about doctrine than about ethics, about polity than about conduct. If they are to live and grow in strength and influence they must not fear to develop and preach the moral principles of the faith they confess, applying them to the questions that are evermore emerging, to the conduct of living men and women, to our divisions, to our class and caste hatreds, to the questions and controversies between capital and labour, to the motives and interests that inspire and guide, or misguide, our home and foreign politics. No society is at liberty to abdicate its own proper functions, or can do so without losing both the right and the power to exercise them. Its failure to put forth its real and patent moral energies has cost our actual Christianity an immense loss in moral influence. It was meant to live a brave and active life, going everywhere with man, ruling Him in all things, in all places, and only as it is made to do so will it have its proper power and do its proper work.

5. But the relations of Modern Faith to Modern Thought must, after all, mainly depend on its living representatives and exponents. A system can act upon an age only through the men in whom it lives and by whom it works. As our Christian thinkers are, so must our Christian thought be. Unless they are as eminent and enlightened as the thinkers they oppose, it is impossible that their opposition can be anything else than feeble and bootless where it is not absolutely absurd. In an age of science it is not possible that ignorance should be power. The religious teachers we need are men of large and living sympathy, sympathy with knowledge, with science and philosophy, with doubt, with the inquiries that often lead to doubt, and, above all, sympathy with the noble minds that are often bewildered by the maze of cross-lights that at once lighten and darken their path in the eager quest

after the highest good. With such teachers Faith cannot die; without them it ought not to live.

If Faith is at once wise, generous, and brave in its conflict with Modern Thought, there need be no fear as to the issue. The nobler is in the long run the stronger, and the more enduring is sure to conquer. Man can never outgrow himself, and he has been made to seek and find his Maker. Human society reposes on religion. Civilization without it would be like the lights that play on the northern sky—a momentary flash upon the face of darkness ere it again settled into eternal night. No age ever needed more than ours a holy and beneficent religion, and such a religion the Christian is, and ought to be made to appear to be. It has fashioned all that is noblest in our modern world; breathes in our atmosphere, pulses in our institutions, glows in our civilizations; and it ought to be so presented to living minds as to be seen as it is: the truth that reconciles reason to reality, that can alone make man noble and set man free.

PART FIRST.

I. *THEISM AND SCIENCE.*
II. *MAN AND RELIGION.*

"*Different therefore from both these sciences [physics and mathematics] is that which deals with the transcendent and immovable, if any such being exists. But of transcendent and immovable being we shall endeavour to prove the existence, and such a nature, if it finds place in the world of reality, may be said to constitute the domain of Deity and to be itself a first and regnant principle.*"—Aristotle: "Metaphysica," x. c. vii.

"*We owe modern atheistic philosophy sincere thanks for having first made us vividly conscious how incomparably great a thing it is to affirm the existence of God.*"—Rothe: "Stille Stunden," p. 43.

"*The true nature and the true good of man, true virtue and true religion, are things inseparable in knowledge.*"—Pascal: "Pensées et Lettres," vol. ii. p. 142 (ed. Faugère).

I.

THEISM AND SCIENCE.[1]

> "*Lord, Thou hast been our dwelling place in all generations. Before the mountains were brought forth, or ever Thou hadst formed the earth and the world, even from everlasting to everlasting, Thou art God.*"—Psalm xc. 1, 2,

I.

THIS is one of the sublimest of the old Hebrew Psalms, fitly expressing the faith Israel gave to the world. It is well said to be "a prayer of Moses, the man of God," for the truth that came by him here proves its inspiration by its power to inspire, to awaken sad contrition, deep reverence, and delighted awe. It sets God, the Eternal, over against man, the mortal, and makes us feel how the very earth that bears and the time that enfolds our race, are but moments in His being, moments that come and pass and perish while He abides. They are because He is; without Him they had not been and could not be. Before, behind, beneath, and beyond all is God, thinking the thoughts that create our world, willing the changes that measure our time and form our history, making our successive generations no aimless march from void to void, from birth to death, but an order constituted by intelligence, penetrated by purpose, and governed

---

[1] Preached in Salem Chapel, York, 4th September, 1881, during the sittings of the British Association.

by righteousness. To the Hebrew there could have been no time without eternity, no man without God; our lives were but the moments which marked His way as He moved from eternity to eternity, from intention to fulfilment.

This faith was the faith of simple men, but the simplicity of the men only helps the more to illustrate the sublimity of the faith. The wonderful thing is, that a belief so large, so rational, so mighty in itself and in its results should have entered into the life of man through men so simple. To describe its action, to recount its history—what it has achieved for man, for civilization, and for religion—would be to tell a tale more marvellous than the most fairy tale of science. But how it has lived, what it has done and caused to be done cannot here be told; our concern is with another and graver question, whether it has any right to continued life, whether any claim on the intellect and faith of our day. That is a question that touches the very bases of our lives, goes down to the roots of all our fair humanities. The need for discussing it is not, indeed, peculiar to our own age. No age has been without its doubts, and faith has never been able to live without a sufficient reason. There are periods when new knowledge seems to make the old reasons for faith invalid, and the time looks critical till the invincible reason, changing its form, stands up in renewed strength. We can better measure the growth of our knowledge than the degree and energy of our ignorance, and doubt derives its force not from what we do know, but from what we do not. What faith has to fear is not the new knowledge, but the new ignorance which the knowledge brings. The more the certainties of science widen, the vaster become the mysteries of being; but every achievement of the scientific intellect leaves the scientific imagination less patient with ignorance, more confident that it can by hypothesis and inference penetrate every secret that lies in the universe within and without. The splendour of a new discovery dazzles the imagination, inspires it with the idea that what has solved one long insoluable problem is capable of solving all, that the light which has suddenly streamed through one dark mystery has but to be turned on the face of nature and into the heart of man to illumine and interpret both. So the progress of science has made the imagination of scientists vivid, and they have indulged in dreams that no ancient theologian or metaphysician in his maddest mood could have surpassed, or even equalled. But there are signs that a saner mood is at hand. Scientific speculation, while wisely audacious in its own province, is with equal wisdom becoming more modest and sober beyond it. It is becoming more conscious of the mystery of being, of the immensity and intricacy of its ultimate problem. Men feel the further from a real the nearer they get to a pan-physical solution; the attempt to state it but shows its utter inadequacy or irrelevance. And so even in presence of the august association that for the moment possesses this city it can seem no impertinent thing to discuss this question, whether science has either superseded or contradicted the ancient belief in the eternal God who made the worlds; in other words, whether, in the face of the doctrines and discoveries of Modern Science, Theism has any claim to live.

1. I will not begin by protesting my love of science.

The theologian, as distinguished from the mere traditional dogmatist, is a man of science, and the sciences form a sisterhood that may know emulation but ought never to know either jealousy or dislike. The distinguished President of the British Association told us the other night the wonderful story of the progress science had made during the past fifty years. But two things he omitted: he omitted to tell us how much theology had contributed to this progress, and how much progress theology itself had made. He said: "To science we owe the idea of progress." He is mistaken, unless theology was the science he meant. The idea of progress in nature, in man, and in history, was the direct creation of theology. That is a fact in the history of thought open to no manner of doubt. Theology, too, was the first to formulate a theory of development, to attempt to interpret nature and man as a growth, though a growth that expressed the unfolding of a purpose, the action of a living will. She was the mother of all our modern sciences, made the minds that created alike the method and the passion for the interpretation of nature. What created these created all they have achieved. Analyse what we may term the mental dynamic forces in science, and you will find them to be creatures of religion, generated as it were out of her very bosom. Zeal for truth is the child of zeal for God; the modern enthusiasm for knowledge was begotten by the spirit of worship, the spirit that laboured to read and know the Mind of the Maker through the things He had made. The man who studies with deepest reverence studies with most success. Reverence can be only where love of truth is and no man who loves truth hates God.

But theology has not only contributed to science the idea of progress and the mental habits and energies that have worked it, she has also proved the reality and vigour of her life by the progress she has made. Within the past fifty years she has enlarged her province and her methods. Theology has her comparative sciences; to her ancient domain there has now been added that field of wonders termed the Science of Religion. No religion is indifferent to her; she seeks to know all, the place each holds in history, its meaning, the work it has done, the way and degree in which it has contributed to the progress, the civilization and the happiness of man. Then she has become more historical, knows better how to handle her sacred books, how to get at the essence and truths of religion; how to interpret, on the one hand, the religious contents of the spirit of man, and on the other, religion to man's spirit. Then, too, theology has enlarged all her conceptions; her idea of God is nobler, her idea of man is worthier, her outlook is immenser, her spirit is sweeter and saner, her notion of the creative method, the Divine order and way of government, of the relations of God, man and the universe has grown at once richer and more comprehensive. Of course, these are very general things to say, and only true of theology, not of all who study or teach it. We speak of the science, not of the multitudes who follow it. All multitudes are of the mixed order. Even the army that marches under the banner of the associated sciences is not all vanguard. Behind it is the vast main body, always critical, often jealous and even distrustful of its brilliant leaders, while in the rear loiters a host of stragglers whose voices now and then reach us as if over a space of fifty years. Progress is never equal, least of all in knowledge; but we measure it from the footprints of the foremost, not from the trail of the last laggard wayfarer.

But while we thus maintain that theology is a science that has well and variously served her sister sciences, we no less cordially confess that these have splendidly enriched and enlarged her province. The sciences that are perfecting our idea of the universe have exalted our idea of God. He has been robed in other and grander attributes since they extended the horizon of human thought into a boundless and peopled immensity, into a busy and immeasurable past. Our notion of the creative process has become truer and sublimer since geology carried us back into its vast successive periods, and showed us the slow and progressive method of the Creator, who fashions worlds as it were by nature, without the aid of miracle, and advances by imperceptible gradations from the meanest beginnings towards the noblest ends. Our conception of the creative action has become clearer and more real since we believed in the conservation of energy, the correlation and conversion of the physical forces, and so were enabled to conceive the causal energy in nature as a unity, indestructible, incapable of increase or decrease, everywhere active, ever changing its form, yet never beginning as never ceasing to be. Then, too, the ideas of order and law in nature have made us more conscious of the unities that govern the Divine action, that bind into harmony the will and method and end of God. A creation without order means that there is no ordering creator. But since science has revealed law everywhere, moulding the tear or the dew-drop as it rounds the star; active in the great forces that guide the rivers, roll the seas, and shape the mountains, as in the apparently tinier forces that gather or disperse the fleecy clouds, and regulate the growth or decay of the smallest flower—man has got the idea of an ordered nature, animated by a great thought, and guided by a great purpose. And the unity of nature suggests the higher unity of its author. The universal reign of law lifts us to the conception of the lawgiving and law-abiding God.

But, while we acknowledge that science has been helpful to our religious ideas, specifically to our conception of God, we must distinctly mark its limits. It has, indeed, done much to ennoble the mind, gladden the life, and ameliorate the sufferings of man. The splendid discoveries of a Jenner have helped to arrest the march of a destructive pestilence; of a Simpson to still the fatal throb of pain. Science has almost infinitely enlarged our command over the resources of nature, over the pernicious and salutary agencies that sleep within and around us. But see how much lies beyond its province. Man has noble instincts and impulses that impel him to seek the true, to admire the lovely, to worship the good, to feel after and find the Infinite Perfection in which the true, and right, and beautiful, blend into a divine and personal Unity. Man has deep moral convictions of rights that are his due, of duties that he owes, of an eternal law he is bound to discover and obey. Man has sad and remorseful experiences, the sense of unfulfilled duties, of wasted hours, of sorrows that have turned the anticipated joys of his life into utter miseries, of mean and unmanly sins against conscience and heart, against man and

God, of losses unredeemed by gain, of the lonely anguish that comes in the hour of bereavement and throws across the life a shadow that no sunshine can pierce. And out of these mingling instincts and impulses, convictions and experiences, rise man's manifold needs, those cravings after rest, those gropings after a strong hand to hold and trust, those cries for pardon, those unutterable groanings after light shed from a Divine face upon his gloom, in which lie at once the greatness and the misery of man. Moments come to the spirit of man when these needs are paramount, and it feels as if nature and her laws were engines to crush the human heart by which we live. And in those supreme moments, whither does man turn? To science? Does not her talk then of nature, and law, and force, and invariable sequence, seem like the sardonic prattle of a tempter persuading to belief in a religion of absolute despair? Those are the hours, known to many a spirit, when the soul breaks through the thin veil of words woven by the spell of man, and seeks to stand face to face with the eternal Father.

2. Let us come, then, to the discussion of our question without the feeling that theology and science are opposed, or in any sense exclusive of each other. That question concerns Theism, the fundamental truth of theology: Does science, the latest and surest knowledge of nature, contradict the belief in a God who made and who rules the world? Now, one point it is here necessary to note—the question is raised not by science, but by scientific speculation. The physicist may think himself the incarnate antithesis of the metaphysician. He is nothing of the sort: he is often the

metaphysician incarnate. The man who handles the ultimate problem of knowing and being deals with metaphysics. He need not speak the language of the schoolmen and discourse of Entities and Quiddities, the Absolute, and Infinite, and Unconditioned; he may use the terms of the latest physics, and speak of Matter and Force, Energy and Motion; but if his problems concern these as known to man and known by man, as the causes of the changes, the factors of the phenomena that constitute our ordered and intelligible world, then he is beyond all question a metaphysician of purest blood, speculative after the manner of his kind. These terms as known to physics have no relevance to our discussion, and so no place in it; before they can have they must be filled with a metaphysical sense, receive from mind or thought as much rational content as will fit them for their office.

What is matter? How do I know it? Has it any being save as known? Subtract mind, and what were matter? Deduct what mind gives to it, and what remains? The physicist may scorn these questions, but his scorn is a sign of his imperfect science. As a matter of fact he cannot, as we shall yet see, be speculative without giving them some sort of answer. We have more than once watched a distinguished scientist work himself into eloquent astonishment over the infructuous abstractions of schoolmen and divines, but only as a prelude to his losing himself in a wilderness of metaphysics, where, becoming enchanted, he has lavished on his physically named metaphysical entities an affection that quite shamed Titania's admiring love of the illustrious weaver, only, unhappily, in his case the disenchantment has not been so clear or so complete.

We repeat then, that we have no dispute with natural science, properly so called, but only with what we may term scientific metaphysics. Now in order to an intelligent discussion one thing is necessary: to simplify the terms as much as possible that we may reach the real points at issue. For the question is, especially on the scientific side, often so stated as to raise false issues and involve a false antagonism. For example, Professor Huxley, on Friday evening, placed in opposition to each other, the belief in evolution and "the belief in innumerable acts of creation repeated innumerable times." The distinction intended is obvious it relates to the creative method, not to the creative cause, but it is so stated that evolution appears as at once a modal and a causal theory of creation. So, too, God and nature are often opposed; He is represented as supernatural, incapable of natural action, so distinct from nature that if He touches it He disturbs its order, interferes with its course; it is represented as independent, self-sufficient, self-sufficing, the home of known and measured forces whose ways and action can be observed and understood. Then combining the notions of a supernatural God and special creations, the two are held to be necessary to each other, while nature and evolution form an opposed unity, capable of performing all it once needed God and miracles to accomplish. As a consequence Theism is identified with one method of creation, science with another. Theism is made to involve, "an endless succession of miraculous creative acts," to assume "the genesis of the heavens and the earth somewhat after the manner in which a workman shapes a piece of furniture;" but science recognises the method of nature, the action of the process it names Evolution. Theism is anthropomorphic, creation by a "process of manufacture," conducted by "a manlike artificer"; but the evolution science loves is natural, the way nature takes to create, multiply and maintain life. The series of antitheses culminates, of course, at the proper point: "the aim and effort of science is to explain the unknown in terms of the known," but theology endeavours to explain the known through the unknown, draws on our ignorance that she may the better interpret in her own interests our knowledge.

But are the assumptions on which these antitheses proceed valid? In what relation does the idea of special creations stand to the belief in God? How are God and nature related? Must we conceive creation by Deity as anthropomorphic? Is evolution a sufficient reason for the being of the order we know? Are matter, motion, force, better known terms than reason and will, and so more suited to state or express our ultimate interpretation of nature? Once we have discussed these questions, we shall be in a better position to discuss this: are there any adequate grounds for the belief in an eternal God who made the world?

II.

In what relation does the idea of special creations and a manlike creator stand to the belief in God? The ideas of special creation and design are thought to be indissolubly related, and alike necessary to Theism. It, they say, must conceive nature as framed by "the technic of a manlike artificer;" and it must conceive him as "acting by broken efforts, as man is seen to act," designing this, fitting it to that, and adapting the finished product to the conditions under which it is to live. The belief in God rose out of the search after causes, or out of the idea that everything had a soul and needed a maker, who in course of time became a Deity. Mr. Herbert Spencer has in his elaborate and painful way resolved the doctrine of special creations into the residuum of the Greek and Hebrew cosmogonies,[1] and the idea of a constructive or architectural Deity, who builds each structure or forms each species according to a special plan, claims a like ancient parentage.[2] And so the conclusion, in effect, is: remove the idea of special creations, and the belief in God loses its basis; deny the existence of design in nature, and there is no evidence of a creating Deity. False ideas of nature have been the proofs of His existence. Science knows the way of nature, but finds in it no trace of God.

Now in the position thus baldly, but not incorrectly stated, there are two distinct questions, one historical, touching the actual genesis and growth of the belief; the other philosophical, touching the form in which it may or must be conceived and expressed. We begin with the historical.

1. Were the ideas that survive in the doctrines of special creations and design the ideas that generated the belief in God? In other words, did men become monotheists because they imagined that as a man was needed to build a house or construct a machine, so a God was needed to build or construct a world? Now one thing is certain, the belief in God existed before

---

[1] "Principles of Biology," vol. i. p. 335.
[2] "First Principles," p. 33.

the idea of creation. God is a primary, creation is a secondary belief. It is a profound mistake to suppose that the primitive theologies or mythologies were cosmogonies. The earliest speech concerning the gods had no concern whatever with creation. Cosmogonic is the very latest phase of mythological speculation; its rise is proof that men have begun to ask concerning the what and whence and whither of themselves and the universe, and men who do that are men over whom the myth is ceasing to reign. Even in the case of the Hebrew, the purest monotheist of antiquity, creation was a comparatively late doctrine. The narrative in Genesis does not record their primitive belief; ages before it was written or dreamed of, the Fathers had believed in *El Shaddai*, the Almighty. And even after they conceived him as the Creator, they did not conceive Him as "a manlike artificer," an anthropomorphic Deity, who as it were laboriously designed and constructed the universe in detail. To Mr. Herbert Spencer, who is as prosaic in handling ancient beliefs as he is imaginative in handling primordial forces, the "Hebrew idea" was "grossly anthropomorphic," representing "God as taking clay and moulding a new creature, as a potter might mould a vessel."[1] But was this the essence of "the Hebrew idea"? or an audacious figure of speech? We must seek its essential characteristic in the words that explain the generic expression, "God created the heavens and the earth." "The Spirit of God moved upon the face of the waters," brooded, a living breath, full of life-giving warmth, over the bosom of the deep. And creation happens when God speaks, when He

[1] "Principles of Biology," vol. i. p. 337.

says, "Let it be." But speech is the symbol of thought and the effect of volition, in it reason and will are alike expressed, and a creation achieved by the speech of God is a creation as it were thought into being. And this underlying notion, as far from anthropomorphism as the latest notion of modern science, is throughout determinative and distinctive of "the Hebrew idea." God is the Unseen, the Unsearchable, "covered with light as with a garment," yet with "clouds and darkness round about Him;" working unperceived on the left hand, hidden on the right, yet knowing the way man takes; far from no one while invisible to all. He is in the heaven above, in the earth beneath, and in the uttermost abyss; He inhabiteth eternity; His name is the Eternal, the dwelling-place of man in all generations. His very name is, if you will allow the phrase, the happiest attempt ever made at de-anthropomorphizing Deity—Iahveh, or as it stands in our version, Jehovah. That term is no common noun, or proper name, or ordinary mode of denoting a familiar or manlike person; it is simply a verbal form expressing "He who is," or "He who brings to pass." It gives Him no name, leaves Him the awful, nameless Eternal Activity, who knows no time, but, changeless amid all our changes, lives the rational energy or will that made and moves the universe. No term could be more entirely free from the taint of anthropomorphism; scientific metaphysics will labour long before they find its fellow.

But it is not enough to deal with "the Hebrew idea"; we must look beyond it. The idea of God is in all the ancient mythologies older than the idea of creation, and it was by a speculative, almost by a scientific act, that the two ideas were brought into causal relations. This relation was not uniformly conceived. Sometimes the creative process was represented as one of emanation, sometimes as one of evolution, sometimes as one of production or construction, architecture or manufacture. The notion rarely assumed the latter form, the other and more natural were the more usual forms. It is an utter and even ignorant mistake to imagine that the idea of design, with its manlike artificer, was a theistic idea; it was in its origin purely scientific or philosophical. The story of its becoming is one of equal interest and instruction. It rose in Greece. The ancient Greek gods were not creators, were all created, had a beginning, were to have an end, stood within the order of nature, lived under the shadow of fate. Hesiod tells us that it was from the union of the " broad-bosomed earth " and " the starry Ouranos " that the gods sprang. One of the Homeric hymns makes earth the spouse of the starlit heaven, the mother of the gods. Pindar made gods and men of one race, sons of one mother. This ancient belief lived long and died slowly, as we may see from the typical question of the inquisitive child, anxious to discover who created the creator (related of Epicurus), " Who made chaos ?" not who made God ? The questions and perplexities occasioned by this belief had much to do with the scientific and philosophical awakening of the Greek mind. The nature it faced was full of mysterious problems which the religion made only the more insoluble. Heaven and earth did not seem the more intelligible for the want of an intelligent creator, they only the more imperatively demanded of the reason the discovery of a sufficient cause. The idea that Zeus was as much a creature as man did not seduce the mind into intellectual quiescence and content, but, on the contrary, stimulated the mind to ask, what had made Zeus and man alike begin to be? Greek philosophy arose in response to these necessities of thought; it was an attempt to answer the questions raised alike by nature and religion. In this attempt it did not seek either to oppose or supplement religion, but simply to satisfy the reason. It was characteristic that the earliest names for the cause were physical—water, air, fire, number or harmony. No man suggested the gods or god, because every man assumed that the primal cause must be cause of the gods as well as of nature and man. The first to suggest that order must have a rational author, was Anaxagoras, but his author was not Deity, was simply mind, ὁ νοῦς. The problem passed on to Plato. His soul loved order and art, saw what it loved everywhere, and he argued that what intellect so enjoyed could not be without intellect, existed by it and for it. The fairest things were the things fullest of reason; and so as the fairest of all things was the cosmos, the eternal reason must have been its maker. So perfect a work of art was inconceivable without a perfect artificer; so harmonious a structure could not have risen without an architect and builder. The heavens were so beautiful a mechanism that they could not have come to be without a mechanic, a Δημιουργός, or Divine handicraftsman, who might most fitly be named God. Plato may be regarded as the inventor of the argument from design, but he invented it for the purposes of science, not in the interests of Theism, to explain nature or complete his philosophy, not to prove the existence of God. Before it, and the notion of creation it involves, were formulated men believed in Deity; and if it has lived long as a buttress to faith, it began to be as a creature of knowledge.

It would, within the limits possible to us here, only burden our argument were we to pursue the point further or illustrate it in fuller detail. All that is needed meanwhile is to note what has been proved: the idea of creation did not create the belief in God. The belief has lived where men had no theory of creation, or one that was not theistic. Further, creation by God need not be construed as the work of a "manlike artificer"; where He has been best conceived, it has been otherwise construed. Again, the idea of contrivance or design in nature was not theistic, but scientific or cosmic in its origin, the discovery of men anxious to explain the universe, not of men anxious to prove the being of God. A change in this idea may affect our cosmic conception, but it should not touch or concern our conception of the Deity. What did not create the belief in God need not destroy it. But to determine this point is only to come face to face with another and more fundamental matter; the way in which we are to conceive God as related to nature, and as active in creation,

2. How are God and nature related? Must we conceive creation by Deity as an anthropomorphic, or "manlike" process, say of architecture or manufacture? This is the philosophical or positive side of our previous question, concerns not the historical relation between the idea of creation and contrivance and the belief in God, but the way in which the reason

may conceive the action of Deity, the mode in which He is related to nature, and acts within or upon it.

It has been already remarked that this relation has been very variously conceived and expressed. Certain peoples have regarded creation as a process of emanation, the procession from the Deity of the whole order of things which existed or was believed to exist. Certain others have expressed their idea by the figure of generation; others again by the figure of incubation; hardly any, certainly no people of the first importance in religion, by the image of the handicraftsman. The Hindus have exhausted the resources of their reason and their speech to represent the nature and action and relations of a Deity who creates by a ceaseless process of alternate evolution and involution. The Hebrew conceived God as a Spirit, who was everywhere present, and active wherever He was. Nature lived, moved, and had its being in Him at every moment, and in every atom depended on Him. He marshalled the hosts of heaven, and called them all by their names; their order was His will. His action was too universal to be conceived as special, too natural and necessary to be regarded as miraculous. The most common processes of nature were acts of God, resultful only as they were His. "He covereth the heaven with clouds, He prepareth rain for the earth, He maketh grass to grow upon the mountains. He giveth to the beast his food, and to the young ravens which cry."[1] The extraordinary and supernatural thing to the Hebrew would have been, not the active presence, but the actual absence of God from nature, or the continued activity of a nature without

---

[1] Psalm cxlvii. 8, 9.

God. This faith was confessed every time he read or repeated the mysterious name. Without Iahveh, "He who causes to happen," there might be chance, but there was no nature or order. The Greek, when he came to speculate as to how the Creator stood related to the creation, found himself face to face with his hardest problem; yet the tendency in the highest minds was towards one solution. Plato did not uniformly conceive Deity as the perfect handicraftsman, his Δημιουργός was but a δεύτερος θεός, a second or minor God. In his sublimest moments he thought of Deity as the Thinker, the Reason which was the home of the ideas, the only eternal realities, which were expressed in the appearances that at once pleased and deceived the senses. At the root of the Platonic philosophy lies the idea that the Creator is related to the creation as the thinker to his thought and to the speech that at once externalizes and embalms it. Aristotle laboured with varied success to express his notion of the causal and creative relation. He thinks that the mover of all things moves them while himself unmoved, just as the object of reason and desire is an unmoved cause of motion. God is the end towards which all things yearn and struggle; His very being is an attraction which creates the motion of each, and regulates the movement of the whole. In a very remarkable passage, Aristotle speaks as if the truth might lie in the union of two ideas, those of transcendence and immanence: transcendence may be represented by the general of an army; immanence by the order or discipline he at once institutes and maintains. As here, so in the universe; the supreme good men call God, may be conceived as both a distinct being and an inherent order. Yet while the two are distinguished they are not divided, the order is created by the being, *is*, not in independence, but in consequence of His existence and action. The highest thought of the Greek mind on the matter that now concerns us may therefore be formulated somewhat thus :—the eternal reason and will which, as God's, are transcendent, created what we call nature, and constitute, so far as expressed and realized in it, its immanent order and law.

This discussion, abstruse though it may have seemed, will have made our problem more intelligible, perhaps also more capable of solution. Men have not been shut up to one mode of conceiving God and His relation to nature, and no more need we. The right conception will be the one truest on the one hand to our notion of nature, and on the other to our notion of God, able, while doing injustice to neither, to unite and harmonize the two. Now at this point there is one thing I must do—entirely dissent from any conception of nature that makes it independent of God, that leaves out the Divine energies, or regards them as so foreign to it as to be capable of action only by interference or miracle. God is in one sense no supernatural being—nature were not natural without Him. Activity is of His very essence; He cannot act without touching nature, and nature cannot be without touching Him. God may be conceived without nature, but not nature without God. Nor can He be conceived otherwise than as everywhere present, and to be present is to Him to be the rational energy of all that moves. He could be inactive only by an act of will, and voluntary inaction could only signify His imperfection, moral and essential. The corporate being, as it were, of God and the world is necessary to both; His transcendental will becomes its immanent energies, that its system may be an order and its course a progress.

This conception of the relation of God and nature harmonizes no less with the new idea of nature than with the old idea of God. Nature used to be conceived as a more or less artful and artificial product, a congeries of wonderful contrivances and adaptations, mechanical and organic. It was a product of mathematical and manual skill; a structure built from the foundation upwards by an architect who planned the whole, designed and fitted together all the parts. Where nature was conceived as a construction, its author had to be conceived as a constructor; the one notion implied the other. But the idea of the Creator as an Architect and Artificer was due to the conception of nature, was not necessitated by the conception of God. Now nature is no longer conceived as a made or manufactured product, but as a system which, alike as a whole and in all its parts, has become by a process of growth or development or evolution. The image which represents the becoming of nature is not a machine like a watch, but an organism like a tree or an animal, which had grown from seed sown somehow in fit soil, If the creative process be conceived as one of evolution, or development, it is evident that the Creator cannot be conceived as a mechanic, or builder, standing without the thing He makes, but as the energy or life working within the process He conducts. The creative power, whether we name it Matter or Reason, Force or Will, must be embodied, or as it were incarnate in nature; in a word, immanent, though not immanent only. Yet this brings us to the very conclusion that has just been insisted on as necessary alike to a complete idea of nature and a true idea of God. If God be conceived as isolated from nature, and nature as independent of God, both are misconceived. I utterly deny that His action can be correctly described as "interference," or "intervention," or "miraculous;" it is natural, constitutes the order of nature, creates progress in history. To speak of God as outside the world, a spectator of its movements and processes, able to get inside only by stopping and deranging the whole machine, is to invert the truth until it becomes utter falsehood. To identify God with the supernatural is to undeify Him; to regard His every act as a miracle is to expel Him from nature and make His omnipotence and omnipresence but empty names. The only supernatural I can conceive is the cessation of the Divine action; the absolute miracle were the inactivity of God.

Of course, this does not mean that nature exhausts the Divine activities, that its history is His life. It means, as we shall yet see, something altogether, even infinitely, different. The immanent implies a transcendent relation, exists through and for it. God is essentially the one, but He is relatively the other. Immanence denotes the mode in which the Divine activities are exercised, not the mode of the Divine existence. He is in nature, but He is not natural. All that it is it is by Him, but it is not all that He is. He is its cause and end, was before it, can be without it, wills its being for purposes that are His and not its. But that it may work His will He works through all its energies, in all its processes. As there is no point in man's body unaffected by his thought, or untouched by his will, so there is no point in the universe without the Divine presence or closed to the Divine action. The new idea of nature has indeed recalled us to a truer idea of God. We can conceive Him now more worthily than before. There was an element of deep unbelief, a shadow of dark denial in the old theistic conception. It placed God afar off; shut man within a nature forsaken of its Maker, and built between the two the dividing wall of blank matter girded and buttressed by inviolable laws. Evolution, in making the doctrine of the Divine immanence a necessity to our idea of nature, has made the doctrine of the Divine presence a new reality in religion and a new inspiration for the soul.

III.

Our discussion so far has been concerned with the false antitheses of our new scientific metaphysics. They must concern us still a little further, but from a changed point of view. Criticism of Theism is conducted in the interests of the new doctrine of nature. The criticism has been mostly of the irrelevant sort, based as we have seen mainly on antiquated pre-suppositions as to what Theism must be, but its design is obvious enough—to demolish whatever blocks the way of the new scientific doctrine of creation. This doctrine may be said to consist of two parts — one formal, the other material; the formal relates to the creative method, the material to the creative cause. The former is the doctrine of evolution, the latter the doctrine of matter and force. The point we have now to determine is this—whether they constitute a really rational and scientific doctrine of creation. Hitherto we have been occupied with the metaphysico-scientific criticism of Theism; we are now to be occupied with the substitutes it offers for God.

1. We begin with Evolution. I need not say there is to be here no attempt either to question or deny it. I have only now argued that the idea of nature it at once implies and expresses is the idea most agreeable to the higher Theism, its rational correlative and counterpart. But to say this is one thing; to regard it as a sufficient explanation of our ordered and living and reasonable world an absolutely different and opposite. What is Evolution? Mr. Huxley said: "the hypothesis that the successive species of animals and plants have arisen, the later by the gradual modification of the earlier." So stated it is simply a theory as to the genesis or origin of species, of the *way* in which they come to be. Professor Tyndall,[1] paraphrasing and interpreting Mr. Herbert Spencer, says: "The doctrine of Evolution derives man, in his totality, from the interaction of organism and environment through countless ages past." This is less cautious, still all that we have is a doctrine as to *how* man became. What then does evolution as so stated signify? To what does it amount? It is a theory of creation, of the origin of species, of the genesis of man. True, but in what sense?—a modal or a causal theory? Does it simply seek to explain the manner or method in which creatures come to be? or does it also seek to explain why they so come? Is it a theory only of the creative process, or also of the creative cause? The distinction is most

[1] Belfast Address. "Fragments of Science," vol. ii. p. 197 (Sixth Ed.).

obvious, but it is fundamental. Mode is one thing, cause another. To describe the process is but to describe the way of working, not the force that works. Grant that by "the interactive play of organism and environment," or in other words, by "the struggle for existence" in which "the fittest survive," nature evolves more perfect forms, and creates new species, what then? Simply the inevitable question: Whence came the primal "organism," "the environment," the existence struggled for, the energies that struggle for it, the nature that is their arena? Speculation as to the process may compel men to speculate as to the cause, but we must not confound a doctrine of mode with a doctrine of essence. Evolution may be a beautiful explanation as to *how* an existing and ordered nature does its creative work, but this must not be taken for a theory as to *what* and *why* this ordered nature is. Evolution is powerful if you make it an absolute gift of nature, ordered, operative, living; but without this it is as helpless and inarticulate as were any orator shut up in a vacuum.

The distinction between a modal and a causal theory of creation is one I must emphasize. Mr. Huxley opposes spontaneous generation and miraculous creation to evolution, but the antithesis is real only on the formal or modal side, on the material or causal it is radically unreal. Evolution must *have* life before it can trace its multiplication and development, must have *both* "organism and environment" before it can show us the genesis of species and the descent of man. Force our evolutionist to come face to face with a universe void of life, with matter inorganic, dead, and to explain whence and why life came, and he must either be silent, or say, by spontaneous generation—which is only a speciously disguised confession of ignorance—or by transcendental creation. Till he has got his primordial germ and the conditions favourable to its growth; that is, till he has a caused and creative universe—he has nothing to say, his theory has no place. He must have a premiss which involves his conclusion before he can evolve it, and by no logical process will it be possible to prove that a conclusion so stupendous as a rational universe was based on a premiss without rational contents.

We come back, then, to our distinction—evolution, in the form in which it is held by science proper, is a modal, not a causal theory of creation. It determines and can determine nothing as to the cause, it simply describes the process. In simplifying the latter it makes the former more rational in nature and in modes of working. The words which conclude Mr. Darwin's "Origin of Species" are very remarkable. "There is a grandeur in this view of life, with its several powers, having originally been breathed by the Creator into a few forms or one, and that while this planet has gone cycling on according to the fixed law of gravity, from so simple a beginning endless forms, most beautiful and most wonderful, have been and are being evolved."[1] Whether there is grandeur in the view depends entirely on the relation between the cause and the process, the Creator and evolution. If His action ceased with His breathing "life into a few forms or one," then He is a Creator who has denied

---

[1] This is a very remarkably worded sentence. Much has been built on it as to Mr. Darwin's own views, but it is most studiously impersonal. He speaks of the "grandeur" of the view of life, but carefully avoids everything that might be construed as a positive expression of belief.

Himself, cut Himself off from His creation, and abandoned it to physical necessity, which is only another name for chance. If His action continued, then evolution is a process He has operated and operates throughout. To admit a Creator at any point, is to admit a Creator at all; He must either never act, or act always and everywhere. Then, as Mr. Darwin states the matter, it depends on the meaning read into "beginning," whether it can be called "simple." If the "few forms or one" be regarded simply as forms, then "simple" describes them happily enough; but if they are regarded as the causes or parents of the future, germs pregnant with all that was to be, then they are not "simple," their seeming simplicity makes them the more exceeding wonderful. They are simple as the first point in an evolutional process, but not as a cause. A process begins with the least, ends with the most complex forms, starts from the lowest, culminates in the highest organisms. But the lowest point in a process is not what a cause is, the sufficient reason of the first and last, and all that lies between. To be so it must be active and operative throughout the process, at all points and moments from beginning to end. If men call in nature or the environment to help the forms in their evolutional struggle, then they but add to the complexity of the process, invoke such a multitude of hostile and conflicting yet concurrent and co-operant forces as mightily exalts our sense of the infinite activity and energy of the cause. The sublimity of the cause is proved by a process which seems so simple and is so complex; the way in which nature makes is her way of declaring the presence of her Maker.

2. Evolution, then, as a modal theory of creation does this for us: it shows us how new forms or new species arise; it does not unveil or reveal the hidden energy or will that conducts the process. It has enabled us the better to understand how the cause works, but it has not opened for us the ultimate mystery— what the cause is. Yet it cannot leave us where it found us; it raises in a more clamant form than ever the old invincible question as to what or who created? Whence the nature that at once evolves and is evolved? Science has made it certain that this earth was once without life, that the history of its life has been a history of progress, of growth from lower and poorer to higher and richer forms. Evolution cannot do without a beginning, and a beginning that contains the end; and simply because it cannot, it compels the question, What made life? What is its cause? What gives me the premiss? What is the premiss from which I start? These necessities of thought, born of the doctrine of evolution, are the parents of our scientific metaphysics, and the material or causal doctrine of creation which these, in order to escape from Theism, have been compelled to formulate, is the matter that now falls to be examined.

"The aim and effort of science," we are told, "is to explain the unknown in terms of the known."[1] Very good; this is what we all aim at, the ultimate cause explained in these terms is science. Let us listen then to the eminent scientist translating the primal and universal cause of our ordered and living world, the phenomena of nature and life and mind, out of the unknown into the known. "By a necessity engendered

[1] Professor Tyndall: Science and Man, "Fragments of Science," vol. ii. p. 356.

and justified by science, I cross the boundary of experimental evidence and discern in that matter which we, in our ignorance of its latent powers, and notwithstanding our professed reverence for its Creator, have hitherto covered with opprobrium, the promise and potency of all terrestrial life."[1]

Matter, then, is the causal factor in evolution, it had, ere organisms were, the promise and potency of all terrestrial life. "Matter" is the known term that explains the unknown. What then is Matter? That question leads us, our eminent scientist being the guide, straight into "the great battle-ground of metaphysics," where we get sadly bewildered by the din of contending metaphysicians. John Stuart Mill reduced external phenomena to "possibilities of sensation." Kant made space and time forms of our own intuitions. Fichte resolved nature and all that it inherits into "an apparition of the mind." To show that doctors differ is a rather perplexing method of diagnosis, apt to confuse the apprehensive and expectant patient, but straightway the confusion grows worse confounded. It is confessed that matter is not directly known; what is known is a state of our own consciousness. That anything exists outside of ourselves, anything except and beyond these states, is acknowledged to be no fact but an inference, whose validity idealists and sceptics are said to combine to deny. So "matter" has become an "inference," our known a thing that may be doubted and even denied. But at this point Mr. Herbert Spencer is called in to help, "With him there is no doubt or question as to the existence of an external world." He thinks "our states of conscious-

[1] Belfast Address: "Fragments of Science," vol. ii. p. 193.

ness are mere *symbols* of an outside entity, which produces them and determines the order of their succession, but the real nature of which we can never know." Did ever search end in a more dismal *caput mortuum?* Matter, the known, as opposed to God, the unknown, has "the promise and potency of all terrestrial life;" but matter is an inference from a state of consciousness, and the inference leaves us ignorant of the real nature of the thing inferred. We argue from symbols which tell us nothing as to the essential character of their cause; and the interpretation of the cause through the symbol leaves us twice removed from real and direct knowledge of the source alike of knowing and being. And so the eloquent interpreter of the unknown in the terms of the known only confesses to the victory of the Nemesis that follows the illogical when he concludes:[1] "In fact, the whole process of evolution is the manifestation of a Power absolutely inscrutable to the intellect of man. As little in our days as in the days of Job, can man by searching find out this Power. Considered fundamentally, then, it is by the operation of an insoluble mystery that life on earth is evolved, species differentiated, and mind unfolded from their prepotent elements in the immeasurable past."

So we find that the material substitute for God, the power which works the process of evolution, is, from the standpoint of scientific metaphysics, "a Power absolutely inscrutable to the intellect of man," and our victorious interpreter of the unknown in terms of the known becomes in face of the ultimate factor of his problem a martyr to the doctrine that "it is by the

[1] "Fragments of Science," vol. ii. p. 195.

operation of an insoluble mystery that life on earth is evolved." Nor was this wonderful; it was simply inevitable. In fact, a constructive interpretation of the universe on any other than a transcendental or heistic basis, is a sheer impossibility. Men who deny that thought or reason is the ultimate reality or cause, have no foundation on which to build. They cannot get face to face with matter; when they name it they are only dealing with a term supplied by their own thought. Subtract thought, and the term vanishes. To make the term create the thought, when there is no term save to thought, is the last infirmity of the physico-metaphysical mind. The men who seek to interpret the ultimate cause in the terms of matter, motion, and force, do the utmost violence to logic and reason. They have to confess that the ultimate objects of knowledge are states of their own consciousness, which simply mean rational acts or thoughts of a rational being. These they do know, their external cause they do not. What it is they may try to infer, but the ability to draw the inference postulates throughout the rationality of the thought that draws it. That thought then is the ultimate thing, and if the universe is to be interpreted at all, it must be in terms that bear the image and superscription of the thought that coins them and gives them alike their reality and worth. The metaphysic that begins its constructive endeavour with the affirmation "matter is the efficient cause of all phenomena," has to end in the confession "matter is unknown." Whether an agnosticism which places a nameless blank at the source of our ordered world is able to hand over an explained order or intelligible world for science to interpret, is a matter we may not, perhaps need not, pause to discuss.

IV.

1. But it is not enough that we subject the material conception of our scientific metaphysics to criticism; we must attempt a constructive argument, adapted to the new idea of nature, in behalf of the ancient belief in the eternal God who made the worlds. This endeavour implies and incorporates our past discussions, grows out of the positions already defined and vindicated. One thing is here specially worthy of note, the quest for a cause is common to Theism and the new metaphysic. It cannot, like the older empiricism, quench the discussion on the threshold by saying "the search for causes is fruitless; as all we can know is antecedence and sequence, the very word 'cause' ought to be banished from philosophy." As a simple matter of fact the search for the cause was never so vigorously, in a sense so hopefully, pursued as now. Evolution has given so strong an impulse to speculation concerning the origin and author of life, that men are forced, even in spite of themselves, to ask after what caused to be. The causal or material conception of our scientific metaphysicians we have just examined. They have not found a material substitute for God, nay, let us roundly and honestly say, they cannot find one. Their attempt to do so becomes suicidal, ends in an agnosticism which can neither affirm nor deny. They are equally unable to say, "Matter did create," and "God did not." Their ultimate and inevitable conclusion is a scepticism more utterly fatal to

science than even to Theism. And the very reason that invalidates the process by which they seek to replace God with matter compels us to displace matter for God. Man is the interpreter of the universe, but he is also its interpretation. The rationality that is the essence of his being is also the essence of its; the thought he brings to it is answered and completed by the thought it brings to him. His intellect faces an intelligible world; what is intelligible to intellect proceeds from intellect, is moved by its energies, is full of its contents. Without the harmony of the outer and inner, the universal and personal reason, man could have no rational consciousness, no sense of order, no ability to interpret the universe, no universe he could interpret. The reason latent in the child can develop into the active reason of the man only as he lives in a rational world. The rationality of the individual could not survive in the presence of the irrationality of the whole. And so we may say, these things involve each other: man as rational, a rational universe; and their mutual rationality reflects and expresses a relation necessary and adapted to their respective natures, an intercourse and mutual speech that makes the particular conscious of the universal reason and of its own dependence on it.

Possibly an illustration may help us to seize some of the more essential points in the argument. Language is intelligible to us because it is a work of intelligence, at once a creation and incarnation of mind. Sounds that did not embody reason could never be to us a language, and no skill of ours could ever extract reason from them. The arrow-headed characters of Assyria were a few years since mere insignificant signs, and men looked at them with a sort of helpless wonder, and the vain desire to know what they might mean. By a series of happy discoveries, used by men of patient genius and rare skill, the insignificant became significant signs, and a long dead and silent language awoke to life and speech. But now one thing was supremely necessary to success, that the signs represent thought, be symbols of reason and rational speech. Had they not been so, they could never have been made intelligible, made to speak to living minds of minds that once lived, and of what they believed and did. One may say, then, that it was the reason immanent in the language that made it rational to us, that unless thought had made it, thought could never have understood, interpreted, and translated it. So the universe is rational to our reason by virtue of the immanent and absolute Reason it articulates; and these two, the outer and the inner Reason, co-existing, alike active, alike related, the universal acting on the particular Reason through nature, through nature the particular reaching, reading and hearing the universal, cannot but create, as it were, by act and articulation, recognition of the fact, a confession and monument of the relation. And this recognition is faith in God, man's discovery of the Reason without and above him through the action of that Reason within and upon him, and, as a consequence, his consciousness of his dependence upon God and his obligations to Him.

Our limits unhappily forbid more than a hurried statement of the principles from which our positive argument must start. Enough to indicate whither it tends: Evolution has supplied us with a standpoint which by transcending unifies the old ontological and cosmological arguments for the existence of Deity. The intelligence of man and the intelligibility of the universe are correlatives, essentially akin, each supplemental of the other and necessary to the other. But this implies that the universe must be interpreted in the terms of the intelligence,—the reason, conscience and will, not in the terms of its antithesis, the unknown interpreted as matter, motion and force. Whatever increases the intelligibility of the universe; in other words, whatever makes the way or method of nature more rational, adds to the validity of this principle, increases the necessity of starting from it in every attempt at a philosophical interpretation of the world and its cause. The more reasonable nature becomes to us, the less we can escape from reason as its source. But not only so, in seeking to get at the nature of this source, we must do it through nature at her fullest, richest, most perfect point. This new necessity is also created by evolution. It is not the stem or the root, but the fruit, which best shows the nature of the seed. It is not one stage in the process, but the end that most clearly shows what was contained in the beginning. Now whatever the moments in the movement may have been, it is unquestionable that evolution terminates in man, and man is mind. But mind cannot be the fruit of nature, unless nature from the first had been the seed-plot of mind. The world that by a strictly natural process grows into reason must stand rooted in reason, the more natural the process the more necessary is reason to the root. What nature evolves had been involved in its terms or premises, the evolution of thought implies the thought to be evolved, the process being as it were none the less dialectical that nature conducts it. Without the prior and parent idealism of nature, we could have no idealism of man.

2. It is the more necessary to insist on this point, as it brings out a necessary contrast—the right method for the study of evolution as a creative process were a wrong method for the study of the creative cause. To know the former, we must study the way nature does her work; to know the latter, we must study the work nature has done. In a process like evolution the cause is not fully revealed till it stands expressed in the most perfect effect. There alone it becomes manifest, there only can its nature be known. What we watch at any lower point is the working of the cause, not the manifestation of its essential character and qualities. Nor is this all; what we watch is what we create. Our beginnings are not nature, they are man carrying back his thoughts of what must have been, are our to-day transported into a yesterday we never knew and so must create. Mr. Darwin's "few forms or one" are Mr. Darwin's, mere abstractions which nature never knew. Mr. Herbert Spencer's beautiful law of evolution is not nature's, is simply Mr. Spencer's, an abstract speculation as to how nature proceeded when she formed inorganic masses, and organic matter and life. These are in reality the end speculating about its own beginnings, thought going back into an immemorial past which exists only to thought, and which has no order save the order thought creates for it. Not at the beginning, which is his own abstract and imaginary creation, must the man who would interpret the nature of the universal cause take

his stand, but at the end, which is nature's most manifest reality, the highest revelation of the creative power. And this reality is man, nature's only interpreter, nature's best interpretation. Can he be explained, can his history be written in "the terms of matter, motion, and force"? Whatever interprets him must interpret the institutions he has formed, the religions he has developed, the societies and states he has founded, the literatures he has created, the systems he has built, the arts he has discovered and perfected, the good he has achieved, the evil he has done, the progress he has made. Have these terms, "institutions," "religions," "societies," "states," "literatures," "arts," "evil," "good," "progress," "achieved," "made," "done," any physical equivalents? Could they be translated into the speech of physics and it remain an intelligible and veracious speech? If such speech be applicable to man, then his history may know motion but not progress, may suffer or escape a breakdown, but not endure or cause evil. If the speech be inapplicable, how did evolution accomplish so extraordinary a revolution as by mechanical laws to change the primordial atoms with which it started into a being whose nature was at once moral and rational, whose conduct was regulated freely from within, whose acts had an ethical quality and were all liable to praise or blame? Can the terms good, righteous, wise, benevolent, be applied to men and nations, and be denied to the Power that has directed the ways of man and reigned over the nations? or, to vary the terms without changing the sense, can man be in any sense a moral being without having his development governed by moral laws? These are questions that go to the root of the matter, that must be settled before we can determine the nature of that cause which is at once primal and ultimate. It is not to be discovered by observations like Mr. Darwin's, or experiments and speculations in physics like Professor Tyndall's, or abstract theories of creation like Mr. Herbert Spencer's; but only as we study nature in all her vast extent and purpose crowned and interpreted by man. Men can use evolution to disprove Theism only when they subtract man from nature; add him, and Theism only the more victoriously lives if the doctrine of evolution be true.

Rightly understood, therefore, evolution mightily strengthens the argument for the being and continued activity of God. It gives not simply a new and truer doctrine of the Creator, but a sublimer and diviner doctrine of Providence. We can no longer think of Him as a Spectator or skilful Mechanic, whose work is done when He has built the world; but as the eternal Presence or Energy or Will which works in and over, through and for us all. He is the first and last, and here the first makes the last, the beginning determines the end. Without the Eternal, time, with all it bears in its bosom, had never been; it rose in obedience to purposes that belong to the Divine reason and the Divine love. Nature, full as she is of living energies that ever struggle for more perfect forms of life, has not her end in herself. She is but a moment in the being of the eternal, but with a meaning and a mission for eternity. Mr. Darwin thought there was grandeur in the view which saw the life, breathed of God into "the few forms or one," evolve or be evolved into the rich and multitudinous forms and kinds of being that fill our world. But there is a grander view still, a view which lifts this home of ours into an eternity beside which the ages of geology shrink into moments, into an immensity before which the spaces of astronomy grow narrow and oppressive, and which sees in it the work and purpose of a Reason whose ends are all eternal and all harmonious, the product of a Will whose energies are infinite, and whose acts are righteousness and truth. Mr. Darwin conceived nature as most wonderful, but as most merciless, the paradise of the strong, but the hell of the feeble. Mere strength prevailed and ruled over all; the fittest, which meant the mightiest, survived, the struggle for life was the sort of Providence that is on the side of the big battalions, a God of war pitiless to the homes of gentleness and love over which he had to pass in his march to victory. If a state of conflict be the basis and beginning of order, the order can only be a state of conquest, where victory and dominion are to the strongest. But the theistic view of life is larger, more generous, has a soul of chivalry to the weak, a fit and beautiful place in its order for the gentle lives that enrich our universe with loveliness and love. The nature which knows Deity does not fear death; the life which comes from the eternal, is eternal life, the creation which rose out of infinite Love guided by infinite wisdom, love will not lose while wisdom will find a way to save. The grace of the eternal God becomes in time the graces of mortal man, and while scientific metaphysics may preach a doctrine that is the death of all intelligence in nature, all reason in man, all order in history, all morality in society, all light and chivalrous gentleness in civilization, let us stand fast in the ancient faith which believes that God has been our dwelling place in all generations; and while rejoicing in the knowledge and wisdom and culture of the present, ceases not to pray, " Let the beauty of the Lord our God be upon us, and establish Thou the work of our hands upon us, yea, the work of our hands, establish Thou it."

II.

MAN AND RELIGION.[1]

> "*And hath made of one blood all nations of men for to dwell on the face of the earth, and hath determined the times before appointed, and the bounds of their habitation; that they should seek the Lord, if haply they might feel after Him, and find Him, though He be not far from every one of us.*"—Acts xvii. 26, 27.

I.

PAUL'S appearance on Mars' Hill is one of the most memorable moments in history. It is one, too, that may well touch our imagination now, as it evidently touched his then. The scene and the man formed a strange contrast. The city was Athens, the home of all that was wisest and most beautiful in the ancient world. The spot where the speaker stood was sacred to justice and to faith. Below him was the blue resplendent sea on which Greece had met and vanquished Persia: beside which Æschylos had wandered, listening to the multitudinous laughter of the waves. Above him was the bright and gladsome heaven, where the gods dwelt who smiled in sunshine and frowned in storm; around him the crystal air through which the Greek went lightly tripping, as in the days of his heroism and fame. On the east of him rose the

[1] Preached before the London Missionary Society, at Christ Church, Westminster Bridge Road, on Monday, May 12th, 1879.

acropolis, glorious alike to sense and spirit, where
piety had transfigured art, and art had exalted piety ;
where the ancient faith lived in forms that had created
man's ideal of beauty, and were to remain beautiful for
evermore. And before him, surrounded by places
consecrated by great names and great deeds, stood the
sons of the men who had made Greece illustrious, the
mother of freedom and science, of poetry and art.
And who was he that formed the centre of this wondrous scene ? A barbarian, a Jew, born of a people
who had no God to place in the Pantheon at Rome,
and no philosopher to be quoted in the schools of
Athens, a man without a commanding presence, the
speaker of a dialect without grace, unable to speak it
gracefully, his worn garments and hard, stained hands
betraying the son of toil rather than the fine and
delicate child of culture. And so to the men about
him, sons of so illustrious sires, he was but a babbling
Hebrew, a person to be wondered at, or made merry
over, or serenely despised. Yet the meaning of the
moment, so tragically hidden from their superfine intellects, stood clear before his strong and exalted spirit.
Paul knew himself the heir of a more splendid inheritance, a sublimer past than even they could boast
of. Abraham, Moses, David, and Isaiah, were names
before which even those of Homer, Solon, Plato, Alexander were destined to grow pale. And the past was
as nothing to the meaning that lived in the present.
He stood there a prophet of the God the Greeks had
not known, but who had known the Greeks, had guided
them, inspired them with a love of freedom, beauty and
truth ; an ambassador, too, for the Christ who had
come to bring the light, the truth the ancient sages

had searched for, but failed to find. And his consciousness of all that lived in the moment, of the death that was working its dread yet beneficent will in the images of beauty around him, of the victorious life that was within the Gospel he preached, lifted Paul into one of his sublimest moods, and enabled him to speak from Mars' Hill to Athens, and through Athens to the ages, words that are the words of the God who seeks that He may save.

Paul's mind lives in his discourse. By means of it we can almost hear the pulsations of his spirit, watch the growth and shaping of the thought that here struggles into speech. Observe how he feels the inspiration of the place. He is no rude and merciless iconoclast. The beauty of the city proves to him its piety; and he praises the citizens as exceedingly devout. This suggests to him a grand question—What was their relation to God in the past? What God's to them, then and now? And he discusses it as a man sensitively open to all that was true and beautiful in Greece, yet as an apostle loyal to all that was Divine and eternal, sovereign and saving in Christ. Though a Jew he cites no Hebrew book, uses no Hebrew image, but plants himself in living sympathy with Athens and the Athenians. The inscription on one of their altars becomes his text; he has come to unveil the Unknown God; to substitute for their confessed ignorance, knowledge. And he does it with the subtlest and most unceasing reference at once to their errors and their truths. The God he reveals is the Creator; no temple can hold Him, no image can represent Him, no gift can increase His honour or His power. And the God who created, reigns—is the sovereign of men and nations. The unity of God involves the unity of man. If there be one God, and He a Creator, all men must have proceeded from Him, and must be ruled by Him. And so every nation of men, sprung from one blood, "He has caused to dwell upon all the face of the earth," that is, He has governed them, made and administered the laws that regulated their coming and their going, their rise and progress, their decline and fall. And He has done this in order that they might "seek Him, if by any chance they might grope after Him and find Him, though He is not far from any one of us." Everywhere His hand is working, and men who grope may well touch it and feel as if it made the darkness light about them. And so to Paul there had been, in Greece and throughout the earth, a double search—God's for man, and man's for God. He had made man for Himself, and man could not rest without Him, or He be satisfied without man. In the light of that truth Paul lived; it transfigured his spirit, made him, though "contemptible in speech," a speaker so eloquent that his words have been to the world as mightiest music, charming it into faith in God and peace with Him. Here was the belief that made Paul the first and greatest of missionaries. He lived to bring God's search for man, and man's search for God to the issue that would gladden earth and glorify heaven.

Now, from this great Pauline idea our discourse will start. God has so made and so ruled man that men must seek Him. They may miss or evade God, but they cannot avoid the search. Man's nature is a nature to which God is a necessity, and which only God can satisfy. God's rule is a rule which has tended everywhere and always to make man conscious of his need, to quicken the longing of the spirit after the Divine Father. And here is the ultimate basis of all missionary enterprise. The nature that has been so made as to need God has, as it were, a right to Him. Those who have the best knowledge of Him, lie under supreme obligations to make Him known. The men who want have rights that the men who possess dare not disregard. The men who possess owe to the men who want duties they cannot leave unfulfilled. To believe as Paul believed is to be bound to act as Paul acted. If our belief is, God made men and rules peoples that they may seek Him, then our duty must be so to help their search as to bring them to the God they need, to their home in His eternal life and love.

II.

Let us begin, then, with a distinct statement of our first principle. God made man to seek Him. The search after God is a thing of nature. In other words, religion is so natural to man that it is simplest truth to say, he is by nature religious. It is not a discovery or invention due to art or artifice, but a holy necessity of nature made by its Maker. No one ever discovered sight or invented hearing. Man saw because he had eyes, heard because he had ears; the sense created the sensations. Speech was no invention or discovery; it grew, and man was hardly conscious of its growth, out of the marvellous alliance in him of the physical ability to utter sounds and the rational ability to think thoughts, until it stood without and lived around him like a subtle, articulated, universalized reason. And religion is as natural as sight, or hearing, or speech—as natural because as native and as essential to his nature. Hence, man gets into religion as into other natural things—his mother-tongue, his home or filial affections—spontaneously, without conscious effort; but to get out of it he has to reason himself into a new and strange position, force his mind to live in a state of watchful antagonism towards its own deepest tendencies. No man is an atheist by nature, only by art; and an art that has to offer to nature ceaseless resistance. The man who claims to be an atheist does not escape from God, only finds an "ideal substitute" for Him; does not relieve himself from religion, only exchanges a reasonable for an absurd form of it. Nature as it exists in man fights against unbelief; and if vanquished on one side is sure to win a terrible victory on the other. This century has seen more than one man relegate God to the limbo of dying superstitions, but only to make the memory of a woman the centre of a religion infinitely lower and less human. Nature as well as time has a whirligig which brings round her revenges, and these are never so fearful as when some strange infirmity of a noble mind ascends the throne of God.

1. Religion being thus native to man, its being is as old as his. It began to be with him: his birth was its. There have been, there are, indeed, men who argue that man's primitive state was one of "superstitious atheism," that our religions are but the transfigured terrors of a savage, that our beliefs are but the surviving though transformed images of his dreams. And they have built an elaborately hypothetical structure which with fine though unconscious irony they call a

science, to show how out of the primitive atheism our noblest theisms have been evolved. But the structure is as imaginary as the state; it rests throughout on a series of unproved and even violent assumptions. For (i.) it requires religion to be generated out of its negation; worship to arise in a state where the ideas that create worship do not exist. If you are ever to have a conclusion, you must first find a premiss; but how is it possible to deduce from "a state of superstitious atheism," a conclusion so stupendous as the religions of the world? Where religious faculties live, where religious tendencies work in the way and degree nature bids, there may be superstition, but there cannot be atheism. Without these faculties and tendencies religion would be a thoroughly inexplicable phenomenon; with them man, in his natural state, may have no instituted worship, while he yet remains radically religious. But (ii.) by what right do our sage ethnologers assume that in the living savages we find the best type of primitive man? The savage is not primitive; he is as to time as remote from the first men as we are, and more remote as to nature. Grant the doctrine of development true, and what then? The nature that does not develop is no real or right type of the primitive germ. A man of twenty years may have only the mind of an infant, but we do not name him an infant, we name him an idiot. The infant of sixty or a hundred years would be the worst of all types of a healthy human child, and the man who built a fine theory on the supposition that he was one could hardly be recognised as wise. And the living savage is but an eternal infant, made by the very fact of his infancy more distant from the primitive man than we are by the fact of our manhood. The faculties that slumber in him reveal less of the aboriginal state than the faculties that live active and creative lives in us. But (iii.) from the dreams, from the ignorant and fantastic terrors of the savage, our religious ideas could not have come. The terrible terrifies, and there is nothing so fatal to healthy moral growth and intellectual progress as terror. But religion has not been, even in its more depraved forms, a terrible thing to man. It has been his comfort in sorrow, his strength in weakness, his inspiration in hard and troublesome endeavours, the light that has cheered him in darkness, the hope that has made him rise victorious over disappointment and defeat. And how can man's loftiest ideals be evolved from his most dismal terrors? If fear had created faith, its death had been the life of civilization; but where it has flourished, there has the fairest culture bloomed; where it has died, there have beauty, truth, and goodness begun to fade and to perish.

Man, then, we hold is essentially religious. Religion is by a Divine necessity of nature natural to him; and, as natural, universal. Wherever man is, it is; coextensive as it has been coeval with the race, and it everywhere represents his quest after God. In his multitudinous faiths he has been, as it were, blindly fulfilling the Divine decree, embodied in his nature, that destined him to seek the Lord, if by any chance he might feel after and find Him. From this point of view the religions of the world have a most touching and tragic import; they show man belated, bewildered, in wandering mazes lost, stumbling darkly on, impelled by his Divine home-sickness, in search of his rest in the eternal. When I think of what these religions symbolize, how they speak of brave endeavours, of anxious faith, and still more anxious doubt, of aspirations that rose to God, of blind desires that stretched imploring hands to a heaven that must descend ere earth could be satisfied, then I feel that I dare not speak of them disdainfully; they plead, with an eloquence that mocks speech, with the men who have a purer faith for a share of it, for a knowledge of it. Where a lower religion is, a higher ought to be; men who are seeking God have the most sacred and indefeasible right to the best service of the men who have found Him. And in the religions that witness at once to the intensity and the reality of the search lies the point where giver and receiver can meet, where, standing face to face, they can recognise their affinity with each other through their common affinity with God. The missionary who confronts an ancient and inveterate idolatry or a savage superstition may feel as if it were altogether evil, and his only possible relation to it one of absolute antagonism. But let him imagine what it would be were he in the presence of a race with no beliefs, which could only mean a race without any capacity to believe, without any God, or any ability to conceive one, without any hopes or fears or ideas that transcended the appetites and the senses, and he will discover that to speak to men who had no faculty for faith were a more desperate labour than to speak to men with the falsest faith possible. But in the heart of the worst lies the possibility of the best; the man who has the one has capacity for the other, and may by it be endowed, as it were, with manhood. The religions of man prophesy of the religion of

Christ, are like voices that rise to heaven as prayers and go sounding across the sea in the old and ceaseless cry, "Come over and help us."

The nature that so divinely demands religion finely responds to it. Man penetrated and pervaded by a true and living religion is man at his noblest and best. Even a bad faith, though an awful calamity, is better than none. It is better that man pursue his quest after God, even though it be through darkness, than that he surrender it in despair. While he believes there is a God he ought to serve, a law he ought to obey, while he conceives that there is a person or power within or above him that makes for righteousness, he lives, as it were, with a sense open to the Divine. We know how bad the world has been with its religions; could we imagine what it had been without them? They may have been, in the degree that they were false, mischievous, but in spite of their falsities they have helped man to live his little life as in the heart of eternity, as in the centre of immensity, feeling, to the measure of his capacity, possessed and inspired by the idea, encompassed and o'er-canopied by the Divine. Hegel said: "All peoples know that the religious consciousness is that wherein they possess the truth: and religion they have ever regarded as their true dignity and the Sabbath of their life." It and it alone, has been able to lift man up, as it were, to the mountain-peak of the Spirit, bathed in the serene yet radiant air of the Eternal and Infinite; and there, conscious of the unchangeable behind the apparent, with the earth beneath, its tumults hushed and harmonized by distance, its very deformities smoothed and its dulness brightened into beauty by the sunlight.

he has heard as from afar the murmur of Divine music, the harmony of the eternal reason softly marching through all our perplexities to its glorious ends. But if religion is thus the point where man touches the Highest, and the Highest penetrates and transfigures man, then it is that which finds, vivifies, and directs the best that is in him, makes him conscious that he has a Maker and Ruler whose ideal he exists to realize, whose end he lives to fulfil. It is only as the nature which has come from God returns to Him that it thinks the wisest, does the noblest, becomes the best.

2. But now let us further note, religion is not only natural and necessary to man, the essential condition of his highest personal good, but it is no less necessary to peoples, is a condition essential to their progress and collective well-being. The idea that Bunsen embodied in his "God in History" was no vain dream. The moment when a people has the noblest conception of God and the strongest faith in Him, in the order He has instituted and the law He administers, in His inflexible righteousness and truth, is also certain to be the moment when its spirit shall be in its sublimest and most heroic mood. Once a sturdy Scot, valiant in speech as in deed, English Ambassador to the Court of Prussia, sat at the table of Frederick the Great, then meditating a war whose sinews were to be mainly formed of English subsidies. Round the table sat French wits of the infidel sort, and they and the King made merry over decadent superstitions, the follies of the ancient faith. Suddenly the talk changed to war and war's alarms. Said the long-silent Scot, " England would, by the help of God,

stand by Prussia." "Ah!" said infidel Frederick, "I did not know you had an Ally of that name;" and the infidel wits smirked applause. "So please your Majesty," was the swift retort, "He is the only Ally to whom we do not send subsidies." There stood the truth confessed. England's best Ally is God; the times of her truest heroism and magnanimity have been the times when she was most obedient to Him. And as with our nation, so with all. A sceptic age is never a great or golden age; an infidel people can never be a noble or creative people. For deed, for achievement in politics or letters, for the highest creations in art, in poetry or sculpture, in architecture or painting, religion is a necessity. In seeking for peoples that know no God, who live without faith or worship, where do our philosophers go? Do they select for their inquiries peoples that have stood on the highest pinnacle of civilization, and do they, while the peoples stand there, point with proud and disdainful finger to the men in whom their culture blossomed into its most splendid flower? Do they go back to the Periclean or Socratic age of Athens and show that Greece in her sublime struggle with Persia had lost faith in her gods; that Æschylos had no belief in a Divine Nemesis, unerring, inflexible, inevitable; that Pheidias had no ideal of deity he could embody in forms so majestic that the men who saw them stood awed, as if looking upon the face of God; that Plato had no consciousness of an eternal truth, beauty, and goodness that sleep in and wait on man, and after which he must ceaselessly aspire? Or, do they go to Italy and show that Rome in her heroic days had no man who believed in the State as the creation and symbol of Divine law; no stalwart sons who dared, in her hour of peril, ask, like "brave Horatius"—

> "How can man die better
> Than in facing fearful odds
> For the ashes of his fathers
> And the temples of his gods?"

Or, do they show that in later and less noble times, Raphael had no faith in Divine innocence and gentleness when there rose beneath his brush those faces of the mother and the Child that the world never wearies of studying, and studies only to love; or that Angelo had no reverence for the invisible and awful majesty of God when he thought into being and touched into beauty the marvellous dome beneath which successive generations have stood to admire and to worship? Or, do they go to Elizabethan and Puritan England, and show that Edmund Spenser believed that man was but a series of sensations— virtue, chastity, holiness, vain or arbitrary or accidental things; that William Shakespeare is a soul bounded by five senses, with no dream of a Divine and Eternal that lies round and glorifies our "little sleep"; or that John Milton is a man blind to "heavenly light," with no faith in an "Eternal Providence," and no desire to "vindicate its ways to man," but is rich in infidel aphorisms and prophetic visions of the happy world that will be when once faith has perished? Do they go to times and men like these and silence us by these or similar results? No, not they. But they go to some cannibal South Sea island, scarce touched by the foot or known to the science of the white man, or to some degraded and wretched African tribe, and then, with these specimens dug from the very heart of the most dismal barbarism, they come forward and cry, "Behold, peoples who acknowledge no God!" Well, then, let us accept the specimen, and only answer, "Compare that atheistic race of yours with our theistic races, and let the distance between cannibalism and Christian culture measure the space that divides peoples who believe in no God, and peoples who believe in Him, and have laboured to follow His Spirit and fulfil His ends."

3. But now one more point will have become evident to you. Since religion is so necessary alike to the man and the nation, to the noblest doing and happiest being of the single person and the collective people, it follows that the higher and purer the religion, the greater will be its power for good, the more plastic and potent the creative and controlling forces within it. A faith strengthens and exalts a people in the degree that it is pure, weakens and depraves in the degree that it is corrupt. History unfolds a wonderful tale to him who has eyes to read it. In India a few thousand Englishmen hold empire over more than two hundred millions of men. The Hindu and the Briton face each other as aliens in blood and speech. Yet, long centuries since, their and our fathers were brothers, lived under the same heavens, watched the same stars rise and set, tilled the same field, worshipped the same gods. Wealth and culture came to them ages before they came to us. While our fathers dwelt in the German forests, serving in their own wild way their own fierce gods; when Rome was still unbuilt, and the Latin tribes dreamed not of universal dominion, when the song of Homer was still unsung, and the clang of Greek arms was centuries distant from

the walls of Troy, the Hindus had settled, conquerors, in their splendid Indian land, and were singing under its brilliant stars and beneath its burning sun their ancient Vedic hymns. Yet how, with that long start on the way to the higher civilization, do they and we now respectively stand? Are not the Aryan cities on the Thames and the Clyde the mistresses of the Aryan cities that stand beside the mightier and more majestic Indus and Ganges? And why? Why has the Hindu declined in power as he grew in multitude, while the late-born Teuton has widened "with the process of the suns," till his culture and his commerce clasp our globe like belts of golden sunlight, though dashed here and there with bands of great and terrible darkness? The faith of the Hindu grew like an iron band round his spirit, became a social system, fatal, inflexible, full of false sanctities and consecrated falsities, from which even death would not allow him to escape; but there came to the Teuton in his brawny and untutored youth a gentle faith, yet strong as gentle, and it moulded him with its soft yet plastic hands, shaped him to new and nobler purposes, breathed into his society a purer spirit, larger ambitions, and loftier aims. And so, while the Hindu feels as if held in the dread bonds of fate, revolving in the cycle of a being that is joyless in its very joys, the Teuton knows himself a son of God, a brother of man, a free and conscious person, sent by Divine love to make earth happier, by Divine righteousness to make man holier. And so the one has stood fixed "in patient, deep, disdain" of change, but the other is ever called by his faith to give glory to God in the highest by creating on earth peace, and among men goodwill.

III.

Let us see now where we have come. Man was made, has been ruled and distributed over the earth, expressly that he might seek God, feel after and find Him. Religion, then, is natural to him; is so, because his nature is religious; was made by God for God. A being so constituted can realize his end only in and through religion, and can be happy only as his end is realized. What is true of persons is true of peoples; what is necessary to the good of the man is as necessary to the weal of the nation. But if religion be the condition essential to the highest well-being alike of persons and peoples, then it must follow, the higher the religion the higher the well-being; they must, as regards kind and quality, throughout correspond. Now this brings us to a new point in the discussion. For if religion be so natural and necessary alike to persons and peoples that all must possess one, if the individual and collective good be throughout determined by the kind and quality of the religion possessed, then it must be a matter of pre-eminent importance, of first and last interest, to know what religion they have, whether it is the best extant, and whether a better be possible. Here, then, is our next inquiry, By what religion can man best find God? best realize the end of his being, reach the happiness for which he was designed?

1. At the outset of this new inquiry, we may divide religions into two great classes, the real and the artificial, or the actual and the fictitious. Real or actual religions are the religions of history or fact, such as have lived, or still live as systems of belief or worship.

Artificial or fictitious religions are those of the individual imagination or reason—schemes or systems proposed as "ideal substitutes" for religion. The title in these cases is one of courtesy, and titles worn by courtesy are seldom well deserved. These ideal religions are the children of recoil and revolution; the creations of men who have broken with an historical faith, and who yet feel faith or worship a necessity. To this class belongs "the Religion of Nature," which played so great a part in the controversies of the eighteenth century, and which was said to be "as old as creation," and as universal as man. But nothing could well have more belied its name. It was in no respect a "religion," or a thing of "nature." It was simply a speculative system, so named that it might the better offend and oppose the religion of Christ. It was never professed anywhere—save by its makers; never existed anywhere save in their minds. The men who made it were not in a state of nature; they were civilized, cultured with the culture of Christian Churches and centuries. Their system was but an attempt to give us Christianity without Christ, and it failed utterly, as every attempt to pluck out the heart, and yet spare the life of a living being, must fail.

(1.) But the failure of the eighteenth century has not dismayed the nineteenth. Even now we may see fictitious religions doing their best to become real. Of these, two may be selected as typical cases—the one an apotheosis of nature, the other of man. David Strauss, in the book that formed so fitting a crown to his tragic career, tried to build on the foundation of our modern physicism a new faith that should supplant the old. To him the universe—the great whole which comprehends and unifies all forces—became the only God. In it there was no room for a personal deity, but only for an impersonal and person-creating all. Before this universe man was to bow, not in dumb resignation but in loving trustfulness. Yet man can only love the good and trust the right, and so Strauss had to invest his universe with the qualities of order and love, reason and goodness. While it ceased to be the work of an absolutely reasonable and good personality, it became the workshop of the reasonable and the good. But what are reason and benevolence, righteousness and goodness? Not qualities of an impersonal energy, but of a personal will—not attributes of an almighty force, but of a living spirit. The rational is the conscious; the silent force moving inevitably to its end is not the benevolent—can be as little touched with pity as fired by revenge. These qualities, then, of reason and righteousness, benevolence and truth, came, not from the impersonal all, but from the personal deity. We cannot spare the attributes and slay the person. Under the name of these Divine qualities, in spite of his brave denials, God victoriously entered the universe of Strauss, so making the very negations of man to praise Him.

(2.) If the apotheosis of nature is vain, what of the apotheosis of man? The religion of Humanity is inspired with an enthusiasm for man. It personifies the race, describes it as *le grand Être*, the immortal, the universal, whose past gave us being, whose present holds us in its bosom, whose future shall receive and absorb us, listening to our voices once we had joined "the choir invisible." And this Humanity is what we have to worship and serve. But why? and how?

What I worship I revere; what cannot claim my reverence cannot command my conscience. The thinker in his study, heir of a splendid inheritance that has been accumulating for ages, full of thoughts that have come to him from Plato and Aristotle, Cicero and Seneca, Augustine and Anselm, Descartes and Spinoza, Locke and Leibnitz; possessed and exalted by ideals he has received from India and Judea, Greece and Rome, Italy and France, Germany and England, may well feel, "How magnificent are the gifts of humanity; how immense the riches bequeathed to me by the generations that have lived and died." But now change the scene; imagine the convict in his cell, or the miserable victim of lust that knows no sunlight save the sickly sunbeam that steals fitfully into her alley, and no comfort but the comfort that comes of stupefying strong drink. He or she may think, "I never knew a father's blessing, or a mother's love. Parents I never knew gave me life, and with it their own bad nature; left me to ignorance, to sin, to be trained by cruel and cunning men in evil courses; and these, the only ways I knew, I have followed to this bad and bitter end." What has Humanity done for those miserable creatures? Does it deserve their reverence? Can it command their obedience? Can it change their natures, making a light glorious as the light of heaven rise within them, transforming their dark and depraved humanity into the likeness of the Son of God? Yet the religion that cannot do this, and more than this, is no religion for man; it may be of humanity, but is not for it. The religion man needs is not a religion that can delight the enlightened and interest the intellectual, but a religion that, while reasonable to the rational, can yet lift the fallen and save the lost; that can be to weak and ignorant men the power and the wisdom of God.

2. We may leave, then, the artificial or fictitious religions, and pass to the real or actual. These may be divided into two classes, the national and the universal, or the religions that belong to a particular nation or people, and those that seek to convert and comprehend the race. Of the national we need hardly speak. They are disqualified by their very nature from ever becoming universal. They are inextricably bound up with the national customs, laws, manners; with the social and political order of their country and time, and could only extend with the extension of the nation. Then, too, their day is past. Once the religions of the foremost nations of the world were national; now they are so no more. Then it was the peoples that had made the religions; now it is a religion that has made the foremost peoples. All round us the ruins of those ancient faiths lie, fallen with the States they once glorified. The religion that through so many centuries reigned over Egypt, that lightened the Nile valley with the hope of immortality, and gave to pyramid and mummy a meaning pathetically unlike the one they bear to us, has perished as utterly as the empire of the Pharaohs. The deities that guided the Phœnician mariner, whom he invoked in peril and praised in prosperity, to whom the Phœnician merchant, selfishly munificent, built magnificent but not beautiful temples, shrines of idols vulgar with ivory and gold, have gone with the ancient kings of the mart and the sea. The faith the genius of Greece made so beautiful, the gods she embalmed in her im-

perishable poetry, and embodied in the immortal creations of her art, live no more, have passed irrevocably, like bright Hellas, into dark and silent death. The beliefs that made the State so august and venerable to the Roman, that made him dream of his City as Eternal, as built by the hands, and after the ideals, and for the ends of the gods, have vanished like the Conscript Fathers or the imperial glories that once crowned the City of the Tiber queen of the world. These national religions are dead, and can revive no more. They reigned over their own peoples and disdained to reign over any others. The gods of the land were for the land; revealed their power in conquest, not in conversions; by might, not by the Spirit. But our world knows religion after another sort. On it has dawned the notion of a universal faith. To us there is only one God, and He has unified man. The nations are many, but humanity is one. And this faith hath created a diviner ambition than the ancient world knew—the ambition to make all men brethren by making them the conscious sons of one Father, subjects of one God. Where this belief has come, the ancient, narrow, national religions can come no more.

(1.) But now let us turn from the dead past and look at the living religions of the world, that we may discover the one man most needs, that has most promise for him, can best help him to fulfil the purpose of his being. In Asia two religions rise before us that are in a sense national, while also far more. Within the Chinese Empire, with its almost five hundred millions of men, there is a great religion. The faiths of Confucius, Lao-tzse, and Buddha there confront and complement each other; but neither singly nor combined do they constitute the religion man needs. The prudential wisdom of Confucius is without the enthusiasm of humanity. It has no large ideals, no exalted hopes, no universal and Divine affinities with which to transform and inspire man. His worship of ancestors means but the despotism of the dead and the bondage of the living, the sacrifice of a progressive and happy future to a narrow and inflexible past. Look at the religion as realized in the people, so quick-witted, yet so stationary, so docile in things of sense and craft, so jealous and slow to learn in things of the spirit, and then imagine what it would be were the world an immense Chinese Empire, enslaved and impoverished by a dead and exhausted past. Nearer to us lies India, and there Brahmanism rules. It is an active, in some senses an aggressive religion, absorbing new tribes, new beliefs, and ever voracious, crying for more. Yet think what it is—the most awful tyranny of custom and caste. Where it goes, its iron distinctions go, making brotherhood, freedom, the happy intercourse of man with man impossible. Morality is unknown to it; it can deify the basest as easily as the best. It reduces personal existence to a calamity, hard to be borne, still harder to be evaded—a ceaseless revolving in the wheel of being that is to be not so much feared as abhorred. Brahmanism universalized could only mean man depraved and sent to wander wearily through time in search of eternal oblivion and peace.

(2.) But these are not the only great religions Asia can show us. Two others claim our attention, more generous and universal, inspired by a moral and missionary spirit. Buddhism is a mighty faith, numerically the mightiest in the world. It is, too, a gentle faith; within it stands a beautiful human personality, which has exercised a sweet and softening influence on its spirit. But even with its admired and admirable ethics, has Buddhism the qualities of the religion man needs? A religion without God is a religion without hope, and a hopeless religion can never do victorious battle against the ills of time. Buddhism is the apotheosis of sorrow and the victory of suffering; man, in order to escape from it, seeking to escape from being—not man resolved that he shall conquer evil, in order that being may be holy and happy. But this cardinal principle makes Buddhism, in spite of its beautiful ethics, radically selfish, and as impotent as selfish. Virtue is cultivated as the way out of sorrow, not as the way to vanquish it. A religion whose highest aim is selfish care for one's own happiness, is a religion of spiritual death. Islam is the very opposite of Buddhism. It humbles man, it magnifies God. Its God is almighty, righteous, merciful, the supreme Sovereign and Judge of man. In it stern Semitic monotheism exists in its sternest form. If fanatical belief in a severe and inflexible deity could make a perfect religion, then Islam had been perfect. But it is only like the truth that it may be the more false to it. The god of Mohammed is a fierce Arab chief invested with the name and attributes of the Almighty. The service he demands is absolute submission, not rational obedience. He spares the sins the Arab loves. A religion that does not purify the home cannot regenerate the race; one that depraves the home is certain to deprave humanity. Motherhood must be sacred if manhood is to be honourable. Spoil the wife of sanctity, and for the man the sanctities of life have perished. And so has it been with Islam. It has reformed and lifted savage tribes; it has depraved and barbarized civilized nations. At the root of its fairest culture a worm has ever lived that has caused its blossoms soon to wither and die. Were Mohammed the hope of man, then his state were hopeless; before him could only lie retrogression, tyranny, and despair.

Where, then, shall we turn for the religion we need? Shall we turn to Judaism? Judea, indeed, has perished, but Judaism survives, seeking to be at home everywhere, not caring to make converts, caring only to be allowed to live. Once, indeed, it was a glorious faith—had poets making psalms that were to be for all after-ages the sacred songs of the world; had prophets speaking of God, and for God, words that were to live like lifegiving spirits; had priests, and a temple, and a worship that were to be to all time symbols of eternal truth. But Judaism was great only as a prophetic religion; once it ceased to be prophetic, it ceased to live; its work was done eighteen centuries ago, and since then its life has been but a reminiscence, an exhausted and spent existence passed in the shadow of its ancient glories.

IV.

From these imperfect faiths, passed in a so hurried review, let us turn to one nearer and more familiar, the faith in which we were born, by which we live, which has created the civilization, the freedom, the intellectual life, the noblest moral qualities of our

Western world. I feel that I hardly dare trust myself in the little time I can now command to speak of the religion of Christ. For what can I say worthy of so great a theme? The most I can do is to ask you to look at it as it confronts you, the religion of civilized man, and man it has civilized. Study it first as regards its ideal contents, and then as regards its actual work or achievements in this world, and then say if there is any religion so complete, so beautiful, so absolutely perfect in the truths it presents to knowledge or to faith, or any that can show so glorious a roll of noble and beneficent service for man. I would it were possible to show the new spirit, the new light and life it brought into the world, and to trace its silent, penetrative, transforming, action in man and society, in the individual and the State. The most that can be done is to indicate in a sentence or two some of the qualities that most distinguish it, first on the ideal side, and secondly on the actual.

1. On the ideal side only three points need be noted—the idea of God, the idea of man, and the relation between man and God instituted and realized in Christ. As regards the first let this be marked: there is no surer measure of the essential character and quality of a religion than the way in which it conceives God. God is, indeed, its creative and all-determining conception, diffusing itself everywhere like a subtle essence. As He is, everything is, from the minutest atom to the mightiest mind. In His works His essential qualities are revealed; the motives from which He creates determine all His actions and relations towards the beings He has created. The world can never be better than its Creator, never happier

than He meant and means it to be. Now think how gloriously Divine is the Being placed by the religion of Christ as the Maker and Ruler of the universe! He creates that He may love and be loved, that He may be a Father to the infinite multitudes of creatures that live in His presence and rejoice in the sunshine of His face. The evil that falls like a shadow over His works His grace pierces, lifts, forces into a background that makes the light of His love only seem the more radiant. He is righteous, too righteous to spare the sin that works misery, but too spiritual to treat moral as if it were physical evil, to be conquered by almighty energies rather than by agencies of grace. Such a God, an eternal Father and Sovereign, infinite personalized love and righteousness, has boundless promise of good and hope for man. He cannot forget, He will not forsake His universe, loves it, watches it, guides it as it moves through its mingled shade and sunshine towards His more perfect day.

And as God is conceived, so is man. The Creator is mirrored in the creature. There is nothing that touches man like the sad mystery of his being. Moments come to us when thought looks out into the immensities above, around, and below, into the eternities behind and before, and in saddest despair we cry, "What am I? Why am I? Whence? O heaven whither?" To these questions what a Divine answer Christ brings! "Ye are God's sons, come out of His love, live in His love, and every moment His love seeks your good." "Like as a father pitieth his children, so the Lord pitieth them that fear Him." But, then, man's soul is not unsullied; the face he lifts to heaven is often red with shame, seamed with passion, dark with guilt, and his cry is, "How can God receive me?" And here the Divine mystery of Christ reveals its wondrous meaning, the grand secret of the new and perfect relation of God to man. In ancient religions God is conceived as a terrible Being, to be appeased by dreadful rites, to be bribed, not into mercy—for mercy He had not—but into partiality and favour. In Christ, God stands forth "reconciling the world unto Himself." The gift is God's; the joy is man's. In the Son, so freely given, God and man meet, the right hand of His divinity binds God to man, the left hand of His humanity binds man to God. Over our weary and sinful earth a spirit of peace was breathed when the words fell and went wandering over it, as from the bosom of the Eternal, "God so loved the world as to give His only begotten Son, that whosoever believeth on Him should not perish, but have everlasting life."

2. And now a word or two as to the actual and active side of our Christian faith. And here let the wondrous way in which the ideal and the active are bound together be noted. It is so in no other religion. The truths of Christianity are moral energies, agencies for the creation of the simplest yet sublimest morality. It exercises this power in the individual and in society. Look around: you confront a civilization that, in all its high, generous, humane elements, was created by the religion of Christ; that has, to all its ignoble, pernicious, and evil elements, in that religion a permanent and merciless foe. Christ is the enemy of all that is sinful and selfish in man and society; and, marvellous though it be, in the conflict He is progressively victorious. Think what an achievement it

is to lead and rule the Western mind. The Oriental does not move like the Occidental. The West describes in days cycles to which the East takes centuries. Where centuries pass without any perceptible change, it is a small thing for a religion to live. The will does not fret to be free, the reason does not so rebel as to recoil into vehement and revolutionary denial. But here our faith faces an intellect that cannot brook ignorance, that is curious to know the secrets of nature and mind, the present and the past, heaven and earth; and claims to control a will that cannot bear restraint, loves to show its independence of authority and to obey its own sweet choice. Yet this reason Christ is powerful to hold, and He is strong to command this will. To live and rule for a thousand years in the West speaks more for the truth of a religion, than undisputed continuance for a thousand thousands in the immobile East. A system that is never doubted can never be believed, and the doubt our faith has overcome and is overcoming is the best proof of its invincible energy and truth. As an actual religion history shows it to be universal, permanent and progressive, able and willing to comprehend mankind, to continue under the most varied forms essentially unchanged, qualified amid the utmost intellectual activity to quicken and lead the march of mind. And its force is always spiritual, moral. To believe it is to be bound to live by it. And it is simple, sober truth to say, its history is the history of the most splendid moral changes the world has known. It has cleansed the heart of the guilty, and changed the sinner into a saint; it has created in every generation a noble army of teachers, reformers, philanthropists; has freed the slave, built the hospital for the diseased and destitute, lightened the horrors of war, tempered justice with mercy, sent conscience and honour into the soul of ignorance and fear. Christ has made man conscious that he was the brother of man the wide world over, conscious, too, that he was the son of God. And so His truth grapples in the most splendid way with our worst ills. Within the soul of the Christian peoples a dread conflict is ever in process. Christ and mammon, Christ and passion, Christ and mad ambition, narrow and demoniac selfishness, do battle there. Now evil has the mastery, and men hasten to sin, or nations rush to battle: but even then the gentle Christ follows, whispers the word that brings penitence to the man, or raises aloft on the battle-field the white banner with the red cross that speaks of woman's tender nursing and man's hand, skilled to cure, swift to heal. O Christ, this world saved by Thee, from the madness of passion, or the still greater madness of despair, can only call Thee blessed.

Here, then, we end our quest. The religion of Christ is the religion man needs; it has come from God that it may bring to God. Here indeed, lies the secret of its pre-eminence. Other religions have risen out of man's search for God; it has come out of God's search for man. In the religion of Christ the redemptive and reconciling energies of God are, as it were, incorporated, sent to live, a beneficent and powerful being, on earth and among men. God created it for man, and man has now a right to God's glorious and universal gift. We dare not intercept it, we who have received only to give. It came to us when we were a savage race; made us the people we are; and now from us it must go out to the old and new peoples of the earth. Africa with her millions, a vast continent opening to us on all sides, for ages spurned by the foot of the white man, or used only for his worst rapacities and lusts; the islands that sleep in the glorious Pacific, rich in varied wealth, with children here fierce as the wild beast, there inoffensive as the lamb; vast spaces of the America that was desolated by the greed and cursed by the cruelties of the pale-faced conqueror; India with her millions held fast in the merciless vice of caste; Central Asia with her moving multitudes praying to a Buddha that cannot hear; China with her crowded cities and teeming valleys and swarming rivers, bent in abject submission before the dead that cannot speak, and a past that cannot inspire; Japan, full of deft and cunning hands, subtle and docile brains, in recoil from her own ancient customs and ways, open to the generous light and wisdom of the West—all these and many more, unconsciously to themselves, stretch over the sea suppliant and helpless hands, and cry, "O England! Queen of the Seas, give us of the secret of your greatness! Let the light that came to you from Christ shine out towards us. Let the Gospel of God's love you received be preached on our shores and through our valleys. Let the power that made you what you are come to us, that the joy and the good and the peace you have may be ours!" In the cry of earth there is the voice of God; and when that voice is heard, the Churches of England must obey.

PART SECOND.

I. GOD AND ISRAEL.
II. THE PROBLEM OF JOB.
III. MAN AND GOD.

"*First, what is a people, or what makes it a people? Certainly not the mere co-existence in space of a greater or smaller number of individuals physically alike; but the community of consciousness between them. This has in the common language only its immediate expression; but where are we to find the community itself or its ground except in a common view of the world? and where, again, can this common view of the world be originally contained or given to any people except in its doctrine of the Divine (Mythologie)?*"—Schelling: "Einleitung in die Philosophie der Mythologie," vol. i. p. 62.

"*There is one notion of freedom in religion and in the State. This one notion is the highest man has, and it is realized by man. The people that has a bad notion of God has also a bad State, bad government, bad laws.*"—Hegel: "Philosophie der Religion," vol. i. p. 241.

"*Among the people of the East who live under a theocratic order, the Hebrews appear to us like sober men among drunkards; though to antiquity they seemed to be dreamers among the awake.*"—Lotze: "Mikrokosmus," vol. iii. p. 147.

"*The great truth known to Israel is that God,—the great truth known to the Greeks is that man,—is a moral, an ethical being. Therefore either cycle of historical development belongs essentially to the other, and that too because both form an essential preparation for Christianity.*"—Rothe: "Stille Stunden," p. 245.

I.

GOD AND ISRAEL.

"*Now Moses kept the flock of Jethro his father-in-law, the priest of Midian: and he led the flock to the backside of the desert, and came to the mountain of God, even to Horeb. And the angel of the Lord appeared unto him in a flame of fire out of the midst of a bush: and he looked, and, behold, the bush burned with fire, and the bush was not consumed. And Moses said, I will now turn aside, and see this great sight, why the bush is not burnt. And when the Lord saw that he turned aside to see, God called unto him out of the midst of the bush, and said, Moses, Moses. And he said, Here am I. And He said, Draw not nigh hither: put off thy shoes from off thy feet, for the place whereon thou standest is holy ground. Moreover He said, I am the God of thy father, the God of Abraham, the God of Isaac, and the God of Jacob. And Moses hid his face; for he was afraid to look upon God. And the Lord said, I have surely seen the affliction of My people which are in Egypt, and have heard their cry by reason of their taskmasters; for I know their sorrows; and I am come down to deliver them out of the hand of the Egyptians, and to bring them up out of that land unto a good land and a large, unto a land flowing with milk and honey; unto the place of the Canaanites, and the Hittites, and the Amorites, and the Perizzites, and the Hivites, and the Jebusites. Now therefore, behold, the cry of the children of Israel is come unto Me: and I have also seen the oppression wherewith the Egyptians oppress them. Come now therefore, and I will send thee unto Pharaoh, that thou mayest bring forth My people the children of Israel out of Egypt. And Moses said unto God, Who am I, that I should go*

> *unto Pharaoh, and that I should bring forth the children of Israel out of Egypt? And He said, Certainly I will be with thee; and this shall be a token unto thee, that I have sent thee; When thou hast brought forth the people out of Egypt, ye shall serve God upon this mountain. And Moses said unto God, Behold, when I come unto the children of Israel, and shall say unto them, The God of your fathers hath sent me unto you; and they shall say to me, What is His name? what shall I say unto them? And God said unto Moses, I AM THAT I AM: and He said, Thus shalt thou say unto the children of Israel, I AM hath sent me unto you. And God said moreover unto Moses, Thus shalt thou say unto the children of Israel, the Lord God of your fathers, the God of Abraham, the God of Isaac, and the God of Jacob, hath sent me unto you: this is My name for ever, and this is My memorial unto all generations."*—Exodus iii. 1-15.

These verses describe a supreme moment alike in the life of Moses and the history of man. In it a state was founded that was not to perish till the kingdom of God had come, a religion was founded that was to live till translated into the revelation of Jesus Christ. If this moment had never come to Moses, nothing would be as it now is—in our history and beliefs, in our politics and our spirits, all had been altogether different. The new name of God made God a new being to man, was to make man in all his generations live with worthier thoughts of God, with soul and conscience more open to the Divine. Yet the moment in its outward aspect subtly concealed its inward glory. The feeblest things in nature may be rich with infinite promise; out of the simplest beginnings have come the sublimest results. That is God's way. Imagine yourself on the shores of the primeval ocean while the hardly cooled earth was still like a monster sleeping in its own thick breath. Amid the ooze at your feet life begins to move so insensuous, so structureless, so feeble, as to be hardly distinguishable from the ooze. Your own highly articulated organism, your sweet and dainty reason, might think this life too low to notice, this moment too mean to be remembered. But let the earth silently travel through immense ages, let the Divine energies active in her do their creative work, and life enlarges, multiplies, intensifies; man comes, makes history, builds his cities and his civilizations, battles with himself, with his destiny, stands up at last the being we know, enriched with all the wealth accumulated from that first moment till now. So this hour of revelation may seem but a mean moment. On a storied and stormy mound, grand only in its solitude, a shepherd stands fronting a bush that burns with a strange light, listening to a voice whether without or within he can hardly tell. In that hour what can lie for the mighty race of man who have come out of one eternity and rest not, pause not, till they have vanished into another? The hour is long past, and were we for an answer to summon from its grave what lies between now and then, think what would come! Israel with his mighty kings and mightier prophets, his sweet singers and priests and scribes; Jesus Christ with His apostles and martyrs, fathers and teachers bearing all the splendid gifts they have given to men; those with many thousands more of kindred persons and things would rise and say, " We were in that hour in the loins of Moses when God met him on Horeb and revealed to him His new but imperishable name."

I.

In order to understand that name and its significance, historical and religious, we must first understand the man through whom it comes, the people to whom it comes. We may assume at once the real historical personality of Moses. It is, in truth, above question or criticism. As has been well said, "You might as well try to cut Israel out of the history of man as to cut Moses out of the history of Israel." Everything distinctive in it runs back into him, with him really begins to be. This can be said in the face of the most recent criticism, and will stand true, however the questions now being so keenly and acutely discussed may be determined. Not simply on the authority of the Pentateuch, but on the combined evidence of the whole history and literature of Israel, Moses was the founder of the Hebrew nation, its first legislator, the parent or source of all its later legislation. His history lives in his work, his biography can be read there. What he does connects him at once with Egypt and Israel, shows him familiar alike with a settled and civilized life, and the fierce, high-handed freedom of the desert. If his work be looked at in the simplest form to which it can be reduced, it still proves him to have known the worth of the civilized state, the conditions under which alone it could be realized, and the means by which these could best be created and developed among the escaped and semi-nomadic tribes he led. In discussing his work and its worth we shall ask no more than is here implied.

Our narrative introduces him as keeping the flock of Jethro, his father-in-law. He had not been always a shepherd. He had reached Midian a fugitive from Egypt, and to him life in the two lands stood out in sharp and painful contrast. As the story is here told it touches us even now. The shepherd, toil-stained, coarse-clad, driving his flock across the blistering desert or tending it on the storm-worn mount of God, appears a being of another and lower race than the dainty "son of Pharaoh's daughter." Jethro, priest of Midian, patriarch of a wandering tribe, formed a strong enough contrast to Pharaoh, monarch of Egypt, heir of many dynasties, master of many lives. The fierce shepherds striving at the well with Jethro's daughters must have looked savage enough to one accustomed to courtiers smooth in manners and in speech, gracefully anticipating every wish of gracious and queenly women. The tent, type of the transitory, adapted to a life that had no luxuries and few necessities, even these being ill supplied, would be a poor home to a man once familiar with the palace, massive-pillared, many-chambered, the centre of the rich and royal city on the banks of the Nile where as boy he had played and as youth he had studied. The contrasts were so violent that neither time nor home reconciled Moses to Midian ; the birth of a son but giving him occasion to express in the child's name, Gershom, the feeling, " a stranger there."

Yet the lost luxury was a splendid gain, but changed for the worse the material conditions of the life that the moral qualities of the man might be changed for the better. Moses forsook Egypt that he might find his vocation. Patriotism has sublimed many a man, has lifted him out of the mean selfhood that knew no universe beyond its own pleasures, into the magnanimity that rejoiced to live or die for the faith of the fathers, the freedom of the brothers, and the future of the sons. The man that does not love his people cannot love his God. The court of Pharaoh tempted Moses to renounce his people; his choice to suffer with them was his election of God. Circumstances can never disinherit the fit heir of a noble past; in him blood is stronger than breeding. His mother gave to Moses more than Egypt could either destroy or control. She ruled, as he little imagined, his happiest and most fruitful hours. The "ark of bulrushes" she made that she might save her child from the Egyptians, which saved him through the Egyptians, was no mere prosaic fact. Like all facts born of an exalted faith, it is as much allegory as fact, speaks of the eternal Providence that works in the humblest lives for the sublimest ends. It was a brave thing to be a Hebrew mother and vindicate the rights of motherhood in those days; and she who dared to be so true to the high vocation of God as not to deny it through fear of a cruel law, could not but live in the son she victoriously struggled to save. And the heroic nature he thus inherited was placed where it could receive fittest training. A weak nature in the court of Pharaoh had been subdued to utter courtiership, had expiated the sin of its Hebrew descent by deeper hate of the Hebrews. But the strong spirit, though tempted to the last apostasy, grew but the stronger for the trial. Pomp awes only those who see it, burdens to weariness, vexes to weakness those who bear it. To see, while no Egyptian, Egyptian society from within, was to see its hollowness; to the free Hebrew spirit its tyranny was hateful, to the nature true born its semblance and its falsehood were abhorrent. To such to be at once the oppressor's favourite and a child of the oppressed was to be cursed with a lot less endurable than slavery. Where the hand that fondles us smites our kin, it twice insults, insults the manhood they gave to us and the affection we gave to them. Duty comes there in its sharpest and most absolute form: to do it may be immensely hard, but what ought to be done is as clear as the finger of God can make it. The soul that has this choice to make is sorely tried, the soul that makes it is highly disciplined. Moses made it, and making it was made fit for nobler things. "By faith he forsook Egypt, not fearing the wrath of the king, for he endured as seeing Him who is invisible."

But Egypt did not only discipline, it educated. Moses was learned in all its wisdom. Wisdom is always good to learn, whose wisdom soever it may be. And Egypt had much to teach, for it had learned much. It had high thoughts of God, though its faith and action were often foolish. It said, God is one, yet it worshipped a multitude of deities no man can now number. It believed in the Invisible throned in Light, yet it adored and honoured with manifold gifts the bull and the crocodile, the ape and the cat. It loved to picture Osiris the Judge, sitting stern, inflexible, administering justice in the Hall of the Two Truths to all who had lived; yet it lived as if God had no concern with the vices of men, thought none the worse of the man who came straight from the beastliest sins, if only he came through the hands of pleased and well-paid priests. Yes, Egypt had much to teach Moses, and Moses was wise enough to learn the best it could teach. He learned that an exalted conception of God badly expressed did not make a good religion; that a debased worship of Deity did not ennoble man or regulate for good his conduct; that a faith administered by priests for the priesthood could only deprave and enslave the people. He so learned what religion ought not to be that he was enabled to understand what it must be made if it was to rule man. The stern Hebrew soul in him recoiled from a faith so soft and indulgent to the strong, so harsh and oppressive to the weak. The high spiritual interior doctrine, so far from justifying, would only the more condemn the sensuous and often sensual practice. Imagine the young man of clean soul, of severe spirit, learning in the schools the high mysteries peculiar to the initiated, the mysteries touching the unity and the indestructibility of life, the Deity who was the one and the all, denoted by a thousand names, expressible by none. He passes from the schools to the temple, watches the priests and the people as they worship the sacred bull clothed in crimson and jewels, or as they bring gifts to the crocodile as it issues from its slimy bed ornamented with fine gold. Or imagine him at the funeral of the Pharaoh he knew, the man whose tyranny, pride, lust, uncleanness, he despised. He hears the ritual of the dead recited, wherein the man is made to tell the judge that he has lived on earth gentle, humble, chaste, clean of hand, pure of heart, possessed of virtues the falsest flattery could never have said were his. Now what would be the thoughts of the young man, by blood an alien, by nurture a native, as he stood face to face with these anomalies, conscious of them as no Egyptian could be? Would they not run thus? "The people know not the God they profess to know. Their worship contradicts their knowledge. Their conduct condemns their faith. If God be one, how can the beasts these men worship be gods? If God be true and good, can He be pleased with bad men who tell the very Eternal Judge to His face that they have been good, or with the priests who recite in praise of the dead the very virtues their vices had made to blush? Whatever this be, it is not religion; in it the thoughts men think of God must find fit expression in worship, must exercise due control over conduct."

These thoughts the young man carried into the wilderness; there they would become ever clearer and more intelligible to him. When he ceased to learn in Egypt he began to learn of God. In the solitudes where nature looked her calmest and most unchangeable, the majesty of Egypt looked but a feverish and passing show, void of the eternal righteousness which alone holds the secret of life. There, too, he came to understand his people, the meaning of their faith, the possibility of a higher mission to man than had come through the conquests or the culture of the Pharaohs. What was the God their fathers had worshipped when they roamed over these plains, lived in the shadows of those mountains, ere famine had driven them to seek the plenty which had become the darkness and bondage of Egypt? They named Him the Almighty, the Most High God, the Lord of heaven and earth. Good; He was then a reality, might and activity and supremacy were of His very essence. He was no shadowy God whose multitude of names but concealed the emptiness of His nature; to believe in Him did not allow men to revere as deities four-footed beasts or scaly monsters of the Nile. To know

Him was to know our Maker, Ruler, Judge, who had made men to serve Him, and could approve no conduct that insulted His majesty and transgressed His law. Could the Hebrews know what the knowledge of this God signified? that it meant a new religion, a new state, a new manhood? Were they absorbed into Egypt they would lose their God, their knowledge of Him would perish; and the hour of their absorption seemed near. Bondage was doing its bitter work; by it they were losing alike their love and their capacity for freedom, and without it their God could not be served. The man who had found God amid the solitude and vastness and silence of the desert, was made of God to know how to found a people that should be His, means to His high ends, bearers and interpreters of the new name that was to create the new religion.

You can see then the meaning of this history. It was no sudden emergence of the supernatural into the life of this man, no forceful or abnormal interference of God with the man, breaking the continuity of his earlier and later life; it was but the fruition of his whole past, the crowning moment of a process which began with his being. This does not banish Providence from the history, nay, it only the more fills it with Providence, by making it the brightest point in an order through which a Divine purpose runs. God does not work by starts and at intervals; He works continuously. In the whole and in all its parts, in every thought of the spirit and in every atom of matter, in the life alike of the collective universe and of every individual, He is present and active. There is no Chance; what men so call is but the Providence they do not understand. Accidents occur nowhere so little as in the lives of the men who have determined the history and progress of man. Just note how it stood with Moses: the nature that came to him by his mother; the passion of love, now touched with fear, now penetrated with joy, in which she suckled him; the affection born of royal fancy that waited on his childhood; the discipline of the king's house, the wise man's school, the priest's temple; the education which came from contact with the void variety of Egyptian civilization and religion; the conflict of the two natures, the native and the acquired, in him; the victory of the Hebrew over the Egyptian; the flight to the wilderness; the impossibility to his cultured spirit of contentment with his ruder lot, or of fellowship with the untutored men of the desert, leaving him to a solitude of soul that became high speech with the Eternal;—these all so combined to educate the man, to fit him for his mission, to lead up to the supreme moment when he met God and heard His new name, that we dare not think of them as otherwise than as the work of the Providence that shapes our ends. Moses, the man of God, was a man made of God for men.

II.

But now we must turn from the man God had so fashioned and disciplined and educated to his work. That work was twofold, political and religious; he created a people and he founded a religion. Yet these two are one: the people were created by and for the religion, the religion was realized in and through the people. The creation of the people was the means;

the realization of the religion the end. To this they were predestined in God's manner, by the nature given, which men anxious to escape the need and notion of Divine action call now a "monotheistic instinct," and now a "genius for religion." This mission they at all periods of their history confessed, naming themselves "the people of Jehovah," called out of Egypt by Him, expressly to be His and to serve Him. This was their distinctive characteristic, made them a peculiar people, elect, precious, a vehicle of Divine ideas, translating them into human speech. Mohammed named them "the people of the Book;" and he named them as he knew them. But it was by becoming "the people of the Book" that they ceased to be "the people of God." Once the only word they had was a written word their mission was ended, for where the word is dead the religion cannot be living. When God ceased to speak in and to and through the people, the people had lost their call or right to speak for God; what had once been special to them had become common to man. But the very word which ceased to be theirs that it might become the world's, remains a witness to this fact,—the very function and destiny of the people was to create this Book, articulate the ideas, work toward the religion it reveals and represents,

So here Moses is sent to do a notable thing, "bring forth the people, the children of Israel, out of Egypt." History is proverbially ignorant of her own beginnings. She loses the people she most loves in mists no eye can pierce, in an antiquity no memory can recall. But here we reach a moment of formation, where we can watch the beginnings of a state which is to be one of the feeblest, while its people are to be one of the mightiest known to time. But what are they? A band of slaves, settled on the borders of Egypt and the desert, hated by their masters, hating them; with the vices of the semi-civilized and the bond; without the freedom of their nomadic fathers, or the virtues, the courage, veracity, resourcefulness, sense of kinship and clanship it breeds; without the arts, the culture, the traditions, the habits of ordered and refined and gracious living that made the civilization of their masters so splendid while so oppressive. Nothing depraves like bondage; enslave the noblest people and they become ignoble, while a people not yet ennobled by centuries of regulated freedom are like matter prepared for the corrupter's hand. And such had Egypt found Israel, the master corrupted the slave, the slave copied the master, only in the manner of the semi-civilized, who ever find it easier to imitate the vices than the arts of the civilized. To lead this people into freedom, to build them into an ordered state, to make them the people of Jehovah, might well seem a hopeless task, one from which Moses, even after his education of God, might reasonably shrink. And he does shrink, asks, "Who am I that I should do this great thing?" But the thing is to be done, not in his own strength, in God's. God is to be with him, and he is to bring forth the people to serve God, where God had spoken to him. Once the men are free, Egypt will be unable to corrupt, and they will come in some measure to understand their mission and their God.

And what Moses was sent to do he did. He led forth the people out of Egypt, constituted them a state, consecrated it to the name and service of Jehovah, We have seen how poor the material he had to use, and with the material the immediate political result, of course, agreed. The state was a poor state, the state of a people half-nomadic, half-settled, with few laws, many barbarous customs, the strong passions that hated restraint and loved swift revenge, driven by the hunger for land and cities to seek by conquest a home in rich and fertile plains. But the extraordinary thing was, this poor state had an end beyond itself, was the bearer of ideas not as yet intelligible to the people, never wholly intelligible, not even to their selectest spirits. In Egypt the religion existed for the state; in Israel the state existed for the religion. Without his faith Israel had no reason to be, did nothing, had nothing he could do. In this respect he stands alone among the nations. Egypt had her culture, her architecture, those wonderful hieroglyphs which became the mother of all our alphabets, her ancient traditions and long maintained empire. Assyria had her cities and palaces, sculptures and writing, wars and conquests, desolating her sister lands, yet helping the onward movement of man. Greece had her literature and art, her philosophies and polities, the forms in which she incorporated her spirit of truth and freedom and beauty, realities to her, to us ideals we fondly dream may yet be realized. Phœnicia had her trade, the industries by which she created wealth, the commerce and colonization by which she distributed it. Rome had her laws and empire, her statesmen and orators, marvellous genius to organize and govern. But amid the crowd Israel stands having only his religion, yet with that possessing more than they all. Mass is not might; it is spirit, not matter, that creates history and determines the destiny of peoples. Little Israel with his religion has done more for the world than China with her teeming millions or the colossal empires of the West with all their political and secular genius.

Now why did feeble Israel accomplish so immense a work? Why does he stand in the sphere of faith, in the region of the spirit, in solitary eminence among the peoples? If order reigns in history, the work of Israel was not due to accident; if reason sits at the heart of things, the place of Israel was no effect of fortuitous causes. His own faith was the most reasonable faith,—called of God for the ends of God, made a people by Jehovah that His name might be magnified. This was not simply a matter of faith; it had its expression or symbol in the world of fact. If you are to understand the genius and mission of a people, you must not simply consider its undistinguished mass. You must study its creative personalities, the men who are at once its dynamic and static forces. Great personalities have this significance—they bear as it were the immanent idea of the people, conceive and express their ideals, relieve and direct the energies that work towards realization. Now there is in Israel a series of the most splendid religious personalities known to any religion. It has no parallel anywhere. The productive power of China seemed exhausted in Confucius and Lao-tzse, the centuries between them and now have been centuries of imitation and recollection. At the source of Parseeism Zoroaster stands, and beside or after him there is no second. Buddha is without a fellow, and Islâm, as it has one God, has only one

Prophet. But it was not so in Israel. There the religion owns one great personality as its father, and personalities almost as great meet us at every stage of its history, making its continued life a continuous development. Behind Moses is Abraham, a grey father standing in the dim dawn of the young world; after him come the men that resume and complete his work. Samuel, David, Elijah, Amos, Hosea, Isaiah, Jeremiah; the nameless Man who writes the one great drama of the Semitic race, the Son of man who dwells among the captives by the river of Chebar, and builds out of the ruins of Israel his ideal state and temple; the Seer that looks out of desolate captivity into the distant future, sees the suffering Servant of God making it glorious, and describes the golden day that tarries so long and yet shall so surely come;—these are but some of the men, a few survivors of the mighty host that in the successive generations of Israel quickened and perfected his religion. While they lived it lived, grew from lower into higher forms, moved from humbler to loftier ideals. And one feature, as extraordinary as singular, marked the whole series—they all marched right onward with faces turned towards the future. The ideals of historical religions lie, as a rule, in the past, their saints are behind them. They live by faith in what has been, admire and imitate the father or teacher, apostle or prophet, who gave them birth. But the ideals of Israel lay all before him. The typical Servant of God was one who had yet to be; the day of Jehovah was a day still to come. The religions that look backward have no hope beyond themselves; the religion that looked forward was prophetic, believed in a God who lived, who had ends and purposes that widened with the process of the suns. And was not Israel, in so living and believing, true alike to our best thoughts of God, and to the Providence that has fulfilled itself in history?

III.

Israel, then, was right in his belief; God did call him out of Egypt, make him a people, the people of God. This series of men was no cycle of happy chances; law reigned in it, and what is law but the order a higher reason institutes and a lower reason perceives? But now this brings us to the second point, the one touching the religion. How was it that Moses made his band of fugitive slaves into a people? By what means did he form them into a state, into what was, indeed, less a state than a church? He did it in the strength of a new Divine Name, a Name that, embodying a new conception of God, invested God with new meaning, made Him, as I have said, a new Being for man. Here are the words that tell how the name came: "And God spake unto Moses and said, I am Iahveh, and I appeared unto Abraham, unto Isaac, and unto Jacob by the name of El Shaddai, but by my name of Iahveh did I not make myself known to them."[1] What this name signified is the matter we must now consider.

Men's names for God are often sad and significant, often beautiful and suggestive monuments of his search after the Divine, the Being he so wishes to find and so fears to love. These show him in this search now wandering in dark perplexity, now resting in calm sun-

[1] Exod. vi. 2, 3.

shine with the light of the eternal gathered round his head. Think what mingled truth and error, awe and fear, loyalty and subservience, were mixed together in those once common and living names, Baal and Moloch. Baal was lord, master, the being who owned and disposed of man, who claimed him as his, and whose claim was admitted. Moloch was king, the being who ruled man, who was his absolute, solitary, rightful sovereign But the names were applied both to God and men who were kings, and the God came to be interpreted through the man. So in that East where kings are tyrants, cruel, bloodthirsty, God was conceived to be as fierce, as pitiless as they, a Being like the human Moloch, to be appeased with blood, pleased to see little children passed through the fire. But now think what toy and peace have come to our common human heart since Jesus taught us to say, "Our Father, which art in heaven." It made God the symbol of infinite love and patience, forethought and tenderness, became the basis and source of the one true religion of humanity. It, as it were, humanized God and deified man, making heaven and earth as of one blood, united in kinship as in affection. The divinest name for the Divine means the divinest religion.

Now the Name that came through Moses was a creative name, destined to work a revolution in the very idea of God, to educe the worthiest, most reasonable and permanent idea ever formed of Him, waiting only the element of fatherhood that came by Jesus Christ to be perfect idea of the perfect God. This Name we represent in our so dissimilar speech by the term Jehovah; our version translates it by the word "Lord," the French by "Eternal." Now what does this Name mean? You will not expect me here to indulge in any recondite philological discussions; such could not be made to any reasonable degree intelligible to you. Yet you must allow a word or two of explanation. The Name is no foreign derivative, no term borrowed or adapted from an alien source, but a product of the Hebrew soil, a native growth of the Hebrew mind and speech. On this point modern scholars may be said to be unanimous; on another the agreement is almost as pronounced, the term is a derivative of the ancient Hebrew verb *to be*. But difference begins here—men are not agreed as to what part, mood and tense, of the verb was the original of the Name. Two main schools of opinion may be noted, one holds it to have come from the simply predicative, the other from the causative form of the Hebrew verb. According to the first, it means, "He who is"; according to the second, "He who causes to happen," or "to be." In either case the term was not, in its primitive sense, a proper name, was the third person singular of a verb so used as to denote one who had not been and could not be named, who was too exalted, too glorious, too universal and eternal in his being and action, to be known by any term or title that had been, or could be, used of created things or mortal men. "He who *is*," "He who *causes* to be," the term is in either case present, ascribes to Him no past, no future, only a *now*, yet a now which is above time and change. For, as the scholar who has done most to revive and recommend the second explanation has specially noted, "He who causes to be," not *has* created, but *is* creating; "He who causes to happen," that is, "He by whom things fall out," who stands by his word or fulfils his promises. Now, it is happily not necessary to decide here between these senses; what alone is necessary is to note this—each implies and involves the other. If the name of God is by pre-eminence "He who is," then, He alone is the Uncreated, and what comes to be comes through Him. If, on the other hand, His distinctive name is "He who causes to happen or to be," then He is the alone Uncaused, the unproduced Producer, who is before He either causes or creates. Either sense yields, perhaps, the most elastic and plastic idea it were possible to embody in a name.

There is a further question I should have liked to discuss—what may be termed the connotation of the Name, what ideas stood associated with it. Was it suggested by celestial phenomena? Did it mean He who causes to rain? or He who makes light and fire descend from heaven? Now here it is necessary to be careful and discriminative. We may distinguish, on the one hand, the innate idea or immanent possibilities of the word, and its primitive history and historical use; and, on the other, the meaning it carried to the mind which revealed it to Israel, and the meaning given to it by Israel. It seems to me that the term must be interpreted through Moses, not through primitive Israel; that while for the history of Israel the primitive associations and use are the most important, for the history of the religion the importance belongs to the innate idea, the immanent possibilities. The power that was in the word the people did not at first perceive. They interpreted it through their old theistic associations, and while they named their God

Iahveh, they thought of *El Shaddai*. The ideas of being, of creation, of the living God, were not new to Moses. He had learned them of old. They had come to him in Egypt, had mastered him in the desert, had been transfigured and personalized by the revelation of Iahveh, and so the Name was rich beyond what Israel could then conceive or believe. But the wealth in the Name did not lie barren, it was a living Name, working life, deepening, enlarging with the life it worked. It was not hard and narrow like *El*, the strong; or *Shaddai*, the mighty, the violent; or *Baal*, the Lord, or *Moloch* the king; it was big with immense suggestiveness, full of infinite possibilities. To think it, to speak it, was an education. It emphasized Being, the Eternal, and mortals who were touched by a tragic tenderness as they thought of the thousand generations behind and the thousand generations before, and the dark, cold, insatiable *Sheol* beneath, which ever receiving was never satisfied, were made to feel the sublime mystery of the God who, without birth, sat in His changeless, eternal Now. It emphasized, too, the creative will, unchangeable as the Being, the God who was so faithful to Himself that all His ways were truth and righteousness, nature and history the mirror of His character. And it emphasized all that was personal in this eternal Creator, placed Him as the supreme and sovereign *Thou* over against man, made Him have pleasure in His people, be gracious unto them as grace became His might and majesty. These splendid possibilities, these Divine latencies were not patent to Israel in the wilderness, or to Israel in Canaan for centuries—it would be the utmost historical unveracity to say they were; but all the same the term contained them, and containing, helped to work their evolution. And the result stands in the literature which describes the ideal, if the unrealized, religion of Israel: in psalms which tell of the eternal God, Cause of all being, the dwelling-place of man in all his changeful generations, of the besetting God, whose presence fills the heaven above and the abyss beneath, and whose eye follows the least as the greatest; in visions that reveal His majesty and show the mightiest creatures awed and humble before His glory; in discourses that declare His righteousness, the secret yet victorious way of His working; in poems that turn all nature into a glorious parable, the animated speech of His reason, the rational expression of His will; in prophecies that describe a golden age achieved by the suffering of His righteous Servant, but by His strength and in fulfilment of His purpose. There is no literature so possessed of God as the Hebrew literature, so penetrated, inspired by the thought of Him as to present a sublime, awed, reverent, reasonable faith in Him. But the loftiest dream lies enfolded in the earliest term. Without the Iahveh of Moses we had never possessed the God of the prophets.

IV.

But the name of God is not our only guide to the Mosaic idea; it is further explicated in the words which describe Jehovah's relation to the people and determine the nature and conditions of theirs to Him. It is not necessary that we here regard any more than the "Ten Words" or Commandments as Mosaic.

No one will deny that they are the heart or kernel of the Hebrew legislation, its aboriginal and as it were parental form. What Jehovah was conceived to be when He became the God of Israel, or rather called Israel to be His people, what He was believed to demand from His people, what His people must be to please Him, stands recorded in these remarkable words. Let us look at them in their simplest form.[1]

Proem.

"I am Iahveh thy God, who brought thee out of the land of Egypt, out of the house of bondage."

Table I.

"Thou shalt have no other gods before Me.
Thou shalt not make to thyself any graven image.
Thou shalt not take up the name of Iahveh thy God for a falsehood.
Thou shalt remember the Sabbath-day, to keep it holy.
Thou shalt honour thy father and mother."

Table II.

"Thou shalt not murder.
Thou shalt not commit adultery.
Thou shalt not steal.
Thou shalt not bear false witness against thy neighbour.
Thou shalt not covet thy neighbour's house."

Now it must be confessed that we have here a very wonderful constitution for a primitive society, a code civil while religious, as complete as it is simple. The first and most notable thing is the relation in which Jehovah and His society are placed to each other. He instituted it—is its Creator. The Rabbins said, "the Ten Words are the pillars of the law and its roots;" but the foundation of the pillars is the proem

[1] Exod. xx. 2-17.

or preface, as it has been called: "I am Iahveh thy God, who delivered thee out of Egypt, out of the house of bondage." Notice: He delivers the people that they may be His; the relation is mutual, but His is causal, theirs dependent. Now, here is a large idea: the society that conceives itself founded by God is a society with wonderful possibilities within it, a church rather than a state, with ideals that transcend itself, the seeds of divinest ambitions; and with this principle underlying all—as is the God, such ought the society to be, with all its ends worthy of Him. But there is more implied: He who creates a people has a real and righteous claim upon the people He creates. The will that gives a society existence is a will the society ought to embody or realize. Hence the exordium naturally underlies the "Ten Words" which declare the will of Jehovah; it does not form the first of these, but is their common basis.

The ten fall into two tables of five each. Of the first table, four directly concern the notion of God, two being concerned with His nature and two with the worship of Him. "Thou shalt have no other gods before Me," and "Thou shalt not make to thyself any graven image." Now these interpret and explain "Iahveh thy God." He is to be Israel's only God: no other is to stand beside Him. This may not be an absolute monotheism, but it *is* a monotheism. The people who believe, "We have only one God," has come very near the conception "there is no other; He is one and alone." But while the first Word refers to the unity, the second refers to the nature: "no graven image." This must be explained through the contemporary conditions. In Egypt the symbolism had swallowed up all the spirituality of the religion. Symbols of God were everywhere; on every wall, in every temple, every tomb. The Deity was hidden by the symbols; the symbols were adored as Deity. In the desert and in Canaan the Semitic tribes had their "images," their household idols, the stones and figures which men revered as gods. Moses said: "There is to be no graven symbol, no carved image here. Jehovah cannot be represented by men's works, is manifested by His own." See how this explicates the Name. Our only God is He who is or causes to be, and He is one whose shape cannot be expressed by the hand or to the eye. He is spiritual, lives to thought, not to sense; an object of faith, not of sight. Imagination dies when it is chained to the senses, but lives when it is winged by the Spirit. The Word that forbade the "graven image" called the possibilities latent in Iahveh into being; the religion which disembodies the Divine idea opens the way to infinity.

The next two Words unfold and enforce the idea of worship involved in the idea of God, while the third represents the coincidence and connection of our primary and fundamental human duty with those owed directly to God. The name of God is not to be used idly or foolishly; speech of Him, therefore, thought about Him, was to be real and reverent, true to the man's own soul, seemly and fit for the one spoken to to hear. The command concerned in an equal degree the sanctity of the Name of God, and the sanctity of all that was said in His Name. Those who know the ancient oriental worships, their extravagances, uncleanness, unveracities, ferocities, the way in which they could be used to consecrate treachery and condone deceit, can alone measure the worth of this Word. The impurities other gods tolerated in acts, Jehovah would not tolerate even in words. Purity in speech meant purity in action, fidelity to God became best fidelity to man. He who broke his vow or violated his oath might surprise his foe, but he offended his God, who would not be the God of the deceitful man. But the worship of one so august and severe could not be left to accident or impulse, opportunity must be made for it. Hence, "Remember the Sabbath-day to keep it holy." One day in seven must be set apart to Jehovah, be His day; on it all the people must think of Him, ask what His will was, whether they had done it, speak to each other of Him, encourage each other so to serve Him that He might be exalted above all gods. But a God like Jehovah could not be satisfied with mere praise or worship. He was not a God afar off, who loved the smoke of the hecatomb, pleased with the blood of rams and the fat of fed beasts. Israel was His, the order in Israel was His order, men must prove their obedience to Him by observing it. The family is the basis of society; no social duty can be fulfilled where the home is despised, its sanctities and sanctions trodden under foot. So the last direct duty to God is the first direct duty to man: "Honour thy father and thy mother." Obedience to parents is the earliest form of reverence for God; through them law first comes to man, and love. This is one of the finest elements in Hebraism; it shows how its stern Deity was most gentle and humane. This Word proves, too, how completely the new had broken with the old religions. Where a command like this was enforced, human sacrifices were condemned.

Honour of parents is possible only where there is respect for children. The counterpart of the Hebrew reverence for parents was the Hebrew regard for offspring; the men who honoured their fathers loved their sons.

The second table is a very rudimentary, yet for a simple people a very exhaustive code of social duties. The underlying idea is clear; the God who called and constituted Israel commands thus and thus. Fulfilment of the duties enjoined in the first table are necessary to Israel continuing His people; fulfilment of the duties enjoined in the second, to the continuance of Israel. All its relations must be penetrated by His Spirit, and regulated according to His will. So there is to be no murder; life is to be sacred; what God gave, man is to protect and reverence. The basis of all social law is the sanctity of man, the inviolable right to liberty and life of the honourable and law-abiding citizen. Then there is to be no adultery; purity is to reign in the home, and where the home is chaste society is pure. The inviolable sanctity of the family, the consecration of the husband to the wife, and the wife to the husband, lies at the basis of all social intercourse, is the cardinal condition for the creation of pure manners, all neighbourliness and nobleness in man. "Thou shalt not steal" declares the sanctity of property, without which wealth and commerce, the culture of the land and the trade of the city, are alike impossible. "Thou shalt not bear false witness" affirms the sanctity of truth and justice. Man must not speak the lie that pains or defames or defrauds a neighbour, must even to his own shame or loss speak the truth that upholds righteousness.

"Thou shalt not covet" goes to the root of all social evil, rebukes sin at its source. It declares the sanctity of one's own soul; it is to be too sacred to be the home of bad desires; as a man thinketh in his heart, so is he; where he does not think evil, he will neither speak nor do it. The end is fit, and worthy of the beginning; the scale ascends from first to last. Murder is the rudest of crimes, but covetousness the subtlest and most easily masked of sins, alike most delicious and most torturing. The law which forbids it forbids not simply evil acts, but the inclinations and tendencies that are the parents of evil; and in so doing proves that it may enforce civil duties, but it does so as a religion.

V.

We must now look at some of the principles and issues involved in our discussion. The name of God which came through Moses was explicated and as it were articulated into a religion by the Ten Words. These show how Jehovah was to be conceived and how He was to be served, what claim He had on Israel and what He claimed from Israel. These things ever tend to correspond. A religion always is as its God is; the thought of the Deity is reflected and realized in the worship and the conduct of the people. No nation is ever better than its conception of God. Where God is badly conceived, the laws and manners of the people are sure to be bad; where He is nobly thought of, the ideal of the people will also be noble, their history a struggle towards higher excellence. We shall, then, in the light of the Ten Words, look at the new notion of God, then at the new notion of religion, and finally at the gift which in these two came through Israel to man.

1. The meaning of the name *Iahveh* has already been discussed and explained. What we are now concerned with is the mode in which the Ten Words interpreted and realized the Name, made its distinctive elements become clear and potent to the confused consciousness of the people. Iahveh is "He who causes to happen," or "brings to pass;" and so the proem introduces Him as the Creator of Israel, his Deliverer, who brings him out of Egypt and bondage into freedom and the desert. And this is done that He may be the people's God and they His people. They are to be for each other. When they speak of Him they are to use a name that belongs to no other God, that no man has appropriated or can appropriate, that denotes His reality, His causality, His changeless being, His ceaseless activity in Israel and for Israel. What would be the influence of a name so derived and so significant to the men who used it? They could not forget its meaning, it was too pure and too peculiar a child of their own speech to allow them to do so; and so to use it was to be forced to think of their God as the true God, the alone real, the alone active. They could not speak of Him without using a term that predicated being and activity of Him, the *He* who needed no proper name stood in an order by Himself, absolutely distinct from the multitude of deities who had nothing but their names to distinguish them. This action of the Name was mightily intensified by the commands which forbade the worship of other gods, the idols or images,

and the idle or false use of the Name. These all stand together, each emphasizing its own element in the idea. "He who is" can never be the fellow or parallel of they who seem to be; to think of God as *Iahveh* forbids that any other being be thought of as God. "He who causes to happen" cannot be imaged in anything man may make; no idol, which is a product of the produced, can express or represent the Producer. And the Name which means so much must never be treated as an idle or empty name, must remain august, awful, a witness to the supremacy of the One it denotes and of the dependence of him who uses it.

But these were not the only elements significant for the Iahvistic idea. The God who had called and created Israel was the author of Israel's law, was therefore the Lawgiver, the Guardian of the law He gave, the supreme Judge. That law was essentially moral, not sacerdotal or ceremonial, enforced the primary and fundamental moralities by the imperial sanctions of religion. But where the law of God is moral, the God whose law it is must Himself be moral; what He so expressly enjoins, must be what He mainly desires to see realized by man and among men. He can have no pleasure in an immoral people; only hatred to an immoral worship. Honour of parents, respect for life, the purity of home, honesty and honour of conduct, veracity and kindliness, generosity and benevolence, the things that promote the happiness of man, the wellbeing and progress of society, are the things He commands His people to do. And the law He makes He administers, the Legislator is Sovereign and Judge. His law is an eternal witness that He is a

God jealous for right, zealous against wrong, a God who loveth righteousness and hateth iniquity.

This fragment, then, of most primitive legislation was charged as it were with forces evolutional of the immanent possibilities, the latent verities of the Divine Name. The Name and the Law of God, which had risen together, were mutual interpreters; the better the Law was understood, the more significant became the Name; the richer the contents of the Name grew, the mightier became the authority of the Law. The people at first did not, could not, know what had come to them. They were like their neighbours, unsettled, sensuous, self-willed, cruel, high-handed, prone to deeds of revenge and blood. They were less civilized than the Egyptians on the one hand, or the men of Canaan on the other. Their customs, beliefs, worship, manners, hopes and fears were on a level with those of the surrounding peoples. But here, into the very heart of Israel, had come a new force of extraordinary magnitude, whose action was to be at once revolutionary and evolutional, disintegrative and organizing, making Israel a peculiar people, working out through Israel a new order and a higher progress for man. They could not think of their God without thinking of their law, could not think of their law without thinking of their God; their God loved and enforced law, their law spoke with the authority of their God. He would not wink at their sins or be bribed by their sacrifices; obedience, right-doing, was the only thing that pleased Him. He would not allow Himself to be compared with other gods, or other gods to stand beside Him; the men that served Him must serve Him alone, and in His way, not in theirs. He would not suffer any man to profane His Name by using it to seal a profitable falsehood, nor would He permit the order He had instituted to be set aside by violence or self-interest; His name could sanction nothing but truth, His authority uphold nothing but righteousness.

The struggle between the new name and the old associations, Jehovah's law and the ancient passions, was long and strong and fierce, but the new force slowly worked its way to supremacy. It seized the great spirits, and they at critical moments guided and formed Israel. In the song of Deborah we can hear how faith in Jehovah and loyalty to His law could gather the people into unity and lead them to victory. Through all the period of the Judges Jehovah and Israel remain the watchwords of order and progress. At its close the development of the Iahvistic idea is the direct cause on the one hand of the attempt at the theocracy, on the other of the rise of prophecy. The great exponents of the idea, Samuel, Nathan, Elijah, Elisha; the great literary prophets, Amos, Hosea, Isaiah, Jeremiah, are typical men, men of severe and exalted spirit, veracious, inflexible, stern, fit speakers for a God whose way is righteous and whose word is true. The word that comes from Jehovah makes the men; the union in them of faith and obedience, their equal love to truth in speech and righteousness in action, their conviction, so variously expressed, that none but a righteous people can serve the righteous God, only repeats and amplifies the Mosaic idea. The greater prophets are indeed the sons of Moses; their high moral and spiritual monotheism but the completed expression of the truths contained in the name and law of his God.

Of course, I know how many burning questions are here lying hot under our feet; these were never intended to be here discussed. All that was meant was to find and state the law or principle that had regulated Israel's religious development. That principle seems to me the idea or conception of God expressed in the name *Iahveh* and explicated by the Ten Words. The God they reveal is a being of a new order, altogether different from any before believed in by man. He is distinguished at once by nature and character: by nature, for He alone is, the one truly real, ever active Being; by character, for He is righteous, holy, the giver and guardian of law, pleased with no service that is not moral. These elements, which we may term respectively the metaphysical and ethical, are contained in the Mosaic idea. The metaphysical is implied in the name, the ethical in the law; and the two so coalesce that they move together when they move at all. The development is equal and common, history making this evident—God is to Israel most truly one when He is most really moral; most sternly moral when He is best conceived as the only eternal and supreme. Intellectual monotheism to be real must be ethical. The god who is not righteous cannot be the one God, may be personified patriotism or passion, blinded by partiality, zealous for his tribe, hostile to man; but the righteous God loveth righteousness more than any people, could befriend no people that forgot it; could forget it only by renouncing Himself. Idolatry ceases to be possible when Deity is believed to be moral; the belief in a God who made and administered a moral law was the death of idolatry and the birth of a victorious and reasonable monotheism.

2. The new idea of God meant a new notion of religion; the coming of a diviner faith made worship humaner and more spiritual. Our notion of religion is so much what Moses has made it that we can hardly conceive what it was before him, or would have been without him. We think of religion as moral, or what ought to be moral, as a law that regulates or ought to regulate the life. But the old idolatries were unmoral, often radically and deplorably immoral. The worships of Canaan were lascivious in the extreme, the religion of Phœnicia was not only corrupt, but a cause of terrible corruption, most disastrous in its influence on Greece and even Rome. The worst immoralities of the ancient world were sanctioned by the religions, which left, too, its worst wrongs unrighted, its deepest miseries unpitied. As was ancient, so is modern heathenism; to it our very notion of religion is unintelligible. We think that the man who believes in a God ought to be a moral man, but the man we describe as a heathen believes no such thing. He does not believe that his god is a moral being or requires moral worship, or thinks any the worse of the man who can lie, or steal, or covet, perhaps all the better of him if he can so do these things as to offer the fatter sacrifices or richer gifts. The worst impiety is not impurity, but neglect of the offerings that persuade the gods.

But the Mosaic idea introduced a nobler conception. God became ethical, a Being of purer eyes than to behold iniquity, the Source of law, the Maker of moral order, inflexible in His justice, rigorous and righteous in His judgment. The supreme thing to Him was not the supremacy of His people, but the reign of righteousness, the prosperity of the good, the humiliation of the wicked. As He was, so must the service of Him be. In a religion that was not moral, in a piety that was not ethical obedience, He could have no delight. A worship that was mere ceremonial could not be worship of Him : a law that was simply sacerdotal could be no law of His. The two notions of religion, the heathen and the Hebraic, stand expressed for us in the words of Micah, placed, too, in living and instructive relation to their respective ideas of God.[1] The people, heathen in heart, ask, like Balak, king of Moab, when he consulted Balaam :—

"Wherewith shall I come before Jehovah, bow myself before the high God ? Shall I come before Him with burnt offerings, with calves of a year old ? Will Jehovah be pleased with thousands of rams, with ten thousands of rivers of oil ? Shall I give my firstborn for my transgression, the fruit of my body fo the sin of my soul ?"

But the prophet, speaking for Jehovah, declares the only service that can satisfy Him, defines the only religion He approves :—

"He hath showed to thee, O man, what is good ; and what doth Jehovah require of thee, but to do justly, and to love mercy, and to walk humbly with thy God ?"

3. In this idea of God, and the consequent notion of religion, lies involved the mission of Israel, the secret he was charged to tell to the world. His possession of this secret gave him his place in history, to speak it was his work. The measure of his success in fulfilling

[1] Micah vi. 6-8.

his mission is the degree in which he has made his faith man's, his secret a message of glad tidings to the world. The result lies written on the broad face of history, lives embodied in the beliefs of civilized mankind. Yet the outward hides through its very magnitude the immensity of the inward result. What the new idea of God and the new notion of religion have done for man we may not attempt to tell. They have changed him within and without, strengthened all his moral qualities, created in him a nobler and sterner ethical spirit, exalted his ideal of manhood, brought elements into his social and collective life that have enormously enriched his best civilizations. Our order is not the Greek cosmos, the beautiful but merciless harmony that man could not but admire, that yet crushed without pity the man who touched it. Our order is moral, the reign of a living and righteous will, which never spares guilt, but is ever merciful to the guilty. Our conception of the universe, of Providence, of the law that is supreme over man and his destiny, is penetrated through and through with moral ideas. From these we cannot escape, we conceive of them as reigning in the time that is our own, in the eternity that is God's, yet reigning as the God who pities, and not as pitiless law. Let these facts and beliefs, with all that they imply, witness that Israel has not lived in vain. Jehovah called Israel out of Egypt to serve Him, and Israel's service of Jehovah has been in the noblest sense service of man.

II.

THE PROBLEM OF JOB.

" And the Lord said unto Satan, Hast thou considered My servant Job, that there is none like him in the earth, a perfect and an upright man, one that feareth God, and escheweth evil?"—Job. i. 8.

THE Book of Job is a work not simply of literary but of living interest, a wonder in that most wonderful body of ancient literature, so deeply studied, so little known, our Hebrew Scriptures. It appeals in an equal degree to the imagination and the reason, to the one as philosophy, the grandest product of the Hebrew wisdom; to the other as poetry, the highest achievement on this field of the Hebrew, or rather of the Semitic spirit, the ripe and fragrant fruit not so much of a man's or a people's genius as of the genius of a race. It stands there the work of a nameless Man; no one can tell who he was, or where and when and how he lived; yet he so lived as to be one of our mightiest immortals, leaving all that made him what he was, the questions that vexed him, the thoughts that possessed him, the faith that consoled him, the hopes that transmuted and glorified his sorrows, set here as to everlasting music. That is an immortality modesty itself need not blush to own: the Man nameless, but his speech and his spirit alive and articulate for evermore.

The Book may be described as a theodicy in poetry, first and still supremest of its kind, parent of an immense offspring. It shows man's despair in the presence of his last perplexity, but shows it that he may be seen to vanquish it in the only noble and sufficient way, by so vindicating the ways of God as to bring man to higher and truer and surer faith in Him. It is a book in the best sense veracious throughout, true alike to the saddest facts of human life and to the loftiest claims of faith, stands as remote from the optimism that seeks to justify God by making light of evil, as from the pessimism that seeks to condemn or deny God by being blind to good. It looks misery full in the face, looks at it where it has least right to be, but where it often most surely is, in the home and heart of the good man; looks at him, not as he is in the ideal region where things are as they ought to be, but as he is in the world of hard and prosaic yet most tragic fact, in contact and conflict with the saddest realities, an innocent sufferer, but held to be a sufferer not innocent, driven by misery and unmerited blame to the doubt, the despair, the anguish that becomes anger at God and man. And then, when it has bravely made us see evil having its will and doing its worst, powerfully helped by the conduct of well-meaning but narrow-minded men, it turns our faces towards the good, brings the light of eternity into time, and makes us hear what God can say to the perplexed and sorrowful, smitten by His hand while obedient to His will. And here the nameless Man shows his courage as much by his silence as by his speech; he is content to leave a shadow on the face of nature, though a shadow that only brightens the light on the face of

God. He leaves us comforted but not satisfied, like men who have seen enough of the dawn to know that the darkness is past and the day at hand, bringing with it the light that makes life radiant with joy. Yet between his first word and his last he has made us know and feel many things, has started questions that deepen the nature, strengthen and purify the spirit, awe and uplift the soul. He has so used evil as to make us think more truly of God, as to touch us with a new sense of the majesty of His being and the mystery of His working, as to inform our worship with reverence and our obedience with reality. He who has never felt the shadow of evil can never know the holiest mysteries of love; he who reveals the saddest perplexities of life creates in man a new sense for God, gives to God a new meaning for man. To conceive Job's problem, and to have our faces turned towards the solution, is to come nearer the heart of all things, the God who is too much the Father of man to leave him an untroubled, undisciplined, and unexercised child.

I.

1. In coming to the problem of Job, we must attempt to come to it as the nameless Author came. It is an old problem now, surrounded by a waste of most arid speculations, dreary even to think of; it was a new problem then, torn, as it were, out of the tribulations of the spirit, wrestled with in the deepest anguish of soul and unto sorest sweat and blood. Within the words we now so calmly read, a heart once throbbed in pain; the man had learned in suffering what he here struggles to teach in song. The history of the

poem is larger than its story, it lives in an atmosphere vaster than the scenes it pourtrays. The man is a people, Israel speaks in Job, his problem is its, proposed, urged, followed through to a solution, that the faith of Israel, raised to a purer and higher form, might be preserved, and not perish before the calamities and confusions of a calamitous and confused time. This is not meant to take the individual significance out of the poem, but rather to emphasize it. The national reposes on the personal sense, the tragedy that was illustrated by the life of the individual was being played out on a more stupendous scale in the life of the people, with such shock and disturbance of spirit as threatened death to the faith in Jehovah. The problem of Job rose out of this conflict between the ideal and the actual alike in the single and the collective life, and the solution was necessary to the reconciliation of faith with history.

The primitive faith of Israel was, as we have seen,[1] simple, suited to a primitive and simple people. Jehovah was Israel's God, Israel was Jehovah's people; He was a righteous God, who rewarded the obedient and punished the disobedient, so righteous that His character and ways always agreed; suffering could not come undeserved, prosperity could not be where penalty was merited. This faith was expressed in the law which was at once the basis and the seal of Israel's freedom; each commandment had for the obedient a promised blessing, for the disobedient a threatened curse. This faith, too, the oldest prophets preached, labouring to persuade the people to faithfulness by disclosing their visions of Jehovah's justice and judg-

[1] See above, pp. 128, ff.

ments. The righteous were to be "like a tree planted by the rivers of water, that bringeth forth his fruit in his season; his leaf also shall not wither;" but the ungodly were to be "like the chaff which the wind driveth away."[1] While fearfulness was to surprise the hypocrite, he who walked righteously and spoke the truth was to dwell on high, safe in the stronghold of rocks, "his bread given unto him, and his water sure."[2]

The more rigorously this faith was held, the more distinctly prosperity became a proof of righteousness, calamity the evidence of ungodliness. Jehovah was active everywhere and in everything; He worked His will in heaven and on earth. Whatever happened, happened through Him and for Him, was either destined to be, or over-ruled in its being, for His ends. His was the will sovereign in history, which but executed or realized His purpose; in His hands were the lives of all flesh, and He so judged that life and lot, character and experience, merit and award, could not but correspond. History was Providence become visible, and Providence could not allow its outward and manifest sign to contradict its inward and real intention. So construed, the faith in Jehovah might well sustain the people in the period of their struggle towards order, might inspire and assure them in their season of conquest and grandeur under David and Solomon, might also strengthen the early prophets in Israel and Judah in their conflict against the idolatries and sins of kings and peoples; but it could not stand in all its stern and simple consistency in the presence of proud wickedness, victorious and invincible,

[1] Ps. i. 3, 4.   [2] Isa. xxxiii. 15, 16.

and godliness overwhelmed by disaster and defeat. Yet these belonged to the surest realities of experience and history. Idolatrous empires, like Egypt and Assyria, became mighty and rich, reaching out towards universal dominion, bringing by their mutual jealousies and collisions trouble to the people of God. The saintliest king that ever reigned in Judah perished in battle with the Egyptians, and with him the bravest attempt yet made to realize the prophetic ideal. The godliest men, too, like Jeremiah, sanctified from the womb, the appointed prophets of Jehovah, had seemed elect to suffering and reproach, hated by the priests, persecuted by the king, disbelieved and mocked by the people, forced to speak the word sent unto them to ears that would not hear, able to obey the God whose speakers they were only as they could bear insult and shame. And amid these fierce conflicts and confusions the most faithful appeared the most defenceless man. Wealth and power came to the violent and unscrupulous, loss and want to the obedient and unselfish. As men contemplated through the ancient faith the desolations and miseries of the time, the wasted cities, the fallen state, lives made burdensome and miserable through their very goodness, they knew not what to think, began to doubt, to despair, to speak as if God had forsaken or deceived them. Thus Jeremiah cries,[1] "Thou, Jehovah, hast deceived, and I let myself be deceived: Thou art stronger than I, and hast prevailed: I am in derision daily, every one mocketh me"; and when he feels the necessity to speak on the one hand and the impotence of his speech on the other, he exclaims[2] "Cursed be the day wherein

[1] Jer. xx. 7.   [2] Jer. xx. 14.

I was born: let not the day wherein my mother bare me be blest." In Psalm lxxiii. we have the reflection of a similar mental struggle, though it has the calmness that comes after victory rather than the pain and tension of conflict. The writer confesses that he had been "envious at the boastful," his steps had well-nigh slipped when he "saw the prosperity of the wicked." The teaching of history seemed this : "Behold those who prosper in the world, they are the ungodly : they increase in riches"; while the lesson of his own experience was, "Verily I have cleansed my heart in vain, and washed my hand in innocency. For all the day long have I been plagued, and chastened every morning."[1] The remembrance of his doubts is bitter; when they had possession of him he had been "brutish and ignorant," but all the same they show the mental conflict through which he had passed, the struggle it had been to him to reconcile his idea and belief of God with the realities of his own experience and the manifest facts of history.

Now, these contradictions of the ideal and the actual, this conflict of faith and experience, of what ought to have been with what was, caused the rise, not so much of one problem, as of a series of problems, of the deepest and most transforming order, within the religion of Israel. Their rise was a great moment, perhaps the greatest since Moses; marked, if not a revolution, a new development in the religion, the birth of a new spirit and new tendencies. It signified that the religion was awaking to the mystery of evil, to the meaning and the mission of suffering, was coming to perceive that a Deity who was simply the conscious

[1] Ps. lxxiii. 2, 3, 12–14.

and active righteousness of the universe was not a Deity sufficient for man's needs, or able to satisfy man's wants. It was indeed a transcendent moment when Israel began dimly to see that suffering was not simply punitive but also remedial, had another and nobler than the old retributive function, might, as suffering of the innocent, be needed to work out his perfection, and through it the greater good of the world. The monument of this transcendent moment is the Book of Job.

2. But we are not yet in a position to appreciate the full significance of the problem. We have looked at the outer conditions or historical occasions of its rise, but we must now attempt to determine another point, whether it rose in obedience to any inner or organic law of development in the religion; that is, whether it was a mere accident, or a matter of vital and natural growth. Well, then, there is one remarkable fact, and from it our new discussion may most fitly start: the experiences or realities which suggested the problem are common to all religions, but the problem is peculiar to the religion of Israel. Suffering is much the same everywhere, evil is most impartially distributed. The good has often been the most deeply afflicted man; the sorrows of virtue and the pleasures of vice have supplied moralists with a theme ever since moralists were. Pain and death early threw a gloom over the bright Hellenic spirit, and made it now wish the quiet of the grave, now sadly ask whence and why they had come. But the question was philosophical, not religious; the good man doomed to sorrow and loss, the bad man living in happiness and wealth, raised problems in speculation, not in theology. Zeus was himself a being

of imperfect morals; he could cheat, lie, lust, enjoyed a sin all the more that it was of the flagrant order, and was all the merrier on Olympus that decency was no virtue of the gods. Where Deity was so conceived, men did not feel any incongruity between the sight of innocence suffering, good smitten and afflicted, and their notion of the Divine. They thought too meanly of their god to think such a matter could concern him. He was almost one of themselves, had had his own troubles, domestic and other, had found it not all sunshine and joy up on Olympus; hatred and jealousy, storm and tempest had raged and ravined there before, and would rage and ravin there again. Greek religion made no serious matter with the mystery of evil, did not even feel it, and where the mystery is no burden to the religion, the religion can neither deepen nor lighten the mystery.

Buddhism, on the other hand, is a religion based on the recognition of sorrow, seems to thrill throughout with the consciousness of suffering. The four " Noble Truths" on which it is built are, the reality of sorrow, its cause, its cure, and the way to the cure. The idea that inspires the Buddha is pity, pity for the world's pain. There is no creature too mean for his compassion; the only being too high for it is the saint who has entered into his everlasting rest. But though Buddhism is so touched and possessed with the miseries of man, it does not know the problem that so troubled Israel. To it sorrow is of the very essence of life, inseparable from it; to be is to suffer. It knows a moral order but no moral Deity, a law that fulfils itself through action, that binds act and issue so indissolubly together that every moment of desire or sin must exact its consequent moment of pain. It does not feel the injustice or wrong of the innocent suffering, for to it there is no innocence; it is not conscious of the evil of guiltless sorrow, for to it all sorrow is guilty, all personal being evil. Pessimism is helpless in the face of the evil it bewails, simply accepts it as necessary to existence, abhors and tries to renounce existence that it may escape from evil.

Now, turn to the faith of Israel as it stood confronted by the sorrowful and calamitous facts of life. The faith said: "Jehovah is righteous; He rewards the good; He punishes the evil, and executes His judgments among men and nations." But the facts said: "Sorrow is often the portion of the good man, joy of the bad; calamity comes to the godly, prosperity to the wicked; the saintly man falls in the very hour of noblest obedience, while the impious celebrates his victory in the very moment of his most insolent defiance of God." And reason, as it compared the faith and the facts, grew restless and critical, then became bewildered and doubtful, and said, "These facts are real, veracious, obdurate, cannot, will not be denied, and do they not contradict the ancient faith? Can it be true that Jehovah rewards the godly when they are the most afflicted, punishes the wicked when they are the most prosperous? The facts we know, Jehovah we believe to be true; yet they do not agree. May there not be some truth concerning Jehovah our fathers did not know or have not told us? Unless there be, our faith must die in the presence of the facts."

Even as stated in this bare and imperfect form, we can see that the problem of evil was far more radical, as it were a mightier anomaly and perplexity to faith, in Israel than in either of the typical religions just named, and it was so because of Israel's stronger ethical spirit, the sublimer moral majesty of his God. The other religions did not feel evil like Israel; it did not stand in such complete antagonism to their idea of the Supreme, the Creator and Sovereign of man, nor in such absolute contradiction to their notion of what ought to be; and so they either reconciled themselves as best they could to the evil that was necessary, or invented means by which men could escape from it by escaping from existence. But it could not be so in Israel, his conception of God would not allow it. Evil was too abhorrent to the character of Jehovah to have any right to be; suffering too offensive to His nature, which loved good and delighted in mercy, to be permitted to reign by any supposed chance or necessity of being. His providence could not be reconciled to what was wrong in life, nor could He so accommodate His action to the manifest course of things as to be indifferent towards victorious guilt or injured goodness. To speak in the language of the schools, Israel's stern monotheism made a moral indifferentism on the one hand, and a pessimism on the other, alike impossible to him. But he could escape these only by a radical modification in his notion of Jehovah, and the relation in which Jehovah stood alike to sin and suffering. These had to be viewed, as it were, from the standpoint of eternity, looked at not simply as they concerned the individual man or nation, in the moment of historical being, but as they concerned the universe, the individual in his immortality, in what was needed to make him become the best possible moral being, most able to do the will and serve the ends of God. Israel perhaps, never quite consciously reached this standpoint, or saw all that even he might have seen from it; but from the moment he conceived the problem, and saw where the solution must lie, his face turned and his step moved towards the light. And as he approached it, Jehovah became quite other than He had been, did not cease to be the righteous Sovereign and rigorous Judge of men, but had these functions transmuted and glorified by becoming a just God and a Saviour, working through suffering redemption from sin. A religion of moral indifference can only leave man unpitied in his guilt, and helpless amid his misery; a religion of pessimism can only preach a gospel of moral cowardice and defeat, a victory of evil so transcendent as to vanquish the very love and reality of life; but a moral Theism so high and holy as the one we owe to Israel has in it the strength that prevails over sin, may start from the idea of a God who punishes the transgressor, but must end in the idea of a God gracious, redemptive, reigning in righteousness that He may subdue guilt, and save the guilty.

II.

The problem the conditions and necessities of whose rise have just been traced, is the problem of Job. That book is an attempt to resolve it, to find for Israel a new and grander line of development, a higher and truer conception of God and His ways. The attempt is significantly enough clothed in poetry; this most complex and mysterious of problems needs for its statement and solution the rich resources of the drama, touches man so deeply that we must look at it as it lives in his very life, moving him to mightiest passion, making him almost godlike in his pain. The book is the noblest poetry, its conception as a whole is magnificent, and is worked out in such "free flowing outlines; grand in its sincerity, in its simplicity, in its epic melody, and repose of reconcilement."[1] It is full of nature, all that was sublimest in the poet's home lives for us in his winged words. We dwell with him in the desert; see the horse, his neck clothed with thunder, the glory of his nostrils terrible, "pawing the valley, rejoicing in his strength, saying among the trumpets Ha, Ha! smelling the battle afar off, the thunder of the captains and the shouting." We stand with him beside the river of Egypt, see the reeds luxuriant on its banks, leviathan sporting in its waters, making "the deep to boil like a pot," "his heart as firm as stone, as hard as the nether millstone," esteeming "iron as straw and brass as rotten wood," in his strength "he laugheth at the shaking of a spear." We stand with him under the orient heaven, the great stars burning in radiant globes above us, feel "the sweet influences of the Pleiades," watch Orion binding his bands, and Arcturus leading forth his sons. Nature is there, vivid as when she stood before his imagination clothed in all her wonders and glorious majesty. But more wonderful than nature is man; he lives the home of that dreadful mystery which he must read or die, tormented by it, fighting it, vanquished by it, victorious over it. The persons that move on the stage, exhibit the action of the mystery in the most varied natures, show it face to face with

[1] Carlyle, "Lectures on Heroes," ii.

spirits purblind through convictions, stiff and formal, held for no reason but their fashion and their age, and with a spirit that can bear affliction but cannot bear untruth, that works its way through fierce vindication of self to deep humiliation before God. The solution of the mystery is expressed in no proposition, but remains in the history of a man set in his relations to God and the ends of God.

In handling his problem one thing is finely characteristic of the poet,—his choice of the persons and scene of his drama. His hero, if we may so call him, is no son of Abraham or child of the covenant; the action does not lie in the Holy Land. The man, the time, and the place are so detached from the historical entanglements, the disasters and confusions that had raised the problem, that it can be treated not simply as Israel's but as man's, untroubled by the passions of the moment or the limitations of the people. It no doubt incarnates the spirit of the time; in its speeches we can listen to its controversies, overhear the debates in the schools of the prophets, the councils of the elders, or the assemblies of the wise men; can feel the agony that possessed the nation, the pain that sat cold in many a heart. We can translate Eliphaz back into his prototype, a hard, traditional, doctrinaire Hebrew, who knows the advantage his years give him, who believes that experience is wisdom, and wisdom what he speaks; a man so used to men as to know how to make policy speak the language of the most gracious consideration, and so consciously prudent that he could more easily imagine God to have erred than himself to have been mistaken. Bildad is a sincere and well-meaning man, less learned in policies, with a touch of human kindliness in him, devoted to his theory, yet very anxious so to speak it as not to bear too hardly on his kind, so to preach his doctrine of judicial righteousness as to make it promise renewed prosperity to the sufferer; while Zophar, intenser, more impetuous, is prone to harsher words and the briefer speech that comes of stronger passions. Honest men all of them, after their sort, of limited views and imperfect sympathies, able to be cruel without meaning it, meaning only to speak the truth, to judge as they believe God does, as God would do were He as they are. These are men the poet in his hour of supreme sorrow may have met—most men who have suffered deeply have met them; but he so places his action that they become ideal and typical rather than historical and actual. They embody a theory of the Divine that stands unveracious and impotent before the saddest facts of a good man's experience; yet it is so embodied that men who hold the theory may feel its untruth without feeling personally affronted or censured. In these men there is judged and condemned every theology which would compel the man who holds it to be cruel to sorrow, able to be true to God only by being false to man.

The book, I have said, is a drama. It is prefaced by a prologue which states the problem, and closed with an epilogue which does not contain the solution: That must be sought for in the drama; in it the Divine oracle speaks. Yet it will become intelligible to us only as we approach it through the prologue; the words that describe the dramatic situation hint the solution of the very problem they state.

1. The Prologue. (Chapters i., ii.)

1. It opens with a description of the hero, the man in whom the mystery is embodied, and through whom it must be cleared up. He must be known that the problem may be understood. He is a "blameless man and upright, one that fears God and eschews evil."[1] With fine poetic insight and truth he is placed in a simple and free society; remote from ancient states or cities with their rigorous laws. In this society, which is yet settled and ordered, familiar with justice and judgment, Job lives an honoured and honourable and bountiful man, just to the guilty, generous to the weak, helpful to all who were in need, happy in his home, grateful to the God who had given him a lot so rich in manifold blessings. In the depth of his sorrow he looked sadly back to the days "when the friendship of God watched over his tent,"[2] and the picture he draws from his memory of this is like the ideal of the good man realized. So honoured is he that giddy youth feels reproved by his presence and in it respected age stands up; before him the princes are silent and the nobles hold their peace, the ear that hears his footstep blesses him, and the eye testifies to a hand ready to deliver the poor and the fatherless and him that had no helper. "The blessing of him that was ready to perish came upon me; and I caused the widow's heart to sing for joy. I put on righteousness, and it clothed me; my justice was as a robe and a diadem. I was eyes to the blind, and feet was I to the lame. I was a father to the poor; and the cause of him which I knew not I searched out."[3]

[1] i. 1.   [2] xxix. 4.   [3] xxix. 13-16.

So had he lived and been loved, a blameless man and an upright, approved of God, honoured of men.

And the good man was prosperous. The wealth a simple society most loves was his, a goodly number of sons and daughters, large substance in flocks and herds which were ever on the increase. Men said: "His prosperity is of God," and what they said he believed. His home and children were consecrated by prayer and burnt offerings; the father was, as the Divine ordinance intended, also the priest of the family, and the joys of the household were sanctified by its faith. In the presence of this good man men lived the better, trusted God the more that Job was so prosperous. He seemed to be a living proof of Providence. So fine a union of godliness and well-being convinced the gainsayers, made evident to every one that a God lived who rewarded every man according to his works.

2. But now the scene changes. We are taken into the presence of the Most High. Satan is there, responsible still, forced, in spite of his rebellion, to give an account of himself and his ways to God. He is asked, "Whence comest thou?" and answers, "From going to and fro in the earth, and walking up and down in it."[1] A random being without rational aims, intent on mischief, watchful of his opportunities, finding everywhere so much of the evil he loves as to have come to the conclusion that the earth is more his than God's. But now here is a fact quite fatal to his conclusion: Job, the blameless man and upright, who fears God and eschews evil. In him Satan has no part or lot, he is altogether and absolutely God's. But Satan is cunning and resourceful enough, and promptly answers, "Doth Job fear God for nought?"[2] No, not

[1] i. 7.   [2] i. 9.

he. Thou hast made him a prosperous man, blessed him with abundance of goods. But put forth Thine hand now and touch all that he hath, and see if he will not bid Thee good-bye to Thy face!" But so perfect is the Divine trust of Job that God's answer is, " Touch not his life, but do with his goods as you will, and so try whether your theory or My judgment be the truth."[1]

The scene then changes to earth, to the house and family of Job, where Satan has his will. The Sabeans carry off his herds of cattle, fire from heaven burns up his flocks of sheep, the Chaldeans make booty of his camels, and a great wind from the wilderness smites the house where his sons and daughters are feasting, and all perish in the ruins. In a moment his wealth vanishes, but the only words the loss can extort from him are words of resignation and reverence: "Naked came I out of my mother's womb, and naked shall I return thither: Jehovah gave, and Jehovah hath taken away; blessed be the name of Jehovah."[2] So far Satan's theory is broken against the facts.

The scene again changes to heaven, where Satan once more appears among the sons of God, and, unabashed, repeats his old answer to the old question.[3] But here is Job more perfect than before, holding fast his integrity though despoiled of his goods. Satan, however, resourceful still, is ready with his retort; "Thou hast spared his health, smite it now, make his existence loathsome, and he will have none of Thee!" The answer is, "Behold now he is in thine hand; only save his life." And so Satan smites Job with "sore boils from the sole of his foot to his crown." Life

[1] i. 12.   [2] i. 21.   [3] ii. 1 ff.

seems now too miserable to be desirable, and his wife, agreeing with Satan, thinks he had better "say farewell to God and die." But the man, still blameless and upright, reproves her as one who speaks the language of the ungodly. "What? shall we receive good at the hand of God, and shall we not receive evil?" And so the prologue ends, showing Job sitting patient in his grief, his three friends sitting silent around, a man who has not sinned with his lips.

3. Now, let us look at the problem as stated in the prologue, and almost solved in the stating. The good man is represented as dear to God, most precious in His sight. God has pleasure in him, knows his worship to be real, his obedience to be sincere and true. Evil may be potent in many, but it has no place in Job; religion may be in others disguised selfishness, in him it is the spontaneous service of the holiest will. While he lives men know that Satan is no god, that the best lives are the lives Jehovah inspires, that the elect of God are the salt of the earth. Now this approval of Jehovah the poet starts from and never forgets; it is to be remembered throughout the whole action of the drama, even where misery seems to touch the faith and quench the reverence of the sufferer. God loves him the more that he has to struggle with an anguish so awfully embittered by a false theology, that he has to bear his sorrow in the face of cruel accusations made by good men who act as if they were judges deputed of God. Honest men who speak falsely of God must always deeply afflict those who truly know Him, most of all when those they speak to are deep in the sufferings that teach obedience. But even then the sympathy of God is deepest; He most loves the man He

tries when those who claim to be His people ply the man with theories that are nearer the doctrine of Satan than the comfort and truth of God.

That doctrine is here finely but briefly stated: "Doth Job fear God for nought?" This stands in remarkable, though far from complete, affinity to the theory of the three friends who appear in the drama. It is their notion of Providence, fitly stripped of its ethical elements, realized in the sphere of religion. If the ultimate truth as to the ways of God be as they state it, then Satan is in the right, religion is service for profit, and the most profitable of services. If the man who best obeys God enjoys the amplest prosperity, then the reward God gives is a motive man may well regard, and worship in view of what he gets. Job does not reach the doctrine of God, though he feels after it and catches sight of it as from afar; but the friends expound, though in most reverent, authoritative and splendid speech, the doctrine here placed in antithesis to the Divine. For as formulated by Satan it stands before us naked and unmasked, and here is what it means: "You think Job perfect, upright, sincere, one who serves God spontaneously, out of love and deepest reverence for truth. There you are altogether wrong; were I God he would serve me as zealously; could I reward as handsomely, his worship of me would be as devoted and unwearied. He fears you because you are the Almighty; were I the stronger and able to give larger rewards, he would fear me instead."

The theory of Providence that may be, however roughly, translated into such a doctrine of religion may be fitly described as devilish rather than Divine. In stating his problem then, the author accentuates the antithesis of good and evil, the antagonism of God and Satan. God loves the man, means and determines his good; Satan does not love the man, distrusts, with the low cunning of the bad, his integrity, means and plots his ill. The beliefs represented in these scenes and interviews are of the noblest and truest order. Good is of God, and good only; evil exists by His permission, but comes from other wills than His, is allowed, for to prevent it He will not uncreate His own creation, but never so allowed as to take the universe or any of its units out of His control; even where evil reigns He so rules as to compel it to praise Him. If He permits evil to come to a good man in the only form in which it can come to him—calamity, loss, ruin, disease, the deepest of temporal sorrows aggravated by the cruelest of human wrongs, use of the name of God to create doubt of the Divine truth, despair of the Divine goodness—He does so in order that He may make it a condition and means of higher good alike to the man and men. Satan has not absolute power over Job, may take away his goods and his health, but not his life, may try but not destroy him. Evil may cause suffering, but cannot compel disobedience; obedience amid suffering is the highest obedience possible. If the good suffer, it is that they may be tried; and the tried are the purified. But there is a higher standpoint still; a good man made better improves all men, raises the moral tone and temper of the world. It is good for Satan to find out that his doctrine is false, that the good man is better and stronger than he thought, that a devil turned almighty were no God, no being fit for a true man's love and worship; and let us say that even he, discovering so much, will be the better for the discovery. It is well indeed that the devil be disillusioned; if it does not improve him, it will save the world some trouble and much unhappiness. Good men, too, of the narrow and uncharitable order, more pleased to exercise judgment than show mercy, may be made to see by a history like Job's that God's ways are larger than their thoughts. But issues like these evoke new elements in the notion, elements that seem to unite the sorrow of the good to the salvation of the world, saying in a dumb way, like a truth just struggling into articulate speech—"The good man must suffer that he may become the best man possible to him, and what makes him the best man he can be makes him of greatest service to humanity, one who helps to redeem it from ignorance and sin to truth and God."

If now in the light of these discussions we attempt to formulate the problem of the prologue, which is the problem of Job, we shall find it run somewhat thus: Grant that in a world which a righteous God governs good men suffer much, the best men most of all, may not this suffering be due to depraved wills, which, while depraved, are yet, as wills, free and responsible, able to act in opposition or disobedience to God; and may they not be allowed, in the Divine righteousness, so to act in order that the good man may be made better, more fitted to do the beneficent will of God, to lessen the error, misery, and sin of the world, to create the conditions of greater holiness on earth and happiness in heaven? The problem so stated carries with it a suggestion of the conclusion, reposes on a richer and more gracious conception of God, implies higher and wider ideas of Providence, man, and sin than had hitherto reigned in Israel. But even as so construed it has only helped us to approach the drama from the standpoint of the author. We are now in a position to read and interpret it with his problem, and the critical moment, with all its conflicts and issues, when it was conceived and formulated, standing clear before our minds.

2. The Drama.

It extends from chap. iii. to chap. xlii. 6, out of which we may omit the speeches of Elihu, chaps. xxxii. to xxxvii. Chaps. iii. to xxxi. are occupied with the dialogue or speeches of Job and his three friends. Chaps. xxxviii. to xli., contain the answer of God to Job's repeated demand that He show and declare Himself. Chap. xlii. 1–6, explains the effect of the Divine interposition on Job, which ends the drama, the verses that follow forming the epilogue. In the speeches of the friends the ancient or traditional view of Providence is expounded. In the speeches of Job its utter inapplicability to his case and consequent unveracity is affirmed, while the conditions necessary to a truer doctrine are made manifest. In the response or speech of God, the relation of God to His works and His works to God is declared in order that Job may be forced to interpret his own particular case through the universal ways of Providence, and the conclusion shows us Job humbled and penitent by the speech and vision of God.

In the dialogue or dialectical speeches the poet does not mean us to regard the friends as altogether wrong or Job as altogether right. Their general doctrine was true, but their particular application false; they erred not so much in principle as in interpretation, their idea of God as the righteous was veracious enough, but their conception of righteousness was too simply judicial or penal, and as a consequence too narrow and violent to allow it to be the exclusive or regnant attribute of the Providence that governs man. The author recognises and emphasizes the truth they have to teach by the splendid way in which they are made to expound and illustrate their doctrine, but he enforces and accentuates the error of their conception or interpretation by making manifest their frightful injustice to Job, an injustice due not at all to the disposition of the men, but altogether to their theory. On the other hand, Job was right in so stoutly maintaining his innocence, in upholding the judgment of his conscience against their interpretation and application of their doctrine, in appealing for vindication and deliverance from their notions of God to God Himself; but he was wrong in not allowing his faith in God to illumine his sufferings, to grow into the confidence that accepted sorrow as the condition or means of higher good. Yet we must not judge the sufferer too harshly. It was necessary to the poet's design that he should be what he is; only so could he be used to illustrate and reveal the higher truth. And he does not stand alone; he is here seen not simply afflicted of God, but also of his friends. The man who is a saint under the hand of God easily becomes a sinner under the tongue of man, and we must not regard indignation against the injustice of the one as anger against the justice of the other. The man's impatience with his friends might almost be construed as a note of saintliness; it was his haste to escape out of their unveracities into the truth of God. But a glance at the speeches will help us somewhat better to understand how the poet works out his solution of the problem.

1. The speeches of the friends. Eliphaz speaks three times—chaps. iv.–v., xv., xxii. So does Bildad—chaps. viii., xviii., xxv.; but Zophar only twice—xi., xx. These men are types, representatives of the traditional theology, persuaded that they speak the wisdom of the ages, very conscious of their own wisdom in speaking it. So Bildad appeals to the former age, and bids Job "attend to that which their fathers have searched out:"[1] while Eliphaz in his second speech reproves Job for "uttering iniquity" and using "the tongue of the crafty," and in the familiar manner of his kind reminds him, "with us are both the grey-headed and very aged men,"[2] quoting, in opposition to the novel and alarming doctrine of the sufferer, the things "which wise men have told from their fathers and have not hid."[3] The view they enforce is simply the old doctrine of the judicial righteousness: suffering is penalty and implies sin, "the wicked man travaileth with pain all his days." Where pain is, men may either argue up to the judgment of God or down to the wickedness of the man. And this is what the friends do as regards Job, at first considerately, with all the kindliness possible to an admonitory spirit doing the disagreeably agreeable duty of candid faithfulness, but later, when provoked by his scornful attitude and words, with almost brutal bluntness. Eliphaz opens with what is meant to be a conciliatory

[1] viii. 8.   [2] xv. 10.   [3] xv. 18.

and sympathetic speech, intended to persuade Job to repentance and to console him with the prospect of renewed prosperity. The man whom God correcteth is happy, and so he is not to despise the chastening of the Almighty.[1] If he does not, all will yet be well, and he shall come to his grave "like as a shock of corn cometh in in his season." But Job refuses alike the comfort and the insinuation, affirms at once his despair and his integrity, and so Bildad uses greater plainness of speech. With the assurance of one deep in the Divine counsels, he asks: "Doth God pervert judgment? or doth the Almighty pervert justice?" and pledges Providence to his doctrine in this fashion: "If thou art pure and upright, surely now He will awake for thee, and make the habitation of thy righteousness prosperous."[2] Job's growing impenitence and insolence under their anxious exhortations exasperates Zophar, who asks, "Should men be silent at this babbling? and when thou mockest, shall no man make thee ashamed? For thou hast said, My doctrine is pure, and I am clean in Thine eyes. But oh that God would speak, and open His lips against thee."[3] And so the speeches as they proceed gather in intensity of passion and blame: the more Job protests his innocence, and appeals to God to vindicate and save him, the stronger become their charges, the more naked their accusations of guilt, till even Eliphaz declares his wickedness great and his iniquities infinite.[4] The end is characteristic. Job out-argues the men, they are silenced, but not convinced; they have not converted him, have not even convicted him of sin, and so they

---

[1] v. 17.   [2] viii. 3, 6.   [3] xi. 3-5.   [4] xxii. 5-11.

will leave him to his conscience and their doctrine, stated in the grandest and most imposing form the most eloquent of them can command,—

> " Dominion and fear are with Him,
> He maketh peace in His high places!
> Is there any number of His armies?
> And whom doth not His light surpass,
> How then can man be righteous before God?
> Or how can one born of woman be clean?
> Behold even the moon,—it shineth not,
> Yea, the stars are not pure in His sight.
> How much less man, a worm?
> And the son of man, a worm?"[1]

Altogether true is this speech of Bildad, but what truth, what special relevance had it for Job? The noblest expression yet given to the righteousness of God is turned into utter falsehood, if used to torment or wrong an innocent man.

2. The speeches of Job. There are three points of view from which these speeches need to be studied. (i.) The sufferer lying stunned, bewildered, shocked under the blows so suddenly and successively dealt by what he believes to be the hand of God. (ii.) The sufferer preached at, admonished and warned by men he knew to be in no sense his superiors, if his equals, in honour and truth, judged by them in the name of God according to a doctrine that he knew did him most grievous wrong. (iii.) The experience and results worked in the sufferer by these combined influences, the change in his faith and attitude to God, the conviction that God must have something to say to him which the old theology had not said, that there must be truths as to God and man which tradition did not

---

[1] xxv. 2-6.

know, and which if they were to be known at all God Himself must now make known. These points of view often blend in a way that only a minute analysis and comparative study of all the speeches would enable us to distinguish, but so far as we can here hold them distinct they give a threefold signification to the words of Job,—a human, which shows the action of heavy and most inexplicable sorrow or suffering on the spirit of the man it had surprised; a polemical, which shows the insufficiency of a traditional but, though true, partial and preparatory theology; and a religious, which brings out the epoch the speeches mark in the history of religion, the moment when the deepened perplexities and needs of man required and received a new revelation of God. On these points our words must be few, the limits of the discussion forbidding any attempt to exhibit their subtle interaction, especially as so darkly conditioned and intensified by the unwise words of the friends.

i. The man in the hands of his sorrow, a surprised and bewildered sufferer. In this aspect the opening speech[1] exhibits him, and it underlies all the others. The seven days of silence had been days of desolation, during which memory and imagination had alike been active. The ruins of his homestead lay round him, the graves of his children were near, the presence of unsympathetic friends made his loneliness deeper. There is nothing so sensitive as a soul in trouble; it does not need speech to tell what the men about it think or how they feel, it knows by an intuition that is almost like the omniscience of God. Then, too, thought had been active in those

[1] Chap. iii.

silent days. The man believed as did his neighbours, conceived God as they did, held Him to be the righteous sovereign, who made the home of the good happy and the habitations of the wicked desolate. He was no wicked man, yet the most awful desolation had come upon him and his house. How then could God be what men had thought Him? What kind of God could He be to permit or take pleasure in ruin like this? So to trouble of heart deepest trouble of soul was added, questionings as to why God had done those things, as to whether the Being who had done them could be a God. Doubt in sorrow is doubt in its deadliest form, bidding consolation depart, despair come, and mocking at the weakness that would wrestle with an Eternal which is not good. So at length the man rose to pour out his spirit in speech, hopeful that comfort might come to him in the gentle and tender ways love can use to soothe sorrow The agony of his soul grew in the presence of the words that described it, but it was too intense to touch the friends; they heard through the medium of their theory, and understood not the man's sorrow because they thought of the man's sin. Their attitude deepened his misery; where consolation was expected only irrelevant and unmerited reproof was found. There is no finer image in poetry than the one Job used to express his disappointments.[1] His friends had been like the torrent beds of the desert, in winter blackish with ice, upon them the snow hideth itself, but in the summer heat ice and snow vanish, the beds are dry and hot, the caravans turn aside for water and perish. " The troops of Tema looked, the companies of Sheba

[1] vi. 15-20.

waited for them. They were confounded because they had hoped; they came hither, and were ashamed." The sufferer denied sympathy where he had hoped to receive it, is indeed like the caravan in the dried torrent's bed, come to find water, but finding only death. Whither shall the man uncomforted by human love now turn? He could not get to God, his friends and their theology stood full in the way. With most wonderful sympathy and insight, the poet exhibits the man bewildered by sorrow, appealing, after the fiercest reproaches, for comfort, for pity, to the friends, who were the more pitiless that they meant to be faithful and kind. He recalls the old happy days, consoles himself with the recollection of what he had been and done. He now abhors himself, and now glories in his integrity; now wishes to die, and again exults in the hope of an immortal life. The man's words are often inconsistent, but the man himself is only the truer to his ideal, the soul in the hands of a sorrow mightier than it can bear, made all the mightier by the contradiction in which its causes stand to the faith by which the soul had lived. There is no grief so great as grief like this, which can find no consolation in the thought of God or the sympathies of man.

ii. The man in the hands of his friends and their doctrine, an uncomforted and wounded sufferer. One point already noticed must here be accentuated. Job did not think of God after the manner of the prologue; on the contrary, he and his friends conceived God alike. His deepest trouble comes from this notion; his history is but his struggle to escape from it. What had been to his spirit highest truth, is broken into fragments against the hard facts of his own experience. While he is feeling all the misery and despair this dissolution of faith brings, his friends make the old belief a deep and agonizing offence to his conscience, a crime against his conscious integrity. They cannot comfort him, for his sorrows are in their eyes the chastenings or judgments of God, repentance, not consolation, is what he needs. To be told that he suffers for his sin, when he knows no sin that he suffers for, is to be confounded and wounded in the sorest part. The men could not say, for they could not think, otherwise, their notion of God being what it was;—suffering was punitive, retributive, impossible without sin, necessary where sin existed. The application of this theory to himself and his case afflicted Job; its presentation in the eloquent and reasoned speeches of the men from whom he had expected consolation, made it a more palpable and terrible thing than it had seemed while floating as it were bodiless in his own confused and troubled consciousness. It stood before him the explanation of his calamities, yet the contradiction of all he knew himself to be. As he sat under its shadow he was now filled with despair at his intolerable wrongs, now roused to anger against masterful injustice. Commentators say, "Job is guilty of defying the Divine Majesty, using the language of insult or reproach to God," and they say not well. The God he defies or reproves is the God of the traditional theory—the Being his friends use as an instrument of injustice or torture, not the God of the truth and his conscience. With this Being or theory he grapples in the strength of despair, with the unceremonious energy of a man who has to conquer or die. He seizes the principle of his friends, but inverts their argument thus: He is guiltless, can he be punished of God?[1] Can God be righteous in punishing him?[2] Nay, as innocent and mocked, an upright man laughed to scorn, he will challenge God to deal justly by him, to appear and vindicate him against his accusers. This is what he has a right to expect, yea, to demand, if God be what these men say. The appeal is vain, God is silent, but the silence is made to prove not the unfaithfulness of God, but the falsity of the doctrine on which the appeal had been based. What they have spoken is not the truth, Providence does not act as they have said, all human life denies it. The wicked do live and are mighty in power, their houses are safe from fear, they spend their days in wealth.[3] Job, when forced to face the theory, does it bravely, so confronts it with reality as to condemn it utterly and reduce its spokesmen to silence. Here he is splendidly victorious; to achieve this victory the poet conceived him. His sufferings and his speeches, if they do nothing else, do this, prove the untruth of the ancient doctrine, and so prepare the way for another and higher, a new stage in the history of revelation, a new development in religion.

iii. The change worked by his sorrows and struggles in the faith and spirit of Job. Here the man is thoroughly typical; his sorrows open his soul to God, so enlarge his spirit that he must receive a new vision of the Eternal to live. But in being prepared for the vision he is grandly instructed, made to see the conditions on which alone his problem can be solved. His notions of man and God become sublimer. He sees that if God is to be justified His Providence must

---

[1] xii. 2; xiii. 22. [2] xix. 6-8. [3] xxi. 7-15.

have an immenser range than earth and time can supply. If man be mortal, no true idea of the Divine righteousness is possible; the immortality of man is implied in the sovereignty of the living God. His Providence viewed within the limits of time is incapable of vindication, within the freedom of its own eternity is justified in all its ways and works. And so here the mouth of the sufferer speaks such words of immortal hope as had not been heard in Israel before: with the new doctrine of Providence rises a new doctrine of Man, bringing such visions of the future as had never yet cheered his spirit. The old idea of the judicial righteousness so magnified time that eternity died before it; the idea which was dawning on Job lifted man into God's eternity, and brightened his hour of deepest gloom with the promise of a nightless day. This hope had come to him like a sudden glad surprise, and he asked—"If a man die, shall he live again?"[1] and fearing to answer all at once, he allowed the hope to grow in silence into a glorious certainty, when it stood forth clothed in fitting speech: "But I know that my Redeemer liveth, and afterwards He shall arise upon the dust; and after this my skin hath been destroyed, without my flesh shall I see God, whom I shall see for myself, and mine eyes shall behold, and not as a stranger; my reins within me are consumed [with desire]."[2] Here the two things are indissolubly blended, the new idea of God and the new idea of man. God is the Redeemer, the man is to be redeemed. Precious in the sight of God is the life of His saint, too precious to be lost in death. The saint shall live and see God, and in the vision of Him be justified and satisfied.

[1] xiv. 14; cf. xvi. 18, 19.   [2] xix. 25-27.

3. The speeches of God. So soon as Job is prepared to hear, God speaks; the revelation comes at the right moment. The man has learned through the things he has suffered. His faith in the ancient theory is dead, he has ceased to judge God according to it. A dim hope has been growing within him into a fixed conviction. This little and troubled life lies in the bosom of eternity, and God acts as one who has eternity before Him, afflicts the righteous mortal that He may redeem him to a more glorious immortality. Is this conviction justified? The more the inequalities, the misjudgments of life, the relations of good and evil in time are looked at, the more necessary does it seem to faith; without it how can belief in the righteousness of the Eternal live? And so with a humbler spirit, and out of deeper necessities Job cries, "Oh that One would hear me! Behold, there is my witness, let the Almighty answer me!"[1] And the Almighty does answer him, Jehovah speaks out of the whirlwind. Here everything is significant, the speeches are a wonderland of poetry and truth. The whirlwind declares the majesty of the Speaker, the might and multitude of the forces He has to control. Job at the outset is lifted to an altitude higher than he had yet dreamed of; his problem is not to be solved in and through himself, even with immortality assured; the universe enters into it. God cannot reign as if the one Sovereign had but one subject; He must deal with the individual as part of a complex whole, yet of a whole that can be governed in wisdom only as the individuals are justly and graciously handled. This is the point the opening of the

[1] xxxi. 35.

speeches emphasizes. Job has interrogated God; God will now interrogate Job. "Who is this that darkeneth counsel by words without knowledge?"[1] The calamities that so perplex, the sufferings that have worked so many sorrows are not accidents; there is a Divine purpose in them. What is confusion to Job is order to God; counsel is in it and wisdom too vast to be comprehended, but true enough to be trusted. For what is the range of man's vision compared with God's? "Where wast thou when I laid the foundations of the earth? declare, if thou hast understanding."[2] Then the story of creation and Providence is told with a stateliness and splendour of imagery that has never been paralleled. Everywhere God acts, every moment He is active. In the eternity behind He laid the corner-stone of the earth, while "the morning stars sang together, and all the sons of God shouted for joy." He shut up the sea with doors, made the cloud its garment and thick darkness its swaddling-band. He has made the morning, and caused the dayspring to know his place. He is the Father of the rain and has begotten the drops of dew. He has bound the stars to their courses, and has sent the lightnings that they may go and say unto man, Here we are. And while His energies are engaged with the mightiest things He does not forget the least, provides for the raven his food, watches "the wild goats of the rock," "the wild ass" of the desert, "the ostrich, which leaveth her eggs in the earth and warmeth them in the dust," the horse that "mocketh at fear and is not affrighted, neither turneth he back from the sword." By His wisdom the hawk

[1] xxxviii. 2.   [2] xxxviii. 2, 4.

flies, and at His command the eagle mounts up and makes his nest on high. And as the sphere of the Divine action is thus made to open into infinity, the Speaker suddenly pauses to ask, "Will the upbraider contend with the Almighty? he that called God to account, let him answer." And Job replies, "Behold, I am vile; what shall I answer Thee? I will lay mine hand upon my mouth. Once have I spoken; but I will not answer (again): yea, twice; but I will proceed no further."[1]

In the second speech even a higher strain is reached. Job is to "gird up his loins like a man."[2] Is he to condemn God that he himself may be righteous? But only a God could judge God, Divine wisdom alone could comprehend and appraise the wisdom of the Divine. Then with a most daring yet magnificent stroke of imagination the poet says: Become in thought God; "deck thyself now with majesty and excellency, and array thyself with glory and beauty." So clothed, use all thy energies to abase the proud and bring the evil to the dust. In that endeavour God will praise thee, for He knows what it is to be God;[3] yet one who only knows what it is to be man judges Him who is God alone! The speech then breaks into a marvellous description of the mighty creatures of the Nile, chiefest of the works of God, the contemplation of which completes the instruction, humbling the sufferer into resignation, yet raising him to a more perfect faith. He confesses: "I have uttered that I understood not, things too wonderful for me which I knew not." He had judged wrongly because he had judged in ignorance. The traditional theory had blinded him;

---

[1] xl. 2-5.   [2] xl. 7.   [3] xl. 10-14.

he had been unable to see God for the doctrines of men. " I had heard of Thee by the hearing of the ear," and so had misjudged; " but now mine eye seeth Thee; therefore I revoke and repent in dust and ashes." [1]

4. Now what is the precise bearing of these speeches on the problem of the book ? What contribution do they make to its solution ? The speeches of Job and his friends prove the insufficiency of the old theory, its inadequacy as a theology of Providence, a true mirror of the ways of God to men. In a world like ours mere penal justice were highest injustice; in view of a case like Job's it cannot be said to be. But this destructive criticism does not stand alone; through it shine beams of sublimer truths bright with the promise of golden hopes. God appears to the afflicted saint as his Redeemer, but to conceive God so is to conceive man immortal. If He redeems man it is an eternal work, begun here perhaps, but perfected under nobler conditions than are here possible. But this, though it comforts, does not satisfy. That the saint is to be happy through eternity, is by itself no reason why he should be miserable in time; nay, it is a reason to the contrary, for if God can make him happy *there*, why not also *here* ? If the man is good in both, why not blessed in both ? The answer comes in the Divine speeches, indirectly indeed, but distinctly. They change the point of view, look at the individual from the standpoint of the universal, at man with the eyes of God. Man is not the universe, and cannot judge Providence as if he were. He belongs to a system immense, complex, infinite, and the Providence that

[1] xlii. 2-6.

does best for the whole will also do best for the parts. Now these speeches bid us consider God's action in the universe. It is His, built by Him from the foundation upwards, its order, its ceaseless activities and inexhaustible energies, its creatures, its manifold forethoughtfulness, its majesty and glorious beauty. And can the God who conceived, created and controls all be forgetful of man, have for him no place, no care, no thought? If into the life of a good man, affliction and ruin come, what do these speeches teach him to say? "God loves order; in the order He loves my sufferings have a function and a work. I may not see the end, may not love the means, but God is Himself the pledge that through these painful means ends most worthy of Him and most blessed for me shall be realized!"

These speeches, then, mark the moment when Israel became conscious of the meaning of God for the universe and of the universe for God. They show that the standpoint of the law has been transcended, that God is conceived not simply as Israel's, but as man's, related to the unit because He seeks through the unit to work out the harmony and completeness of the whole. These speeches are indeed a revelation and interpretation through the universe of what we may call the universalities—of knowledge and will, purpose and action—in God. Where they were comprehended and believed, no man could think of himself as isolated either from or for the care of Providence, no people could consider itself the alone loved of God. But their full significance is not yet apparent; the prologue and the speeches must be looked at together as supplemental and mutually interpretive. In the prologue evil is not of God, it is of Satan, the will that dare to stand and act in opposition to the Divine: in the speeches order and beauty and beneficence are of God, all indeed that makes earth to man majestic, glorious, good. In the prologue God loves the perfect man, has special pleasure in him, watches over him; does not, through very love, spare him pain and sorrow: in the speeches God works in all things and through all creatures, in each according to its kind, yet so as by perfecting the individual to complete and manifest the perfection of the whole. If then we interpret the prologue and the speeches through each other, here are the truths we reach:—The God who loves the order of nature loves the good of man, nature expresses His will, manifests His purpose, and the order He has there achieved He intends man to attain. Man's suffering has a place in God's purpose, is a means to His end. He permits it as a condition of perfection; it comes not because God loves man's sorrow, but because He seeks man's good. Through it He overcomes the disorder which Satan personifies, teaches man obedience, and brings him, a clarified and perfected soul, into the harmony He loves.

III.

It is not easy within our limits to make the full meaning alike of the problem and the solution apparent; but we may say that while the problem was peculiar to Israel the solution was to be of transcendent value both for man and religion. It was not simply an attempt to reconcile the existence of evil with the sovereignty and goodness of God, but also a prophecy of the way in which evil was to be vanquished of the way in which it was to be made an occasion for the manifestation of the Fatherhood of God and the Sonship of Man. It declared that the moral laws of the universe were in the hands of a God who did not reign simply to punish, but to save; that His providence was no mere judicial rule, but a method of discipline, a mode in which remedial and redemptive moral energies worked. It reposed on or rose out of the deep conviction that a moral Deity, a God who loved in an equal degree man and righteousness, could not allow His universe to lie under the shadow and the reproach of sin, and it strenuously laboured to express the belief that the only way in which the shadow could be lifted and the reproach removed was through the painful discipline and victorious obedience of the good man, the man made good by the vision of God, which made him the efficient agent of the Divine will, the highest organ of Divine truth. In the Book of Job the seer struggles towards the only conception of God which has hope for the universe, a conception which, reached, may leave to man many a conflict with evil, but can never leave man to despair.

1. Perhaps the significance of the solution cannot be better indicated than by returning to the contrast of Israel with Greece and India. Greek religion, we have seen,[1] did not feel evil an offence to its notion of Zeus, or Buddhism to its idea of Karma, and so the problem that so troubled Israel they did not know. But to be without the burden of the problem was to be without the joy and hope of the solution; was to allow evil to become too integral a part of the world and its history to be capable of defeat and expulsion.

[1] Ante, pp. 150-152.

The Greek mind, indeed, was too sane and too moral, loved order and freedom and beauty too well, to stand silent and submissive before the awful questions as to crime and its penalties, guilt and its curse; but the form in which they came to it, and the way in which it strove to handle and answer them were characteristic. These questions were the problems of Greek poetry, the dark mysteries that created and inspired Greek tragedy. The Greek drama is the drama of guilt and its inexorable curse, as pitiless to the unconscious as to the conscious sinner, to the man who inherits the crime as to the man who entailed it. The tragic Nemesis has no mercies, is insatiable, pursues with equal and unrelenting passion an adulterous Klutemnestra, whose hands are red with a husband's blood, and a son so noble as Orestes, and a daughter so fair and saintly as Electra, who have been driven to exact vengeance for the double crime. Purification may come, Orestes may by the vote of Pallas escape the Eumenides of his mother, but all the same, the drama exhibits the action of tragic retribution, hardly able to distinguish between acts of awful crime and splendid atonement. And this way of handling its problem Greek poetry owed to Greek religion. It did not conceive the sovereignty of the universe as resting in the hands of a moral deity, but as exercised by an impersonal law or fate which, altogether punitive, crushed the person who dared to violate its order. Under this law Zeus stood as well as man, over both it reigned rigorous and inflexible, almighty to punish, impotent to save. The unequal struggle of will and destiny, man and fate, was the story of the Greek drama, and its moral: Keep within the order of nature, or her laws will break you without mercy. But the story and moral of Job were altogether different. It said: All suffering is not penalty, there may be pain where there has been no crime, yet suffering comes to man through sin. In a world where good and evil live and contend, the good must suffer through the evil, and always in proportion to their goodness. But God is on the side of the right, the mightiest moral energies in the universe are righteous. The blameless man who suffers is a man God is using for the conquest of evil; it can only be overcome through obedience, and obedience is the path of most painful endeavour and achievement. He who follows it does the will that rules for righteousness, and must prevail.

The attitude of Buddhism to suffering was in harmony with its doctrine :—existence is sorrow, misery is inseparable from life. It could only say: "Bear your sorrow in patience, what you complain of is the common lot. Being is hateful: seek to escape from it into Nirvana, where the lamp of life is finally blown out." This is all the consolation, all the direction Buddhism has to give; its comfort is so dismal that the Western mind may well be forgiven if it sees in it only the apotheosis of *ennui*. Its very sweetest stories are intended to make us feel the bitterness of life. One of the finest of Buddha's parables is told of Kisagotami, a young and beautiful woman, a happy wife and mother. Her child died; carrying it in her bosom she went forth to seek some one who might restore it. She came to the Buddha and said: "Lord and master, do you know any medicine that will be good for my child?" "Yes," he said, "bring me a mustard seed from some house where no son or husband or parent or slave has died." She sought patiently from house to house, found seeds enough, but found everywhere death, and returned sadly to the Buddha to speak and hear words that have been finely paraphrased thus : [1]

> "'Ah, sir! I could not find a single house
> Where there was mustard-seed and none had died!
> Therefore I left my child,—who would not suck
> Nor smile,—beneath the wild-vines by the stream,
> To seek thy face and kiss thy feet, and pray
> Where I might find this seed and find no death,
> If now, indeed, my baby be not dead,
> As I do fear, and as they said to me.'
>
> "'My sister! thou hast found,' the master said,
> 'Searching for what none finds,—that bitter balm
> I had to give thee. He thou lovedst slept
> Dead on thy bosom yesterday: to-day
> Thou know'st the whole wide world weeps with thy woe:
> The grief which all hearts share grows less for one.
> Lo! I would pour my blood if it could stay
> Thy tears and win the secret of that curse
> Which makes sweet love our anguish, and which drives
> O'er flowers and pastures to the sacrifice,—
> As these dumb beasts are driven,—men their lords.
> I seek that secret: bury thou thy child!'"

But now compare with this "bitter balm" the consolation of Job, its strong belief in life as good, in God as the beneficent and righteous will that gives order and law to the world, discipline and progress to man; its profound conviction that evil is hateful, a thing alien to being, contrary to the mind of Him who made the beginning, determines the ends, and controls the forces of the universe. Buddhism comforts man amid evil by telling him that evil is universal—" the whole wide

[1] Edwin Arnold, "Light of Asia," pp. 127-128.

world weeps with thy woe"; but Job says—"Evil is, but ought not to be. Sorrow is a discipline meant to bring thee, and through thee thy kind, out of it." The faith that is in Buddha paralyzes, turns its very virtue into vice, its benevolence into a selfish search after the best way out of troubled life into quiet Nirvana; but the faith in the moral Deity of Job invigorates, inspires man with moral purpose, penetrates him with humanest strength, helps him to feel that life is all the nobler for being a battle against evil, all the worthier to be lived, that its Maker has designed that it at once educate and redeem through suffering. By the pessimism of Buddha evil is deified and man sacrificed to the deity, but by this Book of Job moral good is made the sovereign of the universe, and the dark background of its evil is brightened by the glorious arch of promise which spans it. That radiant arch has never since faded from the eye of man, and as his successive generations have continued to march towards it it has brightened and expanded, cheering them with the hope that He who has woven by His own light out of our dark those hues of brilliant promise, will yet change our passing night into His own eternal day.

2. But these discussions have brought us to the threshold of another; which, unhappily, we can barely glance at. The problem and solution of Job mark a new stage in the development of Israel, new elements and ideas enter into his mind, his faith essays a higher flight, his hopes take a wider range. This movement is specially seen in the place given in prophecy to the person and work of the Perfect Man, and in the belief in the universal reign and kingdom God has determined to establish through Him among men. I do not intend

to argue, with certain modern scholars, that Job is the original or prototype of the suffering Servant of God in Deutero-Isaiah,—on the contrary, the critical and exegetical difficulties in the way of such a notion seem to me insuperable. But this I do mean to say, the Deutero-Isaiah carries forward the movement which begins with Job, expounds his problems, develops his truths, incarnates his idea in an ideal person who does in suffering and unto sacrifice the will of God, and so works out the redemption of His people. The solution of Job's problem becomes here the solution of man's, the Servant of Jehovah, His Elect in whom His soul delighteth, is "the Man of sorrows and acquainted with grief." He is to be "despised and rejected of men," esteemed "stricken, smitten of God, and afflicted," but He is not to fail or be discouraged till He has set His law in the earth and the isles wait for His word. Although He should have done no violence, nor had any deceit in His mouth, yet Jehovah was to be pleased to bruise Him, His soul was to be an offering for sin. By His knowledge was the righteous One, Jehovah's Servant, to make the many righteous, and of their iniquities He was to take up the load. In all this we have the fundamental truth of Job as to the function and work of suffering accepted and enlarged, made the bearer of a diviner promise and a still more splendid hope. The righteous Servant of God is made so perfect through sufferings as to become the Captain of our salvation. He comes so gently as not to break the bruised reed or quench the smoking flax, yet comes with the Spirit of Jehovah upon Him, "anointed to preach good tidings unto the meek, to bind up the broken-hearted, to proclaim liberty to the captives, and to comfort all that mourn."[1]

But while the disciplinary and redemptive action of the suffering that becomes in the Perfect Man the bearing the sins of the many, is thus recognised and declared, the corresponding truth as to the aim and scope of the Divine working is no less clearly developed and proclaimed. The truth does not in the Deutero-Isaiah, as in Job, come through the vision of the creative energies in nature, but in what is a form still higher and more agreeable to the idea and mission of the righteous Servant—the vision of the remedial and recreative action of God in man and history. There are no such splendid pictures anywhere of the golden age, of the kingdom of righteousness which is to be the realized beatitude or supreme good of man. Violence is no more to be heard, wasting and destruction are to be unknown, man is to dwell in a city whose walls are Salvation and whose gates are Praise. The sun is no more to go down, nor the moon to withdraw herself; Jehovah is to be our everlasting light, and our God our glory. And then bringing the truths of the perfect sufferer and the reign of God into relations that had been dimly felt after rather than found in Job, the prophet sees that it is through the righteous Servant that the kingdom is to come, that "Jehovah shall cause righteousness and praise to spring forth before all the nations."[2] And so out of the darkest mystery of Providence, sent to trouble that it might teach His people, came the new idea of God and the new conception of suffering that blossomed into the truest and

---

[1] Isaiah xlii. 1-3 ; liii. 3, 4, 5, 9, 10, 11 ; lxi. 1-2.
[2] Isaiah lx. 18-22 ; lxi. 1-3, 11.

sublimest of the prophecies, came, too, the last and highest phase of the preparation in Israel for the advent of the King. After these prophecies much was to be said, but no higher truth was to be spoken till "the only begotten Son who is in the bosom of the Father" came forth "to declare Him."

III.

MAN AND GOD.

"The Eternal God is thy refuge, and underneath are the Everlasting Arms."—Deut. xxxiii. 27.

THESE words, while almost the last, are also among the most memorable in the Psalm so fitly described as "the blessing wherewith Moses, the man of God, blessed the children of Israel before his death." They express one of the sublimest truths of faith—a truth Moses himself had realized in the court of Pharaoh, on the peak of Sinai, in the hurry of flight, and in the calm and glory of the Divine face. He had finished his work, the law was given, the wilderness traversed, the goodly land in sight, and now he had but to be led by the hand of God to the top of Nebo, and thence into great eternity. The voice he knew and loved so well had said to him, "Get thee up into Mount Nebo, and die in the mount whither thou goest up, and be gathered unto thy people." That was a very sweet and soothing command to the weary soul of the old man. His had been a long day; and now, travel-sick, toil-worn, in its mellow autumn twilight, he was to set—

> "As sets the morning star, which goes not down
> Behind the darkened west, nor hides obscured
> Among the tempests of the sky, but melts away
> Into the light of heaven."

But before he goes to the point of evanishment into the everlasting light, he pauses to bless the people; and as he stands on the border-land between time and eternity, feeling his soul in the hands of God, while his body was still in contact with man, he utters this truth of highest, holiest import, "The Eternal God is thy refuge, and underneath are the Everlasting Arms."

The death of Moses seems to me peculiarly beautiful—an ideal death. Away there in the quiet of Nebo, far removed from the plash of tears, or the muffled voices, or the anxious eyes and sad wistful faces of the loved and near, with no crowds of men or city clouds between him and heaven,—watched by angels, tended by God,—the soul was unclothed, and the mortal passed into immortality. That was painless death—death as God, allowed to order it in His own way, makes it—a flight from the highest point of earth to the nearest point of heaven. The most glorious death-bed on earth was Calvary, the next Nebo; because the Christ that died on the one, the Moses that died on the other, alike felt in the hands of the Father rather than in the agonies of death. To die as Moses died, with only God and self present, and while sense closed on an earth sleeping in summer beauty, or a heaven gleaming with stars, soul opened on the unimagined glories of eternity—might well seem the last, highest blessing granted to mortal man. And that or a similar death will be given to every man who lives in the faith in which Moses went to die. "The Eternal God is thy refuge, and underneath are the Everlasting Arms."

Now these words suggest a matter well worthy of

thoughtful consideration, the spiritual value of the simplest and most fundamental religious belief, the belief in a God, Personal and Eternal. It is but right that this matter should concern us while we are in the region of what may be termed Old Testament Faith. There is no truth so simply essential and fundamental in religion as the being and character of God, but there is nothing so little possible as a religion with no other truth, built on or out of a naked and abstract Theism. The Old Testament Faith, whatever it was, was not simply this, was too complex and prophetic to be so described; but underlying its whole historical being was its immense impassioned consciousness of God. Without this it would never have accomplished the work or produced the men it did, or become the historical preparation and basis of the religion of the New Testament. But our modes and forms of worship, the richer speech and elements of our spiritual life, often tend to make us forgetful of the foundation on which our religion reposes, the soil out of which our life has grown. And so it is fit now and then to go down to the roots and ask, What does our faith in God mean? What worth has He for religion and life? Apart from faith in God, I know not where man can find manhood or happiness. With God realized as a conscious, encircling Father, I do not know how man can feel miserable or alone. We cannot worship blind chance. If we believed that we rose out of accident, were surrounded by chance-created beings and events, and were to perish by accident in the end, then we might well live in recklessness and die in despair. Nor can we worship an eternal fate. If we thought that a grim necessity, iron, relentless, made our miseries, destined our disappointments, mocked our wailings and our tears, then might we justly feel like the imprisoned brute, whose only relief is to dash out its being against the walls of its prison. But our faith seizes neither a blind chance nor an iron fate, but a God, who is also a Father, out of whose bosom we came, into whose bosom we return. We have no wish to escape Him—would not, if we could. He alone is good; and to escape from Him is to escape from infinite goodness to absolute evil. While we are His and He ours, we can suffer no ultimate loss; for in God the good, the true, and the blessed are all contained. And so we can be cast down but not destroyed—sorrowful, yet always rejoicing—poor, yet making many rich —dying, and behold we live, while "The Eternal God is our refuge, and underneath are the Everlasting Arms."

I.

1. Now before we can estimate the spiritual value of this simple and primary belief, we must look for a little at the belief itself. What does a man mean when he says, "I believe in God"? "God" is a most elastic term, capable of narrowing to suit the meanest capacity, of expanding to fill the largest. It seems to have a sense intelligible to the simplest mind, while to the profoundest it becomes the symbol of thoughts too high to be spoken, too immense to be comprehended. But though it may signify very different things to different minds, yet, what it signifies does not thereby become unreal. It stands as the symbol of the best and highest Being man can conceive, his idea of the

Being rising with his thought of the good and the high. The notions of the men who first called the being they worshipped God, do not bind the latest; the word may remain while its contents are transfigured, as it were changed from one degree of glory to another. But while later may outgrow the ideas earlier ages expressed by the term God, they do not outgrow the idea which the term represents. The symbol widens to their thought as the firmament has widened to the telescope, telling as it widens secrets before undreamed of, showing such infinite reaches of space, such multitudes and varieties of star clusters, of worlds beyond worlds, as to awe the imagination in its loftiest mood. To dismiss the word, is not to dismiss the truth; *that* is too native to mind to be alienated or expelled by an act of will. The idea of the Supreme is the supreme idea, which asserts its rights not only by living where it has been doomed to death, but by exercising a sovereign influence on all the endeavours and products of thought. And so schools that have denied God have had to coin supersessory and substitutive terms, like "Substance" or "Force," "The Unknown" or "The Unconscious," in order to make their systems seem rational to reason or credible to faith. Indeed, so inalienable are those primary beliefs that demand the word "God" for their expression, so cunningly do they weave themselves into the least theistic theories, that often the last difficulty of philosophical criticism is to make out whether a system that knows no God has no God to know. Nature in her wisdom subtly contrives that what men imagine roundest denials are but confused and darkly disguised affirmations.

We need not here concern ourselves with any of these scholastic substitutes for God. Yet there is one thing we may not pass without remarking—how little any one of these names, or any combination of them, could to the soul and conscience of man take the place of God, how little they could in the supreme moments that are the opportunities of religion satisfy the spirit or control the passions of a man or a people. The Unknown is an abstraction man is unable to worship, that can never be a moral Sovereign exercising the authority of Lawgiver and Judge over man. To be anything in the region of the spirit it must become something known by the intellect; *there* what is beyond knowledge is without influence or reality of being. Men can never say of the Unknown what they have for centuries said of God : " It is love," or that " It is righteous and loveth righteousness," or that " It must be worshipped in spirit and in truth." Yet these are cardinal necessities to religion, for what has no love can awaken none, what has no righteousness can create righteousness in no man. What we may not conceive as either spirit or truth, can demand from us neither sincerity nor veracity of soul. Still less could any one address Force as " Our Father which art in heaven," or speak of the inscrutable Power which is the cause of all phenomena as gracious and merciful, good and true. But these were the very elements that gave to the term God its potency, made God the personalized good, the conscious and voluntary beneficence of the universe. The more highly and purely religious man has become, the less has he thought of the Creator, the more of the Father, the less of the Almighty, the more of the besetting God whose hands were about his spirit, whose eyes were upon his ways, watching how best to lead him out of darkness into light. A great poet, whose words are equally dear to men of letters and of science, tells us " the eternal womanliness draws us ever on ; " that is, the love, the beauty, the sweet and potent gentleness personified in ideal woman, is a ceaseless inspiration to man, wakes him to admiration, wins him to love. But there is one term that embraces everlasting womanliness and infinitely more, the term Eternal Father, or in its simple and beautiful paraphrase, " God is love." Deprive nature of a present God, and you deprive her of all that is moral, ethically beautiful and true. What takes the moralities out of nature, the constitution under which we live and work, takes them out of man ; and without these man is poor indeed. One whose claims on our reverence are of the supremest sort, thought man's last misery was to be " without God in the world," for without Him there could only be victorious evil, broken and vanquished good. The highest dignity, the noblest hopes of man are all conditioned on the being of God, for without Him there can be no immortality, no promise of that growing good that could alone make immortal being desirable. Our manhood is capable of realizing its best only when it becomes conscious of its likeness to God and the possibility of its getting ever nearer Him. Without a humanity penetrated by the idea of Deity an ideal humanity will never be realized.

2. But we must be more specific. When we speak of God do we think of Him as a personal Being, a free and conscious Will ? Now, let it be frankly confessed

that personality seems to me at once the most fundamental and necessary, yet the last and most difficult element in our conception of God. Without it, He is either dissolved into the universe, or evaporated into a mere mental abstraction; yet with it, He seems begirt with limitations, made less than the Infinite and the Absolute. From the standpoint of the speculative reason it might be easy to accept an impersonal God, but from the standpoint of the religious consciousness an impersonal God were none. He might then be conceived as simple Intelligence; but without freedom and the responsibilities freedom involves intelligence loses all majesty and grace, and becomes a necessitated mechanism, that may act cunningly but can be neither good nor wise. If God be impersonal, He can have no heart tender with love, no will moved by swift-footed mercy, regulated by the large righteousness that loves order and deals with the individual through his relations to the whole, no gracious ends for the universe, or energies active in it that may cheer the despondent and help him in his sad struggle with ill. And an impersonal God means a necessitated man, created and ruled by what he may term law, but what is inexorable fate. In seasons of victorious progress men may speak of necessity, and seem only the more to rejoice; but in seasons of adversity and sorrow, necessity is the mother of despair, hatred of life the strong consolation of those who believe themselves compelled to live. Pessimism is no religion, and an almighty author of evil is no God.

Men say—" To describe God as a person is to limit Him, to conceive Him as neither infinite nor absolute, but bounded and relative, confined within an individuality akin to man's." Is it so? What are the elements essential to a person? Two, consciousness and will; or the knowledge by a being that he is, that he knows, that he acts and has reasons for his action; and the power of free or spontaneous, or, simply, rational choice. Where these are, there is a person; where they are not, there is only a thing. Personality is simply the power of ordered and reasonable conduct, whether it be in ruling a world or regulating a life. Now so understood it does not in any real or rational sense involve limitation of being, no more than the attributes of thought and extension limit the Substance of Spinoza, or than the processes of evolution and return limit the Absolute of Hegel. There are no ideas thought to be less personal and limitative than those of "Law" and "Force." Law is everywhere, eternal as being, the universe cannot be without it, without it matter cannot act, or nature do any one of the marvellous things she every moment performs. But law is order, order is simply articulated reason, and the explicit is no more infinite than the implicit, the generative reason can as little be bounded as the generated. Force, too, is said to be universal, indestructible, persistent, continuous, working everywhere and evermore at work. Force so described is not force circumscribed, but rather made infinite and absolute by being made universal. And what does not limit force can still less limit will, its ethical equivalent. For a universal blind force, doing darkly the brightest things, working out without moral character or qualities moral purposes and designs, is less conceivable than a universal will, accomplishing in nature as in man its own high and conscious ends.

Universal force is universal will; what works order and is orderly in its working, has reason behind and within it. If then consciousness and will, the qualities constitutive of personality, can be conceived as universal, the personal God need not be conceived as other than absolute and infinite. Nay, let us now boldly say, without personality He were without perfection. Beatitude can be only where consciousness is; an unconscious were an unblessed God, and the unblessed is incapable of blessing.

3. But the personal God must be ethical, the will that is at once conscious and sovereign must also be moral. The union of the metaphysical and ethical, the harmony of the essential activity and the moral character and action of God was discovered and revealed once for all by Hebraism. What this signified on the historical side to religion, and through it to man in history, has already been discussed: here we have to do with it on its experimental side, its value for man as a being who seeks to know, to love, and to worship God.

Now to conceive God as ethical is to conceive Him as our moral Sovereign, the Source of the moral order and progress in the world. He is good, and the source of all the good that is. The order He institutes He loves, what breaks it He hates. He may, nay, as moral He must, suffer evil to be, but only that He may contend against it with all the resources and energies of His nature. Now, it is here where we touch the essential distinction between a moral order or law and the personal God. In an impersonal order there is no power of moral initiative, of creating new sources and conditions of good. Law can simply act upon what is, not create what ought to be. Necessity mends nothing, breaks what stands in its way, but redeems no man or state. A doctrine like the Buddhist Karma, where law is so inexorable that life is woven into a chain of necessitated acts and results, or its diluted English translation, "the stream of tendency that makes for righteousness," might be a good doctrine for a world of the good, where all acts being holy all results were happy; but no doctrine could be less generous, emptier of hope and comfort, for a state of mingled good and evil. What man needs in such a state is not simply faith in an Eternal that loveth and worketh righteousness, but in an Eternal that loveth men and worketh their good, besetting them behind and before, teaching them His truth, filling them with His Spirit, helping them to attain the righteousness they need to be conformed to His image. Where the sovereign Will is not one of blended love and righteousness, there can be no power of moral initiative working on behalf of men, only an order which fulfils right, but has no cure for wrong. Faith in it may create Stoics, but will not renew or redeem humanity.

When we think of the Eternal God, then, we think of the living Source of good, active at all moments in all lives. He is righteousness, but also love; He is truth, but grace as well. His character determines His ends, His ends justify His ways. His acts become Him, are not accommodated to our deserts, but to His own character and designs. He does not deal with us after our sins, but according to His mercies and in harmony with His own ends. No man is to God an isolated individual, but a unit within a mighty whole, loved as a person, but handled as one whose being was deemed necessary to complete the universe and judged through the ends of Him who means the universe to be complete. And the man who believes in God, believes in One who loved him from eternity, whose love called him into being, designed and prepared a place for him in the system His wisdom ordained and His will maintains. He knows that amid all the shadows and sorrows and shame of life, underneath him and around, are "the Everlasting Arms."

II.

Now that we have reached an approximate notion of what it is to believe in God, we must attempt to determine the spiritual value of this belief. Taken in its whole circumference this were a very large matter to determine, and so we must define the limits within which we are to move. Here then, we restrict our view to man as he lives amid the uncertainties and sorrows of time, a being who looks before and after, sends his thoughts ranging into the eternity behind, his hopes into the eternity before, yet does not know what any day or any moment may bring forth. To man, so regarded, faith in God is of a quite infinite religious significance.

1. His need of the Eternal God seems but too manifest. Weak and mortal, man feels himself a most helpless being. Birth and death are stronger than he; of the one he is the product, of the other the victim. He comes out of a past eternity, in which he had no conscious being; he must go into an eternal future where he is to be—he knows not what. This little

conscious present is all he has, all that sense can discover or intellect disclose. Mind can see, can feel, the lonely sadness of this little life,—can look out into the infinities of space and time, realize their boundlessness and its own minute personality; till it feels like a small self-conscious star twinkling solitary in an immense expanse. In moments when the thought of these infinities, conceived only as such, has been strong in me, I have felt like one standing, and reeling while he stood, on a narrow pillar reared high in space, looking up to a starless sky, out on a boundless immensity, down into a bottomless abyss, till in the despair of utter loneliness the soul has cried, "Oh for the face of the Eternal God above, and the Everlasting Arms below!"

Out of this conscious weakness, out of this utter loneliness, realized even in a living world in moments of supreme trial, rises our need of God. We did not make life, we cannot unmake death; and if in all the universe there is no one mightier than we, what remains to us but the misery of hopes that only dazzle to betray? What are our lives but gleams, that had better never have been, across the face of an awful, eternal darkness? Those infinities of space and time are like boundless deserts, silent, void, till filled with a personal God and Father; but once He lives in and through them, they become warm, vital, throbbing, like hearts pulsing with tides of infinite emotion rushing towards me and breaking into the music of multitudinous laughter and tears. The sky above is no longer space gleaming with stars; but filling it, round the stars, round and through the world, in and about each individual man, is God, daily touching us, daily loving us, giving us life and being in Himself. Those Eternities behind and before us are no longer dark, empty, or, at best, a grim procession of births and deaths; they are a living, loving God, from whom man came, into whom he returns. And that Eternal God makes all things secure, restful, blessed. No moment, either here or hereafter, can ever be without God; therefore in none can the good man be otherwise than happy. What is beyond death is not beyond God. He is there as here; and so, whether we live or die, "the Eternal God is our refuge, and underneath us are the Everlasting Arms."

2. Man's relation to this Eternal God determines his spiritual condition. This encircling, pervasive God, our Refuge; in whose bosom we lie, even when we little dream it, is to our soul what nature is to animal and vegetable life. The animal and the vegetable live only as the vital forces in nature enter into their organisms and become assimilated to their respective substances; so man lives only as the spiritual truths in God pass into his soul and are absorbed into the matter of his being. A dead plant or animal is one out of living connection with nature, unable to receive from the forces that play around it the nutrition they were designed to give, to use its native functions, to drink of the vital streams which bountiful nature pours on and about every living thing. So a dead soul is one out of sympathetic relation to God—one the eternal truths in God surround, but cannot enter, because the living connection has been allowed to cease, the receptive and assimilative functions to die. No soul remains in a dead or paralyzed condition because of poverty in the Divine influences

that vitalize, but only and always because of its own determination not to receive and incorporate these into its substance.

The afflictions that happen to man, while interfering with his domestic happiness or social enjoyment, may yet, as promotive of more intimate and vital relations with God, be blessings, real though hidden. The plant that has withered in a rich and favoured spot of the garden, has often lived and flourished in a quiet and shady nook. Had you met the gardener bearing the plant with its torn and bleeding roots to its new bed, you might have blamed him for thus ruining a thing you loved; or had you seen it soon after it had been transplanted, with drooping and faded leaves, you might have charged him with causing its death. But wait till its roots have struck deep into the new and suitable soil, and the plant that had been heavy and half dead in the garish sunshine blooms into sweet loveliness in the mellow and modest shade. Thus God lifts many a spirit from the soil and society it has loved and plants it away from the passion of life and the fond associations of the past, that it may stand in closer sympathy with Himself and break into a lovelier flower.

What man needs to this intimate and sympathetic relation is a permanent consciousness of the Eternal God as a daily presence, the very atmosphere in which the soul lives, moves, and has its being. To this, two movements are necessary, one from God to man, one from man to God. God's movement is one in fact and essence, though manifold in form and manifestation—Love. There is truth Divine and universal in that saying of the Psalmist—" Thy gentleness hath made me great." All man's greatness comes from God's gentleness. Were He wroth, our spirits would fail before Him; but He remains merciful, and we endure. "Like as a father pitieth his children, so the Lord pitieth them that fear Him." His heart, boundless as space, infinite as eternity, beats with mercy; and the Eternal God around us means simply, Man is enveloped in eternal love. As light must be where the sun is, so where God is present love must be; and as the sun though unseen is not unfelt, so man, though unconscious of God, cannot exclude from his soul the influences that flow from the Divine presence. Earth, when her face is turned to night and the stars, is yet upheld by the flaming hands of the sun; and man is in his spiritual night borne in the arms of Eternal Love. And were not the night within rather than without, did he not suffer from blindness rather than darkness, he might see, even in his night of sorrow, the stars above looking down like the myriad eyes of God in gentleness and pity. The bad as well as the good man stands in the love of God; but, then, it is all without the one, while within as much as without the other, and that makes an altogether infinite difference. He who has become conscious of the Divine love within as well as without, lives in the Eternal God, and has the life of the Eternal realized in him. "This is life eternal, to know Thee, the only true God, and Jesus Christ whom Thou didst send."

But, on the other hand, let us not forget that the movement from man to God is as needful as the movement from God to man. The one, like the other, is a movement of love; yet with a difference. Divine pity moves down to all men; but only from filial hearts does human trust move up to God. The Fatherhood is universal; but only where the sonship is consciously realized can the spirit cry, "Abba, Father!" His loving-kindness falls on us like sunshine by day, that our souls may rise to Him like incense by night. Man, as he is conscious of God and His encircling heart and arms, reposes in these, uses them in his hours of weakness and sorrow. The Divine Father is not the same to all devout men; He is to some more of a daily Presence, more of a permanent Friend; and this larger sense of God rises from a larger need and conscious use of Him in the soul. Vacancies made in the heart are often only rooms in it swept and beautified for God; and His presence at once glorifies the chamber thus prepared, sheds a mellow light back upon the past, and splendid hopes forward upon the future. Were it possible to reduce a pious soul to a consciousness of only two beings—first and pre-eminently, of God, next and feebly, of self—then it were possible to endow that soul with the supremest happiness possible to a creature; and the more nearly any man approaches to that consciousness the more blessed will he be. Of a truth, he is happy who can say, "As for me, I will behold Thy face in righteousness; I shall be satisfied when I awake with Thy likeness."

3. The truths and principles now stated need to be applied to man as he is in time, and as he is to be in eternity. And (1) to man in time. And here let it be noted that the text speaks no transcendental or speculative doctrine of Moses, but simply a fact of his experience. The Eternal God had been *his* refuge. He had known better than most men the extremes of

wealth and poverty, power and weakness, fulness and want. He had known solitude amid the gaieties and glories of the then most splendid court on earth; he had enjoyed Divine society on the sultry and solitary slopes of Horeb. He knew the best Pharaoh could do for him, the worst he could do against him, and had found both to be infinitely little. He had known, in all its anxious and bitter phases, what it was to be the loved and hated, trusted and suspected, praised and blamed leader of a mutinous and murmuring and unstable people. The realities and the semblances, the dreams and the disappointments, the actualities and the illusions of life he had alike experienced; and the grand truth which had amid all given stability, strength, and comfort was, "The Eternal God *my* refuge, and underneath the Everlasting Arms."

Let us ever remember as to ourselves—our strength and comfort in life will be in proportion to the depth and intensity of our consciousness of a present God. The universe in no part of it, time in no section of it, can have any terror to us, so long as we know that the hands of the Everlasting Father are upon our spirits and about our ways. Often as a child I have trembled to cross at night the courtyard of a lonely country mill. Every little object that moonlight or starlight revealed in other than natural proportions was a source of fear—seemed to hide shapes terrible to childish flesh and blood. But if my little hand was laid in the large hand of my father, I could cross the courtyard as gleefully and carelessly at night as at noonday. So, with our spirits held in the hands of the Eternal God, who is above, around, and before, the dark places of Life, Death, and the great For Ever, become light;

and, trusting where we cannot see, our steps are firm, when otherwise they would falter and fail. Without God life is without meaning or end, but with God life has source and purpose and goal. Perhaps you have seen a ship, weather-beaten, wave-worn, with cordage strained and sails rent, amid greeting and acclaim from the shore, answered by glad yet weary hearts on board, glide slowly yet securely into the haven. So returns the trustful soul to God. But can we image a ship, with blasphemy, or revelry, or fatal slumber on board, without compass, without provision, without cordage to spread and tighten its drooping sails, drifting away from the harbour out into the darkness and tempest, where there can be only awful and utter destruction? So floats from misery to misery the man without God. The Eternal is our only refuge; to be without Him is to be without hope.

But, again, it is worthy to be noted that the trials and sorrows of our lives are to be judged by their influence on our capacity for God, and our conscious movement towards Him. Whatever either widens our nature, or so empties it as to make more room in it for Him, may seem a trial, but is a blessing. What God gives, He never recalls. Friends, once ours, are ours for ever. They enter into our hearts while they live with us, and dwell there; and when they die, we lose their presence in our homes, but retain themselves in our hearts as in a shrine. Our dead never die to us. When they have been removed and buried from our sight, God gives them back to us, not as bodily, but as spiritual, to live in our souls for evermore. And in that spiritual presence God is; as it abides, He abides too. Our loved and sainted dead are channels through which Divine influence comes to enlarge our capacity and consciousness of God. In the very measure in which they depart to Him, the less reality attaches to time, the more to eternity. And so, as we ascend the hill of life and friends fall from us by the way, we feel like the traveller who as he climbs the mountain-side sees, while earth expands, its individual objects fade and heaven fill the eye and prospect of his soul. Life is then to us what Nebo was to Moses; and our God, like his God, gives us a refuge in His "Everlasting Arms."

Let me tell you a parable :—A king once planted in his garden a beautiful rose tree, and bade his gardener so tend and train it as to make its flowers the richest and loveliest possible. The tree grew and flourished, and year by year blushed into blossoms of manifold beauty. But it sent out so many shoots, formed so many buds, that its very fertility threatened to injure the quality of its flowers. So the gardener removed the shoots, pruned away the buds, till the tree seemed to bleed all over in loss and pain; but the wounds healed, the sap and the strength ran up to those buds that were spared, and when the season of ripeness was come, the roses were lovelier and sweeter than ever —most meet of all in the garden to be carried into the palace of the great king, to fill its galleries and chambers with delicious and grateful fragrance.

> "God gives us love. Something to love
> He lends us; but, when love is grown
> To ripeness, that on which it throve
> Falls off, and love is left alone."

But it is left alone that it may be the one perfect bond between the human and the Divine, the fragrant sacrifice that rejoices God, the glorious beauty that makes man a source and seat of joy for ever.

(2) Apply those truths to man in eternity. God is there, as here, at every point or moment in it; and so the man who trusts in Him can never be otherwise than blessed. Astronomy has enabled us to conceive how God's presence in this world, and His care for every individual in it, have never withdrawn His hand and mind from the myriad worlds and systems the telescope has revealed. So faith knows that, as God is in time "the treasure of the soul," He will be in eternity "the source of its chiefest joy." The creature is exhaustible; the universe, however immense, must also be exhaustible in the enjoyments it offers to an immortal soul; but the Infinite God must continue to the souls that rest in His arms a perennial fount of happiness. Our dead are in God's keeping. Ah, well, they are better in His than in ours. And though, in moments when intensely conscious of our loss, there may rush to our lips the cry,

> "Oh for the touch of a vanish'd hand
> And the sound of a voice that is still!"

yet, mindful that our dead live in God, we shall assuage our grief by faith in

> "That God who ever lives and loves,
> One faith, one God, one element,
> And one far-off Divine event,
> To which the whole creation moves.

And so our faith in God becomes our hope of immortal life in and with Him. Wordsworth has written a grand Ode on the "Intimations of Immortality from Recollections of early Childhood." Behind the Ode is a history. A "Little Maid," who could think of the dead only as the living, had suggested the problem:

> "A simple child,
> That lightly draws its breath,
> And feels its life in every limb,
> What should it know of death?"

It could know nothing, experience had not contradicted nature, and "Heaven lies about us in our infancy;" for

> "Our birth is but a sleep and a forgetting;
> The soul that rises in us, our life's star,
> Hath had elsewhere its setting,
> And cometh from afar.
> Not in entire forgetfulness,
> And not in utter nakedness,
> But, trailing clouds of glory, do we come
> From God, who is our home."

And what has so lately come from God thinks as God thinks; to its thought, life and immortality are natural, not death. But the Ode needs a companion, one on the intimations of immortality from the hopes of Christian old age. The little child, lately come from God, can think of death only as a mode of life; the aged saint, about to return to Him, can conceive death only as a "going home.". The one has the light in his soul of the glory lately left, the other of the glory soon to be won. Sainted age is a second and holier childhood—the end of life turned back into its beginning—the reminiscence of the one changed into the life of the other, the heaven that lies about the infancy worked by experience into the very texture and essence of the spirit. A life lived in fellowship with God is not lived in vain. He who lives it discovers his affinity with God, knows that he may cease to walk with men, but not to be with and for his Father. To be and to feel loved of the Eternal, is to be assured that His eternity will be ours; to believe that we are sources of joy to Him, is to know that we shall rejoice in Him for ever. Our immortal hope does not then build on the instincts and anticipations of the human soul; it springs, victorious and confident, from our faith in Him who so loves us that He will not lose us from His love, for to lose us were to empty His bosom of its joy, His heaven of its beatitude. Blessed is that old man who has translated the unconscious faith of his childhood into the conscious faith of ripe and chastened age: "The Eternal God is *my* refuge, and underneath *me* are the Everlasting Arms."

PART THIRD.

I. THE JESUS OF HISTORY AND THE CHRIST OF FAITH.

II. CHRIST IN HISTORY.

III. THE RICHES OF CHRIST'S POVERTY.

"*It is characteristic of the omnipotence of the Divine Nature that it should complete its works and manifest itself by some infinite effect. But no mere creature can be said to be an infinite effect, since by its very nature it is finite: in the work of the incarnation alone does there seem to be an infinite effect of the Divine power, which, in the fact of God becoming man, has united things infinitely remote. Also in this work preeminently, the universe seems to be completed by the union of the last creature—man—with the first principle—God.*"—Thomas Aquinas: "Summa," Pars III. Ques. 1, Art. 3.

"*A kind of mutual commutation there is, whereby these concrete names God and Man, when we speak of Christ, do take interchangeably one another's room, so that, for truth of speech, it skilleth not whether we say, that the Son of God hath created the world, and the Son of Man by His death hath saved it; or else, that the Son of Man did create, and the Son of God die to save the world.*

"*If therefore it be demanded what the person of the Son of God hath attained by assuming manhood: surely, the whole sum of all is this, to be as we are, truly, really, and naturally man, by means whereof He is made capable of meaner offices than otherwise His person could have admitted: the only gain He thereby purchased for Himself, was to be capable of loss and detriment for the good of others.*"—Hooker: "Ecclesiastical Polity," Book v. §§ 53, 54.

"*The founding of the Christian Society and the advance of the Church led to the development of those abstract principles which Christianity secures for the secular realm, especially for that side of it which is concerned with the self-consciousness of men. For the religious life presupposes the spirituality of man's nature and his capability of entering upon that life, the capability standing to the life as* δύναμις *to* ἐνέργεια. *By Christianity man is essentially determined as person, and this is the reason why slavery is entirely opposed to its spirit and is in and for itself abolished. For man, according to the Christian notion of him, is an object of the grace and purpose of God: God will have all men to be saved. Quite apart therefore from all special conditions, man in and for himself, and simply as man, has infinite worth; and it is just this infinite worth which abolishes all special claims arising from birth or country.*"—Hegel: "Philosophie der Geschichte," p. 345 (ed. 1837).

I.

THE JESUS OF HISTORY AND THE CHRIST OF FAITH.

> "*Jesus Christ, who was born of the seed of David according to the flesh, who was declared to be the Son of God with power, according to the spirit of holiness, by the resurrection of the dead.*"—Rom. i. 1-4.

CHRISTIANITY is built on Christ. He made it at first, He makes it still. His blood was its seed, and His Spirit creates its flower. Without Him it would never have been, without Him it could not continue to be. The Founder is related to the religion as God to the world; in each case the transcendent passes into an immanent relation; creation becomes Providence—which is simply creative activity become ceaseless and permanent. The person of its Creator is at once the vital strength and primary difficulty of our Faith: its vital strength, because setting as it were the heart of God living and transparent before the face of man, so making Divine love the intensest reality to men feeble and sense-bound; its primary difficulty, because bringing within the forms and conditions of nature a Person and therefore a system essentially supernatural. As a simple matter of fact man's faith in the Fatherhood of God is the direct creation of Christ, never thought of apart from His

Sonship, with no meaning or reality save as seen or construed through it. Deeper knowledge of the Son has been better knowledge of the Father, and the nearer men have drawn to Christ the more have they felt the infinite tenderness and grace of God. But this historical Person has also stirred obstinate questions as to how so great things could be done in so humble a way, and how they could be true, and the invariable order of nature a reality; the reality, too, that to the modern mind underlies and guarantees or verifies all others. The Christ of History brings the cardinal problem of religion down from the clouds of speculation to the world of hard and prosaic and determinable facts, and that is a dangerous place for either things or persons to stand who are not what they seem. Criticism must handle and speak of all who stand there, the more strenuously if they make extraordinary claims on the faith and reverence of all men and times; and the now white now lurid lights it creates enable those piercing and pitiless eyes that love to see the distant past unbury its dread secrets and make confession of its forgotten crimes, to search the period or person on which they fall. That Jesus Christ has so long stood amid those burning lights and before these curious eyes tells an eloquent tale of the quality of His person and the reality of His character. The love of earth has looked at Him till it has grown Divine, the thought of man has studied Him till it has become reverent. The coldest criticism is touched with reverence when it stands before the supreme Person of history, finding Him to be also the supreme Good of man.

Christ's position is indeed extraordinary, unique,

He stands alone, a Person without a fellow. He is the humblest of the sons of men, speaks of Himself "as meek and lowly in heart"; yet, as simply and spontaneously as if it were homeliest and most familiar fact, He describes Himself as the only One who knows the Father, as the Light of the world, the Life of the world, the Saviour and the Judge of men! And His most transcendent claims become Him like His plainest speech. His most majestic are among His simplest words, fall from Him without effort, or any consciousness that He speaks of Himself things too high to be fitly spoken. There is an openness, a sunny simplicity or fine sense of nature about Him when He uses the loftiest words or applies to Himself the divinest names. We may not compare Him with the authors of the historical religions, for the comparisons could be but a series of contrasts. There are, indeed, but three universal religions, those of Mohammed, Buddha, and Christ. The first and the last may not be spoken of together; historical truth will allow neither the founders nor the religions to be compared. With Buddha it may seem otherwise. His, as seen through the traditions of his people, was a beautiful spirit, pious, tender, full of great love, the noblest enthusiasm of humanity, willing at any moment to become a sacrifice that he might lift or lighten the world's pain. Buddhism has produced many excellent virtues, sweet graces, meekness, benevolence, love. But the comparison becomes at every point a fundamental contrast. Buddha has no deity, Buddhism has no real universalities, may be a missionary or aggressive religion, but is not a religion that evokes and satisfies the ideal of man, making him thereby happier, completer and more progressive. The religion of Christ is one of boundless hope, but the religion of Buddha one of absolute despair. Christ came to reveal the Father whence we come, whither we go, and in whom we live; but Buddha reveals only a vacant heaven, a world without a Divine heart to bleed for its sorrows or forgive its sins, with only a moral order to control its destinies, punish its crimes, and, what is to it only a less evil or milder form of penalty, reward its virtues. Jesus loves life, brings it and immortality to light, making the darkness of death only the shadow of eternal day; but Buddha hates life as it now is, as it ever will be, thinks the highest bliss is to escape into everlasting and impersonal quietude. Buddha's is a pitiful, but not a humane religion, is sad and tender over the sorrows of man, but does not awaken, uplift and inspire his manhood. Its spread is the decay of humanity, the death of the virtues that make man the strenuous doer of righteousness, the lover of liberty, the worker of order and progress. Christ's is the opposite of all this; and where the religions so differ how can their founders be compared? And so we again say, Jesus Christ has no fellow, He stands alone. Of the founders of the great historical religions it may be said, they differ as star from star in glory; but of Him who made the only universal religion we must say, He is the Sun whose rising empties heaven of stars by filling it with light.

Now these remarks lead up to a very great question, the relation between the person of Jesus and His religion. Christianity presupposes the religion of Israel, and issues out of the bosom of Judaism, but it is made by Jesus Christ, it lives and does its work ir the world by faith in Him. It incorporates the theistic ideas of Israel, yet its God is much more than the God of the greatest of the prophets. It has absorbed and spiritualized the priestly and ethical ideas of Judaism, yet its notions of law and duty, its ideals of obedience and worship, its truths as to man and humanity, are of another spirit and order than those known to the religion of the Jews. All that differentiates it from what went before, and what stands around it, it owes to Jesus Christ and to its belief in Him, to its Founder and to what it has believed its Founder to be. The relation of Christ to Christianity involves an immense range of questions, critical, historical, philosophical; but the one that is to concern us here relates simply to the personality and its creative action on the religion. So narrowed, the points to be discussed are two, the one concerns the person of the Founder, the other the way in which He has lived in and acted through the society and religion He founded; or, to state the matter otherwise, our discussion is to relate to the Christ *of* history and the Christ *in* history. Our concern meanwhile is with the first of these alone.

I.

As regards this mightiest and most wonderful of the persons who have shared the life of our race, there are two distinct and, to many, incompatible points of view, the historical and the ideal, or the Person as He lived in the region of reality, and the Person as He lives in the region of the Spirit. Hence we speak of the Jesus of History and the Christ of Faith. "The

Jesus of History" is the maker or author of our religion in His actual historical being, as He lived and acted and spoke among men. "The Christ of Faith" is this Jesus as He has been made by the religion, as He exists to the thought and faith of His Church. Now the question for us here is: What is the relation between these two? By what process, or in what manner, did the one become the other?

1. Perhaps it may be as well at the outset of the discussion to be a little more explicit and detailed as to the antithetical phrases we have just used. Well, then, by the Jesus of History we mean the historical Person named Jesus of Nazareth, so far as His life and acts and words are matters of recorded history. That He was of Jewish descent, poor by birth, without culture, as it was then and is now understood; that He lived a Galilean peasant, remained what He had been bred, without social or official rank; that He became a teacher who attempted to reform His religion and nation, yet without ever making the most distant approach to the methods and motives of the political patriot, agitator or revolutionist; that He was followed by a few ignorant fishermen, outcast publicans and obscure women; that He was disbelieved, discredited, and rejected by the official heads, religious and political, of His people, the priests, scribes, and rulers; that in His early manhood, after a ministry of two or at most three years, He was crucified under Pontius Pilate; that out of the few poor people He had taught His doctrines, He constituted a society which His death, so far from breaking up, broadened into the Christian Church, while through it His doctrines became elaborated into the truths of the Christian religion;—all

this is certain enough, unquestioned by the most sceptical criticism, and so for us here unquestionable. Looked at in this naked way, it might well seem as if a life with less promise of universal importance, a person with fewer elements of everlasting fame and influence, of permanent regenerative and ameliorative potency, could hardly anywhere be found. But it is needful that we look at Him in this naked way that we may see Him as He seems to what is called Historical Criticism.

The Christ of Faith appears another and very different person. He stands before us arrayed in all the attributes of Deity, exercising the highest functions of God even while He bears the nature of man. By Him the worlds were made. He is the image of the invisible God, the Logos or Word, who was from the beginning with God and was God, become flesh that He might dwell among men. While His birth was an incarnation, His death was a sacrifice which redeemed man; and by faith in His death men become possessed of the righteousness of God and heirs of eternal life. Though He died, yet He is not dead; He arose from the grave and ascended into heaven, where, as great High Priest, He saves to the uttermost all who come unto Him, and as King of His people He reigns that He may put all His enemies under His feet. So supreme and universal is His authority that all men stand under it; He is Judge of quick and dead, and every man must appear before His judgment-seat and be judged according to his works.

The contrast between the Jesus of History and the Christ of Faith thus seems immense enough, and directly raises our problem : How did the one become the other ? By what process was this historical Person invested with these extraordinary and Divine qualities ? What connection is there between the humble Jesus of Nazareth and the Divine Christ of Faith ? Was it created and established in the manner of mythical apotheosis or rational interpretation ? Was the investiture with such Divine attributes accomplished by a series of happy guesses or strong idealizations by the creative imagination, or by a true and reasonable, which means a necessary, movement of the spirit ? These are our questions, and altogether it would be hard to find any that more nearly touch the heart of the Faith which lives in the churches, and by which the churches live.

2. The questions are historical, yet they imply principles that transcend history and govern its course and development. As historical they must here be dealt with, with only such an occasional glance at the underlying principles as may here and there be necessary. Now to this historical point of view one thing is needful, that we regard the persons concerned as reasonable, doing their best to act as honestly rational beings. This first principle makes it altogether unnecessary to discuss with men who can believe or think they believe that Jesus was the spirit of priestcraft incarnate, or that His disciples were persons in league to represent Him as other than they knew or conceived Him to be. Men who can so think are men of a credulity too vast to be reasoned with. That any designing or crafty spirit should for centuries evoke the reverence of men, inspire their piety, rule their morals, direct their destinies, wake them to their

sublimest deeds of self-denial and sacrifice, is a sheer impossibility. Time is just, and merciless in its justice to idols. Man is often foolish, but he is not permanently insane—which he would be were he able so to believe a lie as to grow wise and good by his belief of it and to deify it out of gratitude. No; whatever Jesus was, He was a reality. What lives and works for righteousness must be righteous; He who has made man true to his ideal self must Himself have been of the truth. And as with the Master, so with the disciples—the attributes in which they clothed Him were to them not fictitious, but most real; expressed their inmost belief, what in very deed they conceived Him to be, not simply what they wished Him to be believed as being. The things we handle are real human beliefs, but whether beliefs of realities is the point to be determined.

3. Now it is evident, as the question is historical, that our first step must be to get as near as possible to the actual Jesus of History, to stand, as it were, in His very presence, face to face with Him as He lived in Galilee before He was arrayed in the attributes of metaphysical Divinity. But this is no easy matter. The freest criticism is often but the handmaid of assumptions that leave it free to negative what they deny, not what they affirm. Dogmatism is not a weakness peculiar to theologians; the anti-theological spirit knows it as well. Strauss, and after him Baur and the Tübingen school, came to the criticism of the life of Jesus with the assumption that miracles are impossible, and so not simply the acts but the personality had to be reduced to the proportions their first principle required. It determined the whole matter

beforehand; all that remained to criticism was to bring history into harmony with the position from which it started. Nature, in the narrower sense, is not the only field for miracles; humanity is one as well. A miracle may be embodied in a person as well as in an act, and to say "belief in one is inadmissible," is but to say, the person to be studied must not be allowed to have transcended the common lot and familiar conditions of humanity. But if that be so, there is no more to be said; the only question that remains is for the curious in psychology, *How* came the men to believe as they did? not what did they believe, and on what grounds? Nor was this primary assumption the only thing that hindered the freer criticism from getting face to face with the facts and the person, the structure that rose on it was a medium that obscured. The mythical theory in the hands of Strauss had neither the method nor the principles of science; it could make history speak any language it pleased, could dissolve the most solid facts as easily as the most fantastic fancies, and where most rigorously applied left everything confused, fluid, indetermined, nothing ascertained or certain. Its attitude, too, to the writings and writers of the New Testament was most violent; in order to find time for the action of the mythical faculty it had to ignore the witness of the apostolical society and of the oldest, most authentic and important of the apostolical epistles. An historical theory constructed in defiance or in utter neglect of the principal sources of the history may be a theory of the imaginative, but is not of the scientific order. Nor was the tendency theory—Tübingen school—more successful. It could explain certain literary phenomena; it could not and did not explain the historical facts which created the men who made the literature. The differences of Peter and Paul are exceedingly interesting from the standpoint of the biographer, but they do not help us to understand the convictions they had in common, the events that made them the men they were. The antagonisms and rivalries of the particular and universal parties in the Church do not cancel the remarkable features in the person and life of Christ, for the most remarkable are the points where they agree, not where they differ. To use the tendencies and parties of the apostolic age to explain Christ instead of Christ to explain them, is to invert the order of history; we get at the meaning of the different tendencies through Him, not at the meaning of Him through the tendencies. Nor do we find an eclectic and egoistic method like Renan's favourable to historical realism; no being like his Jesus ever did live or could live outside the pages of French romance. What is meant for His portrait is but a succession of inconsistent images, shaded according to the humour of the moment, unredeemed from absurdity by the only virtue it possesses, the beautiful French in which it is sketched. I do not know that any one ever stood more remote from the Jesus of History than the Jesus of Monsieur Renan.

II.

1. Let us approach Jesus, then, if possible, without assumptions, either speculative, critical, or historical, anxious only to discover what He was, and how He became what He is to faith. We find Him a Galilean

peasant—poor, obscure, straitened in every way. Education in any tolerable sense was unknown. Such instruction as there was narrowed, did not broaden the man, disciplined and exercised the tribal passions, not the generous and refined humanities. Yet the scornful question, "How knoweth this man letters, having never learned?"[1] seems to mean that even this poor instruction had been denied Him. He had to earn His daily bread by daily toil, and the labour of the hands, especially as the East knows it, has never been friendly to high culture or, indeed, any culture, to a noble and truthful spirit, to a large outlook or exalted ends. His people were most exclusive; their religion had become an idolatry of the tribe, producing hate, evoking hatred. The Gentile held the Jew in abhorrence; the Jew held the Gentile in contempt; loss of freedom intensified the antipathies of race, patriotism embittered without ennobling the hatred of the alien. Conquest, with its insignia of insult and outrage, was everywhere: a Roman governor sat in its halls of judgment, Roman soldiers paraded its streets and possessed its cities; Roman officials levied and collected its taxes, and Roman coins circulated in its markets. The Jews' religion, which the Roman was prepared to respect, would not allow the Jew to respect the Roman; faithfulness to the traditions of the fathers became fanaticism against the foreigner, who was esteemed an infidel reprobated of God. There was nothing in Judea to enlarge, to humanize; the noble universalism of Israel in the days of the greater prophets had perished, and in its place a harsh and bitter particularism reigned. The Roman was

[1] John vii. 15.

made cosmopolitan by his dream, so nearly realized, of universal empire; the Greek by the discipline and truths of his philosophy; but the Jew, who ought to have been made by his religion the most generous of men, had made it the glorification and sanction of all that was most narrow and tribal. The man surrounded by Judaism, nursed on its traditions, breathing its atmosphere, without opportunity of breathing any other, could not be a man for all lands and ages. Nature, and the conditions under which it lived and worked, forbade it.

And Jesus was born a Jew, within this nature, under these conditions. Now it is a first principle of all constructive historical criticism, that a man must be judged in connection with his own country and age. He inherits from his parents, his school, his companions, the entire society in which he lives and thinks, from the customs and traditions, poetry and proverbs, history and spirit of his nation, most of the moral and intellectual elements that constitute his specific type of manhood. If he is a great thinker or discoverer, he is so under the conditions supplied by his circumstances. Genius does not so much create the new as combine the old in a new way. While the living force is in the man, the conditions of development are without and around him. Hence he has what is due to himself—his personal peculiarities, and what is due to his country and age—his national character, his specific kind and quality of culture. Thus, while Plato's splendid imagination and speculative reason were his own, he could never have been the philosopher he was out of Greece. The very form and substance of his philosophy he owed to his Greek birth and education, and an analysis of the previous Greek systems shows how little, save the combination, was Plato's own. Thus, too, our own Bacon, father as he is of the inductive philosophy, could not well have been so in another than his own age. A comparison of his writings with Descartes' reveals a method and style of thought, a relation to the earlier and later philosophies, that has so very much in common as to be capable of explanation only by both living under the same formative and suggestive influences. The discoveries of our Newton had been impossible had he not inherited those of Copernicus and Galileo; and an impartial consideration of the once celebrated controversy as to the priority of his or Leibnitz' invention of the infinitesimal calculus will show that, amid all that was Newton's own, there was also much his in common with the higher spirits of his age. And we have but to mention Coleridge's conscious and unconscious plagiarisms from Schelling, Hamilton's obligations to Kant, Kant's to Hume, Hume's to Berkeley and Locke, to see how much man is rooted in the past, and how much he is fashioned as a thinker, system-builder, or discoverer by inherited and contemporary influences. Hence Christ must be studied in connection with His country and age, that we may discover how much or how little in Him was original, how much or how little derived.

But here we come suddenly upon an extraordinary fact, standing in radical contradiction to the law which all constructive criticism, literary and historical, recognises as the normal law of human development. Jesus was born a Jew, lived and worked as a Jewish peasant, without culture or travel, or the opportunities of intercourse, that would have lifted Him above the narrowness, the illiberal passions and prejudices of such a peasant's lot; and so if the above law has any validity whatever, we should be able so to apply it here as to show Jesus the creation and mirror of Judaism. But this is precisely what He is not. He is the least local, the most universal Person of history, of all men the least the product of His age, the most the Child of Eternity. He in the most absolute sense, in a degree altogether and exclusively His own, transcended the limitations, not simply of His birth, but of His people and time. He had no Jewish characteristic, prejudice or superstition. While destitute alike of Gentile culture and Jewish learning, in His own matters He neither spoke, nor thought, nor acted like a Jew, nor even like a Gentile, but like Himself alone. The Jew thought hatred of the Gentile compatible with his religion, if not implied in it; Jesus that the very essence of religion was supreme love to God, and to man love equal to our love of ourselves. The Jew believed sacred places and prescribed ceremonies necessary to worship; Jesus simply a right condition of the spirit. The Jew imagined that Jehovah was the God of the Hebrews only; Jesus declared Him to be the God and Father of all men. The Jew thought that the kingdom of God was confined to Israel; Jesus that it was designed to comprehend the entire world. The Jew conceived the kingdom as outer and temporal; Jesus taught that it was spiritual and eternal. The Jew trusted much to prayer and fasting; Jesus instructed man to trust in the mercy of God. The Jew regarded the Pharisee as the ideal of goodness; Jesus preferred to him the penitent publican. The Jew believed in the salvation of his own race alone ; Jesus declared that " God sent not His Son into the world to condemn the world, but that the world through Him might be saved."

Of course, I know what can be said as to the likeness of certain precepts of Jesus to certain maxims current in the rabbinical schools. But these and similar things are here altogether without relevance. This is the fundamental matter: the universalism of Jesus Himself. There is no touch or trace of Judaism in His character or personality. He belongs to humanity, not to Israel. Strauss used to speak of His "bright Hellenic spirit," but that was Strauss' way of describing His universalism, for a Jew who was essentially Greek was no Jew. Yet He was as little Hellenic as Hebrew; was indeed, though the "Man of sorrows," radiant enough in soul to be the brightest Greek ; but His gentle yet most massive moral strength, His love of man, the purity that enabled Him to mix with sinners without feeling the defilement of sin ; the patience that could bear to be smitten without being provoked to smite, so wonderfully combined with the elevation that never allowed men to think His forbearance weakness; the grace that made Him beautiful even amid His sufferings ; the gracious magnanimity that could forgive crafty and pitiless enemies in the very moment of their insolent triumph, were so His own as to be direct creations of His will, lifting Him above the Greek as above the Jew, and making Him the embodied ideal of humanity, the solitary Son of man. History has confessed this universalism of His in its own victorious way ; the ideal of manhood He created became and remains the regnant ideal of man, the humanest men being the men who realize it.

2. This, then, is the first remarkable characteristic of the historical Jesus—His moral and ideal universalism. In emphasizing it, we are not emphasizing anything esteemed miraculous, simply noting what is independent of His so-called miracles, and belongs to the very essence of His personality. The second distinctive feature stands connected with the first, but it must be viewed in relation to His ministry rather than His birth. That ministry was no serene and placid season : it was trouble and sorrow. It involved conflict with the men His people most respected ; condemnation of the customs and institutions they most revered. It brought about, too, relations and circumstances full of the gravest dangers, fruitful of the severest trials. For a person of moral purity to mix with sinners in order to save them, was a new thing in the history of man, intelligible to none save the sinners themselves. For doing this, Jesus was suspected, despised, hated by the piously respectable of His people, and they did their best by misjudgment, by the exercise of the social and religious ban, to shut up the Saviour of sinners to the fellowship of sin. The hazard of His position is hard to realize ; the lowliness of His birth, the simplicity of His life, His unfamiliarity with men and affairs enormously increased it. He was condemned by a name, " the Friend of publicans and sinners," watched by suspicious eyes, while ears anxious to mishear waited for His every word, charged with evil on account of His very goodness, met at every point by the antagonism of the men who claimed best to know and obey the law of God. Their antagonism soon had a most tragic issue. What the Pharisees feared to do the

priests did not scruple at; and Jesus, though "a just Person" to the judge who tried Him, was scourged and crucified, insulted in the very hour and article of death by the men who had wronged Him.

Now look at the idea of Himself that He, while so situated and misconstrued, so misjudged and ill-fated, yet conveyed to the men who knew Him best. They thought Him sinless, a Being solitary in His moral perfection, separate from sinners while their Friend. Nothing in the outer conditions and relations of His life tended to create this idea; everything was against it. The society of the guilty is not the soil most favourable either for the growth or the fame of holiness. To be suspected by the men of recognised sanctity was not the happiest way to secure the reputation of sinlessness. And to be seen throughout His public career, which had no years of honourable and commanding service behind it, in conflict with the men who were the interpreters of the Divine law, the depositaries of the ancestral wisdom, the heroes alike of politics and religion; to be crushed, too, in collision with the priests who guarded the temple, performed the worship, and exalted the name of God, was certainly to be placed under the conditions that most invited severity of judgment, and would best exhibit every error of manner and conduct, every infirmity of temper and will. But the remarkable thing is that the men who knew Him believe and speak and act as if He were throughout perfect in character, motive, and action,—a Man without sin. Not that they were men of mean moral ideas; they had a consciousness of evil so intense as to be an enthusiasm against it; nay, one of their most marvellous achievements was to universalize their consciousness, and, as it were, stamp their sense of sin into the very soul of the world. Yet these men thought Jesus without sin; nay, it was their knowledge of what He had been that created their idea of human guilt. It was the light shed by His holiness that made man seem so dark; in the shadow of His goodness human evil appeared more and worse than before. And this new conscience of theirs did not simply concern the treatment Jesus had received; it concerned even more themselves and their conduct. They judged none, not even the enemies of the Master, so severely as they judged themselves. They became conscious of their own exceeding sinfulness through the sinlessness of Jesus. There is no more significant fact in the region of religion, no mightier proof of His holiness, than the tremendous force of this creation of His, the conscience for sin. Nor must we forget the quality of the men in whom and through whom He created it. They were not finely susceptible sons of genius and culture, imaginative men, capable of acts of splendid idealization. They were unlearned, ignorant men, transformed and inspired by the sheer might of His extraordinary influence, made through the knowledge of Him conscious of what they themselves were. And so they live before us in their own epistles as men possessed by a sense of evil, made fearful, wretched by it, yet sure that good is mightier and more masterful, though the strength that works its victory lives in Jesus, and comes to man through faith in Him.

Here, then, we have our feet on facts. The historical Jesus so lives as to create, in spite of unhappiest circumstances, a new ideal of holiness, a holiness so perfect as to awaken in the men who knew Him a new sense of sin, a conscience for it, an enthusiasm against it which nothing but the victory of His good can satisfy. Now, how is this to be explained? Whence this quickening sinlessness,—this creative holiness, realized amid conditions so provocative as almost to necessitate guilt? The law of heredity does not explain it, for this is the law the fact traverses; nor can any theory of development, for to every such theory it stands in radical contradiction; nor can His education, for between any education possible to Him and the result there is not only disproportion but positive opposition. The cause cannot be found without,—must be sought within. Circumstances may develop qualities, but they do not create characters. Sinlessness is impossible without a sinless will, holiness without a whole and holy nature. But if so, then the perfection of Jesus is the creation of Jesus—His own work, not another's, least of all His people's and His time's. Yet to be the creator of His character is to be the creator of all it has effected and achieved, the source of the moral forces which it discharged upon the world. But see where this brings us—face to face with a miracle in morals, a creative or, if you please, supernatural act in the region of spirit, that kingdom of personality which transcends the nature of the physicist as thought transcends matter. And if Jesus, viewed apart from all deeds of physical power, becomes in the hands of historical analysis a miracle in the sphere of morals and personality, how shall we think and speak of Him?—in harmony with modern ideas of a nature which honours no supernatural, or with the facts of His person and history?

3. But now we must advance another step. The ministry that was so troubled and tragic was also very brief; it could hardly have been briefer. It was so short that the marvel is that it accomplished anything whatever, especially as He came to it so unprepared and unannounced that men could ask in wonder : " Is not this the carpenter, the son of Mary ?"[1] We may almost say, His is the briefest ministry on record, certainly by far the briefest of those that have affected the religions of man. It lies at the utmost within a period of three years, the duration of the actual and exercised ministry being probably much less. But however short, it was long enough to allow Him to become the supreme Teacher of time. His words have been the wonder of the world ; the more they are understood the more they are admired. Age has not dimmed their light, lessened their sweetness, or diminished their force. Familiarity has not spoiled their freshness or their fragrance ; life, though it has become richer and more varied, has not outgrown their wisdom, or superseded by fulfilling their ideals. Time and culture have called into the field of thought the wealth of many centuries and lands, but no rival to the words of Jesus has come. They shine peerless as ever, the sweetest, calmest, simplest, wisest words ever spoken by man to men. So true are they, so mighty in their energy, so soft in their strength, so reasonable, so fitted to make life peaceful, gentle, happy, holy, that men who have wished not to believe the Christian religion have often refused to part with the truths and consolations of Jesus. And He so wove His person and His truth together that men cannot hold

---

[1] Mark vi. 3 ; *cf.* Matt. xiii. 55.

by it without holding by Him. His character lends their highest charm to His words; His words find their most perfect mirror and illustration in His character. No one ever possessed as He did that hardest and noblest veracity which consists in the absolute agreement of doing and saying, being and expression. What He said of His Father in heaven becomes intelligible to us through the way in which He lived as the Son. The universal neighbourliness and brotherhood He enforced and declared found their highest sanction and example, not in His parable of the Good Samaritan, but in His own spirit and conduct, the brotherliness He embodied. The law of forgiveness He proclaimed He fulfilled, and the prayer on the cross, "Father, forgive them," has made more men relent and be merciful than the command, "until seventy times seven." The truth of the words reflects the truth of the person. They are imperishable because He is universal, and what speaks of Him may not die.

But now let us put together the Speaker and His words, Jesus and His truth. He is humble, born in the home of a race distinguished for its passionate jealousy and hatred of other races; yet, without education or travel or intercourse with distant peoples, He speaks the highest wisdom, the truths of sweetest, yet strongest and most universal import that have yet come to man. His career was troubled, sorrowful, tragic. He was disowned by the men esteemed patriots and saints, crucified by the priests, who claimed to know the right place and way of approaching God; yet His words are as calm, His spirit as serene and radiant, as if He had been at rest in the bosom of the Eternal Father. His ministry was brief, briefest on record; yet His words are the mightiest of all ever spoken to man, the most imperishable in their influence and might. What does this mean? Let us see if history will make it more intelligible to us.

Let us compare Jesus with a great natural genius who had every possible advantage, say Plato. Plato was well-born. Noble and wise Athenians were among his ancestors. He was born in the most brilliant age of the most brilliant country of antiquity, and was, perhaps, its greatest man, certainly its greatest thinker. His genius—speculative, imaginative, religious—was splendid. The year of his birth was the year of Perikles' death, and the sunset splendour of the Periklean age shone on his boyhood and around his youth. The Persian War was near enough to awaken enthusiasm for its heroes and their victories; the passion of patriotism it had inspired was not yet dead. The ambition to discover the polity that could best preserve and realize her loved liberties possessed the mind of Greece. The tragedies of Æschylos had quickened in it a new and awful consciousness of the righteous and retributive forces that ruled the world. The sculptures of Pheidias were just beginning to make the Hellenic spirit conscious of its most perfect ideal, the sense of the beautiful it was to create in man. The schools were grappling strenuously with the problems of young and adventurous thought, were asking where the solution might lie, whether with the fire and flux of Herakleitos, or the atoms of Demokritos, or the mind of Anaxagoras, or the dialectic and doubt of Protagoras. To be educated in a city where so many and so splendid moral and intellectual forces

met and acted was to be educated indeed, was to
breathe an air whose every inspiration was genius.
And Plato's education was the very best Athens could
furnish. Neither body nor mind was neglected.
Reason, imagination, taste, were equally cultured.
While yet young he became a disciple of Sokrates, and
the dialectic and educative skill of the great disputant
were used to develop all that was excellent and philosophical in the young man. In his master's school
he met the most illustrious spirits of the age. The
splendid but erratic genius Alkibiades; the brave and
solid Xenophon; Euripides, the poet; Criton, the
philosopher and ideal friend; the most brilliant orators
and statesmen of that most brilliant time; and that rare
and rich society could not but awaken and educe all
that was highest and deepest in a man. And everywhere outside the school there was culture. The wit
of Aristophanes now convulsed the Athenians into
laughter, the tragedy of Sophokles now touched them
by its moral grandeur, now melted them by its mellowed
sorrow into tears. The poetry and philosophy of the
past, the thought and activity and glory of the present,
contributed to the rich endowments of this rarely-gifted
soul. Then, he travelled, studied under Eukleides at
Megara, under Theodoros at Cyrene, under the Pytha-
goreans at Tarentum; studied in Egypt the mysteries
and rites of its ancient faith. And this man, the incarnation as it were of the philosophy and faith of his age,
opens his academy at Athens, teaches for many years
the finest spirits of his time, lives in contact with
the greatest men then living, and dies at a ripe old
age, leaving his highest and truest thoughts on record,
and a school to perpetuate his philosophy and name.

But the conditions under which Jesus lived and worked stand in absolute contrast to Plato's—descent, birth, people, country, time, circumstances, education, opportunities, all were as opposite as they could be, and disadvantageous in the degree that they were opposite. The free air of Athens was not His, nor the joy, which makes the teacher creative, of susceptible and sympathetic disciples. Time grudged Him His brief ministry, sent want and suspicion and hatred to vex Him, loaded Him with sorrow, burdened Him with disciples slow of heart and dull of wit. And He lived as one whose work was to suffer rather than to teach. He made no book, wrote no word, caused no word to be written; but with a confidence calm and steadfast as if He had been the Eternal casting into immensity the seeds of the worlds yet to be, He spoke His words into the listening air, that they might thence fall as words of life into the hearts of men. And then came the miracle of their creative action, the work which makes them so mighty a contrast to the Platonism which was so splendid in its promise, but has been so poor in its achievements. For it is here where the contrast between the speakers finds a sudden reversal. Suppose some one had gone to the most lucid critic of those days, and said, " Compare the words of Jesus and Plato, and tell us which has most importance for man," and can you doubt the answer? With fine lucidity, analysing and distinguishing the two, he would decide thus: " Culture has the promise of the future; whatever is not of culture is not of light. Plato's system is so comprehensive and elevated, is recommended by a dialectic so dexterous, adorned by an imagination so splendid, covers so completely the life of the individual and the state, that it cannot but win commanding authority over man; while the system of Jesus, if system it can be called, bears disappointment and defeat in its lack of all literary form and æsthetic quality." But no apostle of culture can judge for man; his soul knows the truths it needs, knows when these satisfy him, proves his satisfaction by the progress they enable him to make, the order they cause him to achieve. And the words of Jesus have been, in a sense absolutely their own, man's; ever since they were spoken they have formed the best part of his life, been the healthiest and most wholesome moral influence in his world. Why? The universalism of the person has its counterpart in the universalism of the words; the ideal for all men speaks the truth for all minds. The nature perfectly realized in Jesus proclaims the truth that is to realize the perfect nature in man. But this universalism of person and truth is no accident, no happy stroke of chance; it is of God, who alone knows and possesses the secret through which His creation is to be perfected. Jesus must then be the supreme work of Providence, for through Him the mystery of creation enters on that grandest stage which men call redemption. But even so, has not the Jesus of History become the mightiest and most mysterious person history has to show?

4. But to the humble birth, and, alike in this ethnical, ethical, and intellectual sense, parsimonious conditions, to the troubled and brief ministry another feature has now to be added: the ministry was obscure while troubled, as narrow and confined as it was brief. It moved on a small and mean stage, was exercised among simple and untutored men, absolutely without

the mind or the culture that could invent or appreciate large aims. Galilee was a poor field for any work of wide issues, the fishermen of its small inland sea poor scholars for a Teacher of sublime ideals and truths. Yet on this field and among these men Jesus for a few months carried on His mighty ministry. His fame spread as far as Jerusalem and throughout Judea, but no farther; on the wider stage of the capital He may now and then have appeared, and there at last He went to suffer and to die. But even there the arena was of the smallest, watched by the narrowest passions, beset by the meanest issues, with no outlook to a larger atmosphere and freer world. Altogether deepest obscurity marked His ministry, poverty, prejudice, and insusceptibility of soul the men among whom it was exercised.

Now, in this obscure ministry, so meanly circumstanced, Jesus proved Himself in the strict sense a Creator; He created a society or state which was at once a new ideal and order for mankind. No one doubts that the idea of the kingdom of Heaven or of God was His peculiar creation. He did not make the phrase, but He made the thing. What He meant stood in direct antithesis and contradiction to what the Jews had understood the words to mean. Speaking with all moderation, His idea as to humanity was the grandest that had ever come to the spirit or consciousness of man, had most promise in it of universal good, of unity, freedom, fraternity, justice, truth. It was the reign of God in man, a state of righteousness, peace, love. The good it promised to all it was to accomplish by making all good. It did not seek to create happiness through kings or statesmen as such.

but to create everywhere happy men, whose joy it should be to enlarge the happiness of man. It was not revolutionary in the political sense, yet it was the most radical of all political revolutions. It assailed no existing order, yet its aim was to create an absolutely new order by the creation of a new mankind. It abolished not simply the old priesthood, but all official priesthoods for ever; for it made it every man's right and sovereign duty to draw near to God for himself as a son of the eternal Father, as a subject of the everlasting King. It refused to recognise any of its citizens as kings, for all were subjects, and there was no respect of persons or classes with God. This was then, and remains still, the most splendid dream of universal empire that has visited our race; but it is an empire which aggrandizes no man, for it is God's and exalts God alone, abases no man, for its purpose is to lift all into the dignity of citizenship in the city of the great King. It is hard in presence of this glorious ideal to speak calmly, yet it is necessary to speak the truth. And it is simple truth to say, the hour when this kingdom was revealed and instituted was and is the supreme hour in the history of man, the greatest of all that stand between the day of his creation and this. For through it was made manifest what he was meant to be, what ever since he has been striving to become. The ideal of Jesus was the ideal of God. He revealed to man the Divine possibilities and purposes immanent in his nature, made humanity know what it was to be one, unified by the reign of God in each, the Fatherhood of God over all.

And this splendid ideal we owe to the briefest, obscurest, most tragic ministry on record. In the ministry there was nothing to suggest or evoke the ideal, everything to suppress or quench any dim feeling that groped or looked towards it. It was a direct creation of Jesus, could be nothing less or else, for He alone explains it, while it in turn helps to explain Him. It stands in essential connection with the characteristics before noted; provides, as it were, for the realization in humanity of what they had manifested to be in Jesus and to have come into the world through Him. What has been described as His universalism, signifies that manhood in Him became what its Maker designed it to be; His was neither tribal nor racial, neither national nor temporal, but universal, man as conceived by God translated into an actual being known to men. His sinlessness is the ethical expression of His perfection, His holiness its positive realization in the sphere of religious relationships and duties. The speech that unfolds the elements or qualities of his ideal, the principles underlying and creating His manhood, incarnates His truth, communicates the secret of His being to men. And it is because He gave this secret to His words that they might bear and distil it everywhere, that they have so rich a grace, so infinite a charm. In loving them men love the ideal of their own humanity; they touch us, for they are as the voice of the eternal Father speaking to the lost but not perished sonship in man, and so they have a sweetness which is like the reminiscence of a past too distant to be remembered, yet so real as to survive in unconscious memories. And what the words are for the individual, the kingdom is to be for the race; it is an ideal for collective humanity, a means, too, for its realization.

Isolated units can never be perfect, the perfecting of men and of man must go hand in hand, the regeneration of persons being incomplete till they are incorporated in a regenerated society, a renewed mankind. And so we may say, this obscurest of ministries was the most glorious of revelations, and, must we not also add? why it was so is the foremost problem of history.

5. But now the unity and relation of these facts and truths as to the historical Jesus brings us to another point : the position He Himself occupied in the realization of His ideals, personal and universal. That position was cardinal, all turned on Him. Without Him nothing was possible ; He had come expressly that these sublime ends of His might be reached and made real. We must recollect what He seemed, and we must now see what He claimed to be. He was " the Son of man," not of any person or people, but of humanity, and so of its God,[1] and as such able to forgive sins. He came to fulfil the law and the prophets;[2] they testified of Him, He was their end ; all history was a preparation for Him. He was the Lord of the Sabbath,[3] had the right and the power to abolish or create religious institutions. He came to seek and save the lost,[4] to restore sight to the blind, liberty to the captive, life to the dead.[5] He invited all that laboured and were heavy laden to come to Him and He would give them rest; to take His yoke upon them and learn of Him, and they would have peace of soul.[6] The kingdom He had instituted was a kingdom of the truth ; its citizens were the men who heard His voice,

---

[1] Matt. ix. 6; xii. 37, 41 ; xvi. 13.
[2] Matt. v. 17.
[3] Matt. xii. 8 ; Mark ii. 28 ; Luke vi. 5.
[4] Luke xix. 10.
[5] Luke iv. 18.
[6] Matt. xi. 28, 29.

and confessed, He is the Christ, the King.[1] No man ever made claims like these; yet Jesus makes them calmly, as if unconscious of the immense issues and the immenser dignities they imply. He is confessedly the humblest, meekest, purest, truthfulest Speaker and Teacher man in all the centuries of his existence has come to know; yet He speaks these great things of Himself as simply as if it were not Himself He was speaking of, and had not the great ends He wished to see accomplished full in view. And in the presence of these sayings, what are we to think? Can we think that they are other than the transcript of His inmost consciousness, the mirror of the truth He knew Himself to be? It seems to be a thing of last incredibility that Jesus, being what we have seen Him to be, could be mistaken as to His own meaning and mission, could have erred in the interpretation of His own person, His place and work in the redemption of humanity. The truth of Jesus becomes the supreme testimony to the Christ; we follow Him, hear Him, learn what He is, what He comes to do, what He has done, and confess, " Thou art the Son of God, Thou art the King of Israel."

III.

Our discussion has hitherto been concerned with the Jesus of History, but it has resulted in His becoming the Christ of Faith. The problem with which we started seems to have been solved in the process of our historical analysis; the person known to history appears to have turned out the very person

[1] John xviii. 36, 37.

known to faith. The relation is necessary and inseparable, the two being in reality one. The connection is so essential that to apprehend the religious significance of Jesus is to discover that He is the Christ. It is this religious significance alone that has been here discussed. His so-called supernatural acts have in no respect influenced the argument or entered into the material analysed. Yet we find that Jesus has only become the more wonderful, with all the better right to claim our admiration and our faith. But this does not end the discussion. The conclusion must be verified and further vindicated by an appeal to the history of the literature concerned, an attempt to discover the relation between the oldest knowledge of Jesus and the faith in the Christ.

And here a most notable and suggestive fact meets us. Our oldest, most indubitably authentic Christian literature is devoted to the exhibition of Jesus as the Christ. In the order of time the historical Jesus is first; but in the matter of literary presentation the first place is occupied by the Christ who claims our faith. The great Pauline Epistles are older than our Gospels. In these Epistles Jesus is the Christ, "the Son of David according to the flesh, but the Son of God according to the Spirit."[1] He is the Second Adam, the Lord from heaven.[2] He is the Own Son whom God did not spare, but delivered up to the death for us all.[3] He is the end of the law for righteousness to every one who believeth.[4] He was delivered for our offences, and raised again for our justification.[5] He is Christ crucified, the Lord of glory,

[1] Rom. i. 3, 4. [2] 1 Cor. xv. 45, 47. [3] Rom. viii. 32.
[4] Rom. x. 4. [5] Rom. iv. 25.

made of God unto us wisdom, and righteousness, and sanctification, and redemption.[1] Of His grace, though He was rich, yet for our sakes He became poor.[2] When He rose from the dead, He became the firstfruits of them that slept, and so by Him came resurrection, and in Him shall all be made alive. And the risen Christ is to reign "till He hath put all His enemies under His feet."[3] And as He reigns He judges; all must appear before His judgment seat.[4]

Now from the literary and critical point of view these are our oldest and most authentic words concerning Jesus, which means that when He first, through His apostles, appears to claim our consideration and regard, it is as clothed in all the attributes of the Christ. And this fact does not stand alone, and so is not to be explained by any idiosyncrasy peculiar to Paul. The Apocalypse and the Epistle to the Hebrews are very unlike each other, and also very unlike Paul, and they are both, if not older than the oldest, at least older than two, possibly than three, of our Gospels. In the Apocalypse Jesus is the Christ, the Son of man, Alpha and Omega, the First and the Last, He that liveth and was dead, and is alive for evermore.[5] The throne of God is also the throne of the Lamb,[6] who died that He might make His people kings and priests unto God. He is the root and the offspring of David, the bright and the Morning Star, the Judge who cometh to give to every man according to his works.[7] In the Epistle to the Hebrews He is the Son of God, who made the worlds, the bright-

---

[1] 1 Cor. ii. 2, 8; i. 30.
[2] 2 Cor. viii. 9.
[3] 1 Cor. xv. 20–25.
[4] 2 Cor. v. 10.
[5] Rev. i. 13, 11, 18.
[6] Rev. xxii. 3.
[7] Rev. xxii. 16, 12.

ness of the Father's glory, the impression or very image of His substance.[1] He is the Captain of salvation, the Son who learned obedience by suffering, the High Priest who ever liveth to make intercession for man, who appeared to put away sin by the sacrifice of Himself.[2] Once more we find that the doctrine as to the person of Christ is as old as Christian literature,—is not surpassed in age by the books which present us with the historical portraiture of Jesus.

Now what does this fact or series of facts mean? It does not mean that the doctrine preceded the history, for the doctrine everywhere implies the history as its basis or object for interpretation; but it does mean that the history and the doctrine stood so essentially and organically related that the Person was, as it were, aboriginally transcendental, came to thought clothed through act and speech and realized personality in all the attributes of the Christ. History and doctrine had their common root in the Person. The history could not be written without the doctrine, the doctrine could not be stated without the history implied as something known and understood. Without this organic and aboriginal connection alike of history and doctrine with the person of Jesus, we can explain neither the creation, nor the faith, nor the achievements of early Christianity. With this, these are traced back to their source in the creative personality whose historical significance we have been here attempting to interpret. The Jesus of History is the sufficient reason for all these effects. To know Him is to believe in the Christ.

But it is not enough that we answer the question

---

[1] Heb. i. 2, 3.   [2] Heb. ii. 10; v. 8; vii. 25-27; ix. 26.

with which we started; it is necessary that we see the reasonableness of the apostolic belief. For the belief was reasonable to the Apostles, the Christ was to them also ὁ λόγος, which is the Reason as well as the Word, the Word as the symbol and garment of reason. Jesus was no accident—ever since the birth and fall of man the generations had been now more, now less unconsciously marching towards Him. Christ had built the worlds, they expressed His thought; man incarnated His idea, had been made in His image. It was fit that the Creator should be the Redeemer. He who gave the image could not allow the image to be marred and broken. The nature He made trusted Him who made it, and so man before He came travailed with the hope of His appearing. But through Israel came a diviner voice breaking into distincter speech, and the people Jehovah called lived to bear the Christ, once they had borne Him dying, in order that He might the more victoriously do His work. If the speech of our modern schools were here allowed us, we might say that the name "Christ" represented to the Apostles a philosophy of God, of Nature, and of Man. The philosophy of God was the fundamental, a sublime and noble doctrine. It conceived God as essentially love and righteousness, a Being who was never without love, who contained in Himself both the subject and the object love always implies; a Being so righteous that He could not bear the presence or the reign of wrong. And so when sin came where holiness ought to be He could not leave it alone, loved the man, hated the sin, and so sent the Christ to condemn the sin and save the man. The philosophy of Nature made it live for

God, made it, too, alive with God, the arena of His Providence, the field on which His judgment against sin and His love for man might be splendidly manifested. The philosophy of Man was vast and profound, contained doctrines as to the organic being and collective responsibility of the race, which yet only intensified the individuality and responsibility of its constituent units, as to the order and movement of man in history, as to his nature, his origin, his life here and his life hereafter. The man who has most worked himself into the heart of the apostolic thought will most wonder, if we may so speak, at its daring completeness, at the splendid courage with which it embraces God and man, time and eternity in one immense and harmonious system. And this system is as it were epitomized in Christ; it all stood together in Him, a universe whose unity was its head. The doctrine can only be understood through the system. An exposition of the system were the best apology for the doctrine. For the man who would understand it must never forget, that the men who proclaimed to the world the faith in the Christ believed that it was needed not simply to explain the Jesus of History but also the whole problem of life, the deepest mysteries of the universe, of man and of God.

And here our discussion, incomplete as it is, must end. Enough that we have traced the organic connection between the Jesus of History and the Christ of Faith, and indicated the lines along which thought must move to comprehend and construe the latter. The Apostles might be simple men, but their faith was not the faith of the simple, was indeed the wisest and the largest reading of his last mysteries which has yet come to man. And what shall we say of Jesus the Christ, who so opened the universe, so declared the Father to these men? He stands alone, in a Divine and most significant solitude. Why? Why have we only one Christ? We have had many philosophers, and neither to Sokrates, nor Plato, nor Aristotle among the ancients, neither to Bacon, nor Descartes, nor Spinoza, nor Kant, nor Schelling, nor Hegel, among the moderns, could the palm of solitary, indisputable superiority be given. We have had many poets, and neither to Homer, nor Dante, nor Shakespeare, nor Milton, nor Goethe could the praise of unique and unapproachable excellence be awarded. We have had many soldiers, and neither to Alexander, nor Hannibal, nor Cæsar, nor Charlemagne, nor to any of the mediæval and modern commanders could absolutely unequalled military genius be attributed. And so in every other department of human thought and action. No man is entirely unique. Every man has many compeers; Christ, and Christ alone, and that in the highest department, the religious, is unique, solitary, incomparable; and our question is, why? Why has the Creator of men created only one Christ, while He has created myriads of all other kinds of men? That Creator is infinitely benevolent; He loves His creatures, He seeks their highest well-being. That well-being Christ has promoted not only more than any other man, but more than all other men that have ever lived. If one Christ has been so mighty for good, what would a multitude have accomplished? Yet God has given to our poor humanity only one, and if we persist in asking, Why? can we find a fitter answer than the answer that stands written in the history of the Word made flesh? God in giving *one* gave His all: "God so loved the world, that He gave His only begotten Son, that whosoever believeth in Him should not perish, but have everlasting life."[1]

> "Morality to the uttermost,
> Supreme in Christ as we all confess,
> Why need we prove would avail no jot
> To make Him God, if God He were not?
> What is the point where Himself lays stress?
> Does the precept run, 'Believe in good,
> In justice, truth, now understood
> For the first time'? or 'Believe in Me,
> Who lived and died, yet essentially
> Am Lord of Life'? Whoever can take
> The same to his heart and for mere love's sake
> Conceive of the love,—that man obtains
> A new truth; no conviction gains
> Of an old one only, made intense
> By a fresh appeal to his faded sense."[2]

> "I say, the acknowledgment of God in Christ
> Accepted by thy reason, solves for thee
> All questions in the earth and out of it,
> And has so far advanced thee to be wise.
> Wouldst thou unprove this to re-prove the proved?
> In life's mere minute, with power to use that proof,
> Leave knowledge and revert to how it sprung?
> Thou hast it; use it, and forthwith, or die."[3]

[1] John iii. 16.
[2] Browning: "Christmas Eve and Easter Day." Poetical Works, vol. v. 154
[3] Browning: "A Death in the Desert." Poetical Works, vol. vi. 127.

II.

CHRIST IN HISTORY.[1]

"Jesus Christ, the same yesterday, to-day, and for ever."—Heb. xiii. 8.

IN this verse the writer states what may be regarded as the thesis of his epistle, the truth it was written to prove. The Christ who had come is a Christ who had ever been present with man, the hidden thought or reason that made the religious customs and institutions of the past intelligible prophecies of good things to come. The religion of the Hebrews, their priesthood, law, temple, sacrifices, were without Him unmeaning "shadows," but by His presence they were changed into vehicles of living light. Without Him Hebrew history had no Divine purpose or promise in it, but with Him the people and their past became eloquent of the truths God best loves to speak and man most needs to hear. Yet the most demonstrative at once proofs and symbols of His presence with man were not things, they were persons. It was not the priesthood, whether of Melchizedek or Aaron; nor the law, whether of Moses or the priests; nor the temple, nor the sacrifices that had from generation to generation been there offered; but it was the Men of

[1] Sermon preached at Liverpool before the Congregational Union of England and Wales, October 14th, 1878.

faith that had been the most illustrious witnesses to His presence. He made them the men they were; they lived by Him and for Him. Their faith was faith in the Christliness of the Eternal, or rather in the Christ whose home is the bosom of the Eternal God, and their lives had reality only as He was real. The men of God who lived by faith were God's chosen witnesses to the faith by which they lived. As Christ had been in the past, so was He in the present, changed in form, unchanged in essence, speaking the truth of God, creating by His speech the life of God in the spirit of man, gathering the men He quickened into new societies, making new peoples with fathers and founders even more illustrious than the heroes of the ancient faith. And as He had been and then was, so was He ever to be—a creative and saving Presence, the Maker and Ruler of a humanity conformed to the Divine ideal, the leader of the men who were to lead the world, "Jesus Christ, the same yesterday, to-day, and for ever,"

The apparent and the real, the actual and the ideal in Christ seem to face each other like the sharpest contradictions. The faith built on Him stands in most marvellous contrast to His historical appearance. His person is the power of Christianity, the greatest force for good of all kinds in the greatest religion that has ever penetrated, possessed, and ruled the spirit of man; yet it cannot be said that while He lived He escaped obscurity. He was the child of a hated people, known only to be despised. He was poor, humble, unbefriended by rank and power. He did none of the great deeds that smite the eye and awaken the wonder of the world. His name in His lifetime did not travel beyond His own land. Rome did not hear of Him, or Greece. The only Roman known to history who saw Him thought Him a person to be pitied, innocent indeed, but not important enough to be saved from the fury of a disappointed and vindictive mob; and He died hated, despised, deserted by all save the very few whose love was stronger than death or shame. Yet by the righteous irony of the Providence which is ever most ironical when it seems most mocked, this Person, so obscure and lowly, so friendless and forsaken, has been proved to be the sublimest and the divinest Person in history, the one Man who has been to the civilized world for centuries the Very God. Imagine Pilate, as at noon of the fatal day he seeks rest after the irritation and humiliations of the morning, suddenly possessed by a vision, in which he sees the Jesus his coarse soldiers have scourged, whom he has scornfully abandoned to the cross, whom the Jews are in the very act of crucifying, raised to honours such as no Grecian god or Roman emperor ever received, believed to be the very Son and image of the invisible God, confessed to be the supreme Person of history, swaying over men and peoples the sceptre of the grace that saves, of the righteousness that judges—and would he not, as the successive scenes opened before him, begin to feel as if this were too marvellous even for a vision, and wake with a consciousness of mingled horror and amused amazement from what he might call the maddest of mad dreams? Yet what had seemed to him a series of absurdest impossibilities stands before us a series of realities accomplished. The crucified Christ is a centre whose circumference is Christianity, and a centre to which the innumerable hearts which form the living stream of the Christian centuries have turned for peace, light, love, for the comfort and cheer the thought of the humanities in God can send into the feeble and despondent spirit. Above these centuries as they have come and gone He has stood, "Jesus Christ, the same yesterday, to-day, and for ever."

There is a Christ *of* history and a Christ *in* history, and we may say, if the one seems to face our faith like a contradiction, the other faces it like a victorious vindication. If experience has proved anything it is this, the necessity of Christ to the moral well-being and spiritual rest of mankind. It were as impossible to count the spirits to whom He is a supreme necessity and a splendid joy, as it would be to resolve the stars that lie beyond the reach of the most powerful telescope. As the stars of the milky way are able from their very multitude, while singly indistinguishable, to girdle heaven with a zone of light, so a cloud of witnesses no man can number forms the glorious pathway of Christ down the ages, most luminous where the night seems darkest, most beautiful where it melts into the light of day. The glory that lies about His path adds beauty to Him who walks in it, and He comes towards us clothed in the radiant garments woven for Him by a faith stronger than time, by a love mightier than death, "Jesus Christ, the same yesterday, to-day, and for ever."

I.

Now here we come face to face with what seems a most fitting subject for our consideration; this viz., what Christ meant to do, what He has done, and why He has been able to do it. And this we must consider, not as a question in historical criticism, but as a matter of vital religion and practical politics, as a means of discovering what our living Christianity ought to be and ought to do and aim at doing. The ideal and the actual elements in Christ are not contradictory, the one only clothes and expresses the other; but the actual in Christianity is often a radical contradiction to the ideal in Christ. Yet these ought to be harmonized, nay, must be harmonized if the Christian religion is ever to become the religion of Christ. To live for Christ is to carry out His purposes and ideals, to fulfil the work He has been doing in and through man, and is still seeking to do. What the Churches supremely need is a return to His spirit and ideal and method; these they must follow that they may accomplish their own ends. His achievements are our inspiration. The grand deeds of the past ought to brace the present to action, do not save it from the trouble of acting, only help it the more nobly to act. It were an ill logic that made a noble and heroic father the apology for an ignoble and cowardly son. Power unexercised is power lost; energy unused is energy wasted. Christianity cannot rest on its laurels without losing them, without confessing that its work is done and its end near. A faith that lives on the credit of its past is not a living faith; a religion unable to do valiant and righteous work in the present is a religion the world can very easily spare.

Let us confess that we are confronted by hostile forces of enormous strength, by evils of immense magnitude. There is unbelief, aggressive, belligerent, most dogmatic where most sceptical, most omniscient where most agnostic, attempting by professing not to know to put down divinest knowledge. There is a superfine worldliness, the materialism that comes of comfortable material conditions, charitable to evil, incredulous of good, indulging its cynicism by declaring that all religions are for the cultured—equally false, for the ignorant and superstitious—equally good and useful. There are sins clothed in æsthetic and refined vices, the more mischievous that they are so subtle; and there are sins clothed in gross and bestial passions, facing with awful power the strength, the zeal, the piety of all our Churches. But what does this confession mean? That our work is only well begun, and is not to be easily completed. For a brave man to know that an evil is, is simply to know that it has to be vanquished. Our work is to seek to see the face of our foe in the darkness, that we may the better close with him in a struggle that may at once evolve strength and ensure victory. The idea of a state without struggle, without high strain and brave endeavour, is but the idea of a fool's paradise. Our faith lives by conflict. God's great law is this,— in conflict truth becomes purer, mightier, the more capable to live because the more able to command and possess a man. So "greater is He who is for us than all they who are against us"; the thought, sin, passion, which are but of yesterday or to-day, what are they alongside "Jesus Christ, the same yesterday, to-day, and for ever"?

But if we are to understand what Christianity has done and what the Christian religion ought to be and to do, it must be through Christ Himself and what

He aimed at achieving in man and history. His ideal ought to be ours; only as it is so have we any right to bear His name. Well, then, His aim was twofold, individual and universal, personal and social, particular and collective. Its intense individuality no man can question. He came "to seek and save that which was lost." His symbol is the Shepherd returning from the wilderness with the strayed lamb He had found. To Him a soul transcends in worth a world. Over its repentance there is joy among the angels of God. Yet the salvation of the individual is only a means to the great social and collective end. Christ came to create a society, to found a state, to make and rule the kingdom of God on earth. That kingdom was to be spiritual, a kingdom of spirits, the home of high and holy beatitude, working out righteousness, peace, joy among men. God was to rule in the conscience; He was to be its King, it was to be His seat. Where it was realized in the Spirit, God's ideal was realized; once it had fully come on earth, earth would be as heaven, completely obedient to God's will. That kingdom might seem to leave the ancient kingdoms of the world standing where of old they stood. But, in truth, it was the end of their reign; the new Man made the world new. Christ formed a new order by the new spirits He formed, changed the state by changing its units; did not attempt the absurd and impossible task of changing the units by simply changing the forms of the state. He came to build the city of God out of living spirits, making it the home of the men He saved; lifting each man He saved above the narrowness and impotence of time by making him a citizen of the city whose Builder and Maker is God. The kingdom as spiritual could be realized only in and through spirits, while as of God it was too immense, too Divine, to be embodied in any single form of life or polity. It was meant to penetrate, pervade, inspire all, but all could not adequately incorporate or express it. The kingdom was man and all his societies, histories, civilization; all his arts, sciences, polities, translated into a complete articulation of the will of God. To this collective end the individual was necessary, for it he existed, for it was saved. Men were to be converted that they might be kings and priests unto God; through them He was to reign; through them Christ was to work His mediation, the reconciliation of the world to God, even the Father.

Now this double aim, individual and collective, was not only Christ's; it passed from Him to His apostles. Paul preached "repentance toward God and faith toward our Lord Jesus Christ," but he so preached not simply in order to save persons, but to build up the Church of the living God, the temple of the Spirit, to form the commonwealth of Israel, or the citizenship of saints, where men ceased to be Jews or Greeks, and became the family of God. Peter preached to the multitudes that he might help to create a state religious, divine, "a spiritual house," "an holy priesthood," "a new heaven and a new earth," wherein righteousness was to dwell. John watched and prayed for a new Jerusalem that was to supplant the old, the holy city that was to come down out of heaven from God, adorned as a bride for her husband. And the times when this double aim has been most vividly before the Church have been the times of noblest power. If there are moments of inveterate worldliness, it is when men sink the individual in the social end; if moments of impotent *other*-worldliness it is when they sink the social end in the individual. Lose the individual, and you have a relentless tyranny, religion reduced to an organized and supercilious ecclesiasticism; lose the social in the individual, and you have a spiritual atomism, religion reduced to a short and easy expedient for winning peace in death and happiness with God, religion made impotent to make men religious and holy and true as citizens on earth or in heaven. The time when the Christian Society has been possessed by the thought of a reigning Christ, of creating a humanity that was a brotherhood obedient to God, articulating and expressing His will in all forms and modes alike of its individual and collective life, has ever been a time of Christian heroes, of men who lived not only to do God's will themselves, but to persuade all men in all states to come and obey it, that they might have an earth which, living to God's glory, created man's highest good.

II.

1. Such then was Christ's ideal. But how was it to be realized? Whose were the creative energies? Where did they live and how were they to be exercised? It is enough meanwhile to note simply this point: Christ Himself was the centre and seat of the creative energies; in Him they existed, as it were personalized, made active, living, powerful, by being compacted, or organized, into a great personality. That the forces that created Christianity proceeded from Christ is open to no manner of question, is sure indubitable fact.

Men may seek to explain what He was, or how He became it, but one thing they cannot deny, that Christ made Christianity; that its being is due to Him. He is as a simple matter of fact the greatest personality in history. The forces that lived in Him are the divinest forces that ever penetrated and possessed the spirit of man. They have effected the grandest and most civilizing revolutions in his history, have exercised over him the mightiest, most commanding influence. Men may seek to resolve the Christ of our Gospels into the child of the myth-making Oriental imagination, made creative by the enthusiasm of a great love, or to explain Him as the last result of the exaggerative spirit and polemical interests of rival parties, tendencies that advance through conflict and antithesis to synthesis and harmony. But then these attempts only prove this: the Person who inspired those imaginations, who called into being these parties, did, in so doing, create Christianity. The fact of His creative action is not changed, nor the wonder lessened, but much rather increased, for just in proportion as the Creator is made less marvellous, the creation becomes the more. To conceive the effect as so extraordinary is only the less to allow any one to argue an ordinary cause. Then, too, the theories are inconsistent with the experience of the men who frame them, for every student of our Gospels confesses the power, commanding, authoritative, of the Christ. In Him there dwells a wondrous fascination. The coldest critic feels warmed into love of Him; in His presence the most daring thinker feels his soul touched with beautiful reverence. The Divinity within Him proves its presence and reality by the admiration it commands, the devotion it creates. To

Spinoza He was the temple of man, where God stood most perfectly revealed, the Divine word or eternal reason become incarnate. Rousseau, in his extravagant way, contrasted Christ and Sokrates, and concluded that while the one died like a philosopher, the other died like a god. Goethe thought that progress was possible on all sides save one—the moral majesty, the spiritual culture expressed and exhibited in the Gospels could never be excelled. Schiller named the religion of Christ in its purest form the incarnation of the holy, Jesus Himself being to him incarnate holiness. Strauss praised Him as the supreme religious genius of time, who had created and impersonated the ideal or absolute religion. Renan confesses that He merits Divine rank, that to Him belongs the unique honour of having founded the true religion, leaving it to us to be at our best only His disciples and continuators.

And from other sides no less eloquent and conclusive testimonies come. The splendid cycle of thinkers that began with Kant and ended with Hegel, made Christ the last problem of their philosophies; to explain Him was to explain at once religion and man, mind and history. It is a rare yet remarkable fact, that while He is the pre-eminent problem of historical and critical thought, the most hotly debated, the most variously solved, no reasonable man ever doubts His sincerity, or the blameless, solitary, and radiant beauty of His character and life. There is no surer measure of the essential spiritual quality of an age than its estimate of Christ. A time of moral degradation is marked by insensibility to His character, His purposes and aims; a time of moral elevation and heroism is marked by an enthusiasm for Him and His purposes born of the most splendid love. A power so imperishable and immense can never have been at its root an unreal, or unrighteous power. Eternal law has made it impossible that the false should ever create the true, or a bad ideal form and inspire a good reality. While Christ remains the personality creative of all that is best and noblest in man, let Him live, " the same yesterday, to-day, and for ever."

2. But now, why has Christ been so pre-eminent and creative a personality? Why has He so long remained one? What was the secret, what were the sources of His transcendent might? These are large questions, and it is possible here and now only in the faintest way to indicate some of the lines along which the answers lie. Let this at the outset be noted: what He brought with Him as His absolute gift to faith—an idea or thought of God that made God an absolutely new being to our race. The theological significance of Christ's person is simply infinite. He is in the most absolute sense a revelation of God to men. Man's thought of God, of the cause and end alike of his own being and of the universe, is his most commanding thought; make it, and you make the man. And Christ was here a supreme Creator. He made our thought of God; made His God ours. Since He lived men have felt, and do feel—if God is, then He must be as He is revealed in Jesus Christ. A God like this does explain the world; the world without Him were no home for man.

Now consider what this signifies. Men cannot escape God. Reason, feeling, imagination, conscience, drive us towards the Divine, the Eternal. The attempt to escape Him is an impossible attempt.

Impulse is stronger than will. Where the choice is not to find Him the impulse conquers the choice. Agnosticism is abhorrent to man. A professed agnostic is still a person who knows, and indeed in a quite infinite degree. His passion is a knowledge so absolute that he knows what things cannot be known. Against his own will the agnostic becomes a seeker after God. It is significant that the most distinguished of our living agnostics, the man whose fundamental principle is that the Infinite, the First and Ultimate Cause, cannot be known, is yet the author of our most comprehensive and omniscient system of philosophy, a system that attempts to explain all things in heaven and earth, alike as to their whence and whither, their genesis, behaviour, and end. If the Ultimate Cause, which simply means the true reason of things, cannot be known, then it is impossible to have any philosophy, for what is philosophy but the search after the true reason of things, conducted in the sure belief that such reason exists and can be found? And so Agnosticism is as fatal to science as to religion, for to attempt to explain the becoming of the world on the basis of absolute nescience as to the primary and efficient cause, is to attempt to make science stand upon a principle that declares knowledge vain, and therefore science impossible.

And as in the case of the individual, who in spite of his agnostic self is driven into gnosticism, so in the history of man. Everywhere he has made most diligent search for God. Everywhere the great goal of thought has been, Who was the First, who is to be the Last? Why came I into being? Why this world? What is the end of our being? The tragedy of the human spirit, and there is no tragedy like it, its search after truth, its failure to find it, its strenuous belief in it as still to be found, is all summed up in its quest after God. Just look at the history of Indian thought. When ancient Brahmanism ruled supreme, men thought God a kind of unending circle, a great revolving Force that everywhere and always sent into existence units that vanished only to return in other forms; and Buddha, feeling life to be altogether miserable, seeing no escape from the eternal circle of being while the Brahmanical deity was allowed to live, seeing, too, that at no point was the circle blessed, everywhere pain, shame, misery—declared, God is not, no Deity lives. To base a great faith on atheism seems awful to us. Yet it was blessed to India. Buddha's evangel was, there is no God, and the evangel was real, for God had been so misconceived as to be a horror to the spirit. Only by his divine denial of the Divine could the hope of escape from the merciless cycle of being come to the Hindu mind; to it man's greatest boon in time was loss of God; man's last beatitude, *nirvana*, loss of being, the passing into absolute quiescence. Buddhism is the grand logical result, worked out on the most stupendous scale, of Pantheism. Deny the personality of God, and the best thing for the race is to deny God; the best thing for the person, escape from personal to those impersonal modes of being which are the dreariest everlasting death. Rightly read, our whole past, our whole present, becomes but the splendid example of man's search for Deity, his need of God made the more significant by the mad endeavour, if he cannot reach the truth, to break away and live without the very God and Father he must find if he is to escape the paralysis of despair.

Now, note, how into this world, with its chaotic thought of God, yet its equal necessity for Him, Christ came. He came and declared that the First Cause, the Final End of the world, viewed in relation to man, is an Eternal Spirit which can be represented by no name but the name of "Father." The Father must be in an equal degree Love and Righteousness, as Love seeking the good of His children, as Righteousness seeking their good through an eternal law of truth and right. Love is eternal, had no beginning, can have no end in God. Love, too, is social, can exist only as there is the subject and the object of love. Love made God happy; love craved to create happiness; wished, as the ever-blessed God was blessed in Himself, to fill the silent places of the universe with glad voices, with happy souls. Man is not a necessity to God, but God needed man, needed man to satisfy His infinite love, the large and eternal emotion, of His own great spirit; and as God needed man, man rose obedient to God's need. But the need was not simply creative, it was redemptive as well. Love must aim at the good of the child it caused, and labour for it; as the individual rises out of love, love ever continues to work his good, to seek his weal. Ill to a child is ill to a parent; sin in man is suffering in God. Out of man's ill came God's suffering, revealed, realized, made to the universe for ever apparent in the Person, in the sacrifice of Christ. It became the God who is eternal to make Him perfect through suffering. God so loved the world that He gave His only begotten Son, love itself involving sacrifice. That thought of the Eternal Father ruling in love through righteousness towards lovely and righteous ends; that thought of the Eternal brooding in ceaseless pity, working in untiring energy in all the units for the good alike of the single person and the collective race, was the splendid gift of Christ to man. And so as we think of it there comes to us, as to Karshish the Arab physician, bewildered for the moment by the mysterious grandeur of the new conception which had come to him through his unexpected meeting with Lazarus, the man the Christ had raised from the dead, the vision of a diviner Deity than any philosophy or religion of the peoples had as yet known:

> "The very God! think Abib, dost thou think?
> So, the All-Great were the All-Loving too—
> So, through the thunder comes a human voice
> Saying, "O heart I made, a heart beats here!
> Face My hands fashioned, see it in Myself;
> Thou hast no power nor may'st conceive of Mine,
> But Love I gave thee, with Myself to love,
> And thou must love Me who have died for thee."[1]

3. Now this new thought of God, this creation of the divinest elements in our conception of Him, was an absolute gift, so absolute that it can be neither renounced nor recalled. It has so entered into and possessed the spirit of man that he cannot expel it, or escape from it. It is now his, even in spite of himself, for ever. It would have been pleasant, had it been here possible, to show how the ideas of Christ have gone into the very bone and marrow of living mind, penetrated the very soul and substance of our newest and most characteristic modern thought,

[1] Browning: Poetical Works, vol. v. 228-9.

making it essentially unlike ancient thought, classical or oriental. It is strange, for example, that the Buddhism of the East has appeared in the West. Buddha's great doctrine of Karma, the law or impersonal moral order, which goes on for ever fulfilling itself by binding choice and action, action and result indissolubly together, has been introduced into this home of the Philistines by the modern master of phrases, and baptized "Stream of tendency." But then, while Buddhism has appeared in its great fontal thought as a stream of tendency, Christ has come in and added the idea "that works for righteousness," and the man who would have been a Buddhist, had Christ not been, finds himself steeped in a circle of Christian ideas from which he cannot, and would not if he could, purge his consciousness. Lucretius long ago constructed a system purely material, made the universe the home and arena of forces altogether physical, with God and Providence, religion and worship banished as altogether hateful things, every variety and form and quality of life being the work of a nature self-evolved. David Strauss tried to formulate in our own day what was to be the faith of the future. It was to be faith in the majestic cosmos, in the mighty unordered, all-ordering order, expressed in worship, the feeling of reverence for the *universum* so immense and so harmonious. But his universe was no longer the universe of Lucretius, it was a universe of love, with benevolence and righteousness built into its order and expressed in all its laws, a universe, as it were, baptized into Christ. And so men like Strauss, who stand up in all the serene and conscious wisdom of this nineteenth century to ask, "Have we any faith?" answer themselves. They stand in borrowed plumes, arrayed in ideas most indubitably Christ's, yet arguing as if it were a possible problem,—" Are we still Christians?" With an unconsciousness that is only a mightier testimony to His truth they speak ideas that are His, and hold them the noblest and most necessary elements of the law by which men ought to order their lives. In so doing they witness to this—that Christ Himself, His words, His meaning, His mission, and all His purposes, have so passed into the thought and spirit and blood of the world that the world can never more escape from Him. He is the soul of its noblest thinking, the motive and mainspring of its humanest action. "Jesus Christ, the same yesterday, to-day, and for ever."

III.

But this brings us to another point. We must consider not simply what He brought and gave, but what He was. Any attempt to discuss from the doctrinal point of view what He was, would raise immense theological questions; but I wish meanwhile to discuss the matter under one aspect only—the relation of Christ's person to the realization of His ideal, particular and collective, as the source and vehicle of the energies that were to create His society and direct its work.

1. Notice, then, Christ's was a pre-eminently fair, perfect, beautiful humanity. He was God's ideal of man realized, made manifest, actual, active. Now this humanest of all historical personalities can be studied under three relations suitable to our present theme, the relation to eternal law, to man, and to God.

As to the first, the relation to law, Christ was personalized righteousness, our human virtues articulated, revealed, made to live a life ideally perfect, while entirely real. He was truth, chastity, gentleness, love, faith, hope; all the graces law most loves and man most admires, active, vital, and embodied. In relation to man, He was simply incarnate beneficence, an embodiment of the love that can bear, and dare, and do all things that it may promote human good. He was the spirit of human brotherhood personalized. The men who sinned against Him did not provoke Him into retaliatory sinning, their hatred only evoked His pity, their vengeance but supplied occasion for the exercise of His forgiving love. The great things that possessed His spirit, the sorrows that broke His heart, did not turn Him from the service of His kind. As He was in all His thoughts benevolent, He was in all His actions beneficent. For man He lived, and for man He died. Then in relation to God He was perfectly obedient; the first-born Son of the Eternal. He came to do His Father's will, and He did it. He suffered indeed, but only that He might the more learn and manifest obedience, and stand to all time as one who possessed and made manifest a double Sonship, at once "Son of God" and "Son of Man."

Now think how these elements of His personality have acted upon the thought of man, have influenced and affected the life of the world within as without the Christian society. His relation to law has constituted a new and more perfect moral ideal for the race, has created a new order of beneficent virtues, has made the noblest to be not simply the bravest man, but the gentlest, the humanest, the chastest, and the most charitable. It exalted conscience, it ennobled freedom, making men feel that whatever touched man's conscience and stood between him and his duty, or the law of his God, was an attempt at an unholy bondage of the spirit. His relation to man, with the brotherhood it expressed, created the idea of fraternity, ended the deep degradation of the slave, the deeper degradation of the autocrat, introduced the time when man was to be the brother of man the world over, and all lands and distant isles of the sea were to be bound in sympathy and love. The great thought of our humanity as a brotherhood, and all the beneficent work it has done in the world, has been His. Then out of his relation to God came the idea of man's common sonship and the equality of all the sons before the eternal Father; and the glory of the equality that came through Him is this—it did not abase, it exalted; it did not simply humble the proud, it lifted the lowly, thrilling the poorest with the idea of kinship with God. It is in traits like these that the quality of Christ's conception stands revealed. It was an almost infinite elevation of the idea of man. It levelled nothing but the evil or vain; it raised the highest to a loftier height than he had ever dreamed of. Mankind became consciously a family, with God as their common Father; men found the distinctions of earth vanish before the sublime equality which came of their common sonship to Heaven.

2. And these have not been allowed to be barren ideas; the energies of their Creator have made them our most potent spiritual forces. For one thing His person showed them in organic unity; in harmonious and reciprocal activity. He made it evident that law exists for man inside and in behalf of humanity; our

best obedience is true beneficence. Then His love of God was expressed in service of man; His service of man was obedience to God. And this, while it widened the range, exalted the end of human service. Men in serving man served God; good was done to our kind for the greater glory of God. And this worked a wonderful change alike in the motives and objects of action; it made the most ideal duties practicable. You have found love of man one of the hardest things possible; there are men it is impossible to love. You cannot love badness—how can you love the person who incorporates it? A lie is hateful; is the liar loveable? You cannot love a mean act; can you love the man who incarnates meanness? You hate lust; can you love the lustful, the man whose uncleanness makes the very atmosphere around him an offence and a shame to you? Christ brings an answer to these questions. It is not the actual man you love, it is God's ideal. You do not seek to save him for his own sake merely, but for the sake of the God that made him, and made him to be good, and means him still to become what He made him to be. The size of the ruin proves the grandeur of the ruined nature. You love the nature the ruin marred. In every actual devil there is a possible god. Christ made us to see the possible god in the actual devil, made us so to see it that we might love this Divine image, though lost, yet latent in the very worst, and labour that it might be restored. Once love of God becomes love of humanity, religion becomes a mass of ameliorative energies, the civilized agencies of the world concentrated, organized, glorified. Missionary enterprise, home and foreign, becomes possible, for to us the savage, however debased, is more akin to the angel than to the brute, the man possessed of passions that are but demons may yet be the home of holiest enthusiasms. So we do and must believe while Jesus Christ remains "the same yesterday, to-day, and for ever."

3. As with his thought of God, so with his realization of the ideal of man—the world cannot escape from it, cannot expel the ideas, the inspiration, the consciousness it has created. It holds and commands the men who think they have most completely superseded Christ. There lives in our midst a so-called religion of humanity, which seems the very negation of the Christian. It knows no Creator; its only God is *le Grand Être*, the collective race. Yet the race it has deified it seeks to love, to serve, to make more godlike in its good, less demoniac in its evil, to build into a mighty organism whose every unit shall contribute to the good of the whole, and the good of the whole become the possession and the joy of all the units. Yet whence came the thought of humanity as a whole, a delicate yet stupendous organism, a concrete and finely articulated being, with all its component units in ceaseless interactivity, so subtly and sympathetically related that no good or ill could come to one without touching and affecting all? Many centuries before Comte there lived a man named Paul, the most famed interpreter of the Christ. He thought of Adam as so bound to the race, and the race as so bound to Adam, that the good of the one, or the evil of the one, was the good or evil of all; thought, too, of Christ as so bound to humanity, and humanity as so bound to Christ, that He represented, incarnated, contained it, that it lived, moved, acted through Him.

His good was its; its good His. To serve Him was service of man; and every man He saved helped to sanctify humanity. And so Paul thought that by living for Christ he only the more lived for man. To work for Him was not to work for transient reforms, or variable and imperfect policies, but for the ends of the Creator, the eternal purpose of God regarding man. To obey His law was not to be guided by the generalized experiences of the race, but to follow out the plan after which humanity had been built, that the mind of the Builder might be perfectly fulfilled. And he conceived his action and the action of every other individual as affecting not simply man and man's whole future, but also the immense universe that sleeps in the bosom of space, the principalities and powers in heavenly places that learn through the Church the manifold wisdom of God. That was an idea of related and interactive being such as never glimmered on the soul of Comte; and if Positivism says: " See how noble and humane our religion; it bids you worship and serve humanity as *le Grand Être*," we shall only make answer—" We have a grander and sublimer truth. To us humanity articulates the thought of God, and we worship God by serving man, according to the ideal of Him realized in Jesus Christ, who is 'the same yesterday, to-day, and for ever.' "

IV.

1. So much for Christ's ideal and the energies, all contained in and proceeding from Himself, that were to realize it. But the discussion of these questions has brought us to another—" How, or in what way did

He proceed to realize His ideal? What was His method?" It was to work from within outward, from the one to the many, the unit to the mass. He proceeded by calling individuals, for their own sakes indeed, yet not for their own sakes only, but for man's as well. Christ, in order that the truth and life in Him might live and work, created out of the men He called and saved a society, the kingdom of heaven, the city of God. It was like a vehicle of the ideas He incarnated, a seedplot of the life He possessed. The saved were saved that they might be agents of salvation. The society of the saved was intended to be a society of the healed, working like a great healthful balm in the sick heart of humanity. That balm was to be after its nature an invisible fragrance shed from the visible societies of saintly men. Those societies were allowed to determine their own outer being, the specific shape they were to wear. Christ did not make for His society a policy that was everywhere and always to stand unchanged and the same; did not bind it under immutable formal laws—*that* had been to swaddle it in iron bands that had soon worked its death; but while He made His society, and was to live in it an everlasting Presence, He allowed the life immanent in it to regulate its outer form of being, its great modes of action. That society of His has had various ideals. There is the Papal or autocratic; there is the Episcopal or aristocratico-monarchical; there is the republican or Presbyterian; there is the democratic or Congregational. The ideas are different in each; the ideals are different, too. The Papal system aims at unity, but thinks it can best secure unity by keeping all the men of the society children, bound in absolute obedience to an authority decreed to be above the human liability to err. The Episcopal attempts to imitate a constitutional monarchy, thinks that a political uniformity, with its drilled and graded orders, is better than the freedom of the spirit, or the spontaneous and concordant action of a loving and trustful brotherhood. Then the Presbyterian is a republic, ruled by the elect, the spirits considered the wisest and the best; ruled by the few for the good of the many, yet with the power ultimately in the hands of the multitude, who are educated, disciplined, ennobled by the power they exercise. Then the Congregational system regards privilege and duty as co-ordinate, believes that no man can be within Christ's society who is not a saved, and so a saintly, and therefore a sane man, believes, too, that every man within the society has been called to exercise the privileges and the rights, and fulfil the duties of Christian manhood. It assumes the ideal ripeness or perfection, or the struggle towards it—to be helped, not hindered, by the functions of active citizenship—of all the units constituting the specific society.

With the comparative qualities and warrants of these polities I am not here concerned: enough to say, the one that does least justice to the manhood of the saved, is most alien to the ideals and ends of the society; while the one that confers on them most freedom, most of the privileges and duties of citizenship, is most in harmony with Christ's ideal alike of the citizen and the kingdom. And so it is but what was to be expected when we find that the men nearest to Him, who best understood His mind, His own disciples and apostles, followed the Congregational way. It was the freest, the most elastic, allowed most room to the men who loved "the liberty of the spirit" and "of prophesying," made it impossible to sacrifice the reign of God to a human polity, certain to be most faulty where it most claimed to be infallible. But all this lies beyond our immediate purpose. Here we have but to recognise this truth—the Christian society is greater than any Church, another and infinitely nobler thing than any Church polity. The society exists in all the Churches, but is contained in none, is not exhausted by all. The polities exist to help the realization of the kingdom, but no polity has realized it as completely as it needs and admits of realization. Each in its own place and in its own way seeks how best it can fulfil the great purposes of Christ as it conceives them and wishes them to be conceived, in order that His kingdom may come, and His will may be done by all men everywhere.

2. This society, then—with its power of creating its own forms, some less, others more perfect; some good, others in various ways mischievous — was launched upon the great tide of life. It looked frail, feeble, impotent enough, without the promise of the strength or skill that could outride the storm. Yet it was an absolutely new thing in the history of man, wonderful alike in its simplicity and wealth, the plastic forces within it, its ability to suit all men in all places. It was a new religion, yet was like no old religion, it had no temple, no priesthood, no ritual, no method of propitiating Deity, no Deity that needed propitiating; it was spirit and power, a religion that lived by the truth but through the simplest agencies, men seeking to persuade man to be reconciled to God. No

religion is like this, independent of form and independent of place. You cannot call Christianity an oriental or an occidental religion, an Eastern or a Western institution. It is neither; it is both; it belongs to man, it claims the whole earth. You cannot transplant Brahmanism; it is Indian throughout, was born in India, must live in India, is, outside of India, unintelligible, impracticable, impossible. You could not naturalize Buddhism in Europe; it would die of the process, broken by its very contact with the climate, the freedom, the institutions, the energies, the wholesome nature of the brawny and healthful West. Islam is an oriental faith; is at once too stern and indulgent, too simple and inflexible, too much bound to rude custom and half-savage institutions, to sacred places and barbarous rites, to breathe our Western air or suit our Western mind. But Christianity is universal, capable of being naturalized in any land, of living on any soil. She is bound to no place, wedded to no custom, carries no rites, is embodied in no institutions that must be, or indeed can be, localized. She is a kingdom of the truth, a temple of the Spirit, a city of souls who live by faith in the truth, and spread by speech the truth by which they live. The only things in Christianity cardinal, essential, eternal, are her truths. These she lives to teach, and the more she teaches the more she lives. The religion that is truth is universal; the faith that is a polity is local, perishable, destined to an unstable life, sure of an unlamented death.

Christ's society, then, was constituted by the truth, as it had been instituted for it. It was a kingdom of the truth, and men became its citizens through faith in that truth. The call to believe was an invitation to enter the society, to become a fellow-citizen with the saints. The call was thus necessarily individual; the conversion of persons was the extension of the society. The results looked at singly and in themselves were small enough; looked at collectively and in their issues most wonderful. The called were found to become new men, made according to the mind of Christ. His power as a maker of men proved Him to be a Creator, able to realize in others the ideal He had incarnated in Himself. His creative energy took many forms, received most varied expression. First and pre-eminently, He had, as no one else has had, power to make common men heroes, common persons persons of universal importance, foremost forces in history. The men He selected to do His work seemed the least likely men. From the shores of Gennesaret, from the fishermen's boat, from the receipt of custom, from the ploughed field, from the weaver's loom, He called men —men the world had despised, or held as at most fitted for their crafts—and He made these men His apostles, creators of a new faith, builders of a new humanity. Perhaps no enterprise ever promised as little as the work undertaken by the apostles, certainly no men ever promised less. Yet, let the Christian centuries witness to the kind and quality of the work they undertook, to the kind and quality of the men who accomplished it. Celsus, the earliest literary assailant of our faith, a very wise man, a physician and a philosopher, a true child of culture, proud of the manners, the speech, the daintiness and delicacy of the cultivated, said, "See what a set of men these Christians are! The teachers of our noble philosophies in our academies are cultivated gentlemen, acquainted with the best thoughts of the best thinkers, and able to give them fit because elegant expression; but these Christian preachers, why they are fishermen, and publicans, and weavers, and cobblers, the porters that stand on our quays and run on our errands, ignorant Jews, illiterate Greeks, the veriest barbarians, enthusiasts without the gift of refined thought or cultured speech." But now, let us take Celsus at his word, accepting his testimony as true, and what then? Does he not become one of our oldest, though most unconscious, witnesses to the power of Christ? It was a new thing in the history and experience of man that men such as Celsus described should become grander and mightier than any known to his academies, possessed of ideas as to God, as to men and society and the state, sublimer than Plato had ever imagined—men wiser in their notions of civil rights and political duties than Solon, dreaming of more splendid conquests than had ever dawned on the soul of Alexander or Cæsar, working at the foundations of a city infinitely nobler in ideal, as it was to be incomparably grander in history, than the city Athene loved and shielded, or the city Romulus founded and Jove guided to universal empire. To make these men out of what they were into what they became was to do a Divine work. Their call was the regeneration of man, their change the renovation of the world. Their preaching created the kingdom of the Spirit, broke the idol of the tribe, replaced it by the idea of humanity, and taught men to live for man by living for God. He who created the apostles and fathers of the Church recreated humanity.

3. But this was only one aspect of His action; the men He called to faith He also called to virtue. He

bound together belief and conduct, religion and morals as they had never been bound before. Men had been taught in the schools to know, but not to practise, virtue; Christ made the common people virtuous, and with a virtue finer in quality, nobler in range than the best of the schools had ever thought of. The result was extraordinary, but the simplicity of the means that achieved it was more extraordinary still. Christ made a grand discovery; He discovered the power of pure and simple human love. Before Him Love, Eros, Amor, had been known to the poets. They had sung its praises, its pleasures, its pains, the mighty passion with which it craved one earth, one heaven, one immortality; yet their love was but passion, a search after joys dear to the poorer self, living to be indulged, dying of indulgence. But Christ lifted love into a diviner atmosphere by giving it a new object, made it a new thing, mightiest and most propulsive of spiritual forces. Love of Christ was no sensuous passion; it was affection purified by the purity of the person it embraced. And while most intensely personal, it was as strongly universal, for love of Christ is love of man, of all the ends, purposes, agencies he embodies. To love Christ is not simply to love an individual; it is to love the race, the humanity He personalized. There is no affection like it, so universal yet so concrete, so diffused yet so concentrated, so broadly human yet so special in its aims, so direct in its action. The universalism in Christ's person universalizes the love, makes it seek to attain a manhood as pure as His, to become a benevolence as broad as His, to form a society correspondent to Him. No man can love Christ and spare the ill He hated, or despise the men He died to redeem. In loving Him we love mankind, in loving man we love Him and all He represents and contains.

The love of Christ was thus for the whole life moral and social, alike of the individual and the race, both a statical and a dynamical force. It created, as it were, a true centre of gravity for collective man, which was at once to maintain the equilibrium of all his native moral forces, regulate their action and determine their development. The humanity of Christ is an inexhaustible ideal for the race. It has so bound it to God, so penetrated mankind with theistic associations and relations, so transfigured it with the hopes and aims and ideals that spring out of its Divine kinship and destiny, so, in a word, worked the filiation of earth and heaven that no corporate unity or collective immortality can satisfy our notion of man; he has in him capabilities of indefinite progress, before him the hope of realizing the ideal dreamed by the Creator when He thought into being the world of free and rational spirit. It is this boundless significance of the person of Christ for humanity that makes love of Him a dynamical force so persistent and mighty. Love of Him can never be satisfied with what has been achieved, for His ideal is, as it were, insatiable, demands a perfection that the nearer it is approached only the more retreats. Yet the perfection that so eludes us is not illusive; every step forward is a step in real attainment, brings us nearer the goal of a perfected humanity, personal and collective. While His history lies behind us, He Himself is an ideal that moves ever before, and to love Him is to be drawn towards a good whose infinite promise is the mother of all our noblest performance.

4. But we cannot rightly apprehend all that is meant by Christ's power to create and control the men He called, and the society they formed, till we have studied its action in history. Through these men and this society He has acted and still acts on man. His action is at once collective and individual, through the whole society and through each of its component units. By what He has done through this twofold agency, He has profoundly modified the history and development of man, been the most potent and plastic spirit in our modern civilization. Just take one phase of His historical action,—what He has accomplished through great personalities. Were He dropped out of history, with all the historical personalities He has fashioned, it is hardly possible to conceive what to-day would be. The mightiest civilizing agencies are persons; the mightiest civilizing persons have been Christian men. No man in the ancient world, be he poet or philosopher, warrior or statesman, did as much to create the permanent humaner and higher elements of our civilization as Peter, and John, and Paul, men altogether obscure and commonplace till touched by the creative hand of Christ. The men who have most thoroughly understood Him have been centres of the noblest dynamical and moral forces in history, Athanasius, Augustine, Anselm, Aquinas. But select one century and let it suffice, say the sixteenth. It was the century that achieved our freedom, that vindicated the rights of reason, the supremacy of the conscience, the duty of the intellect to know for itself God and the truth of God. But what made the sixteenth a so pre-eminent century? Not Leo X., the pagan disguised as pope; not Charles V., heir of

many dynasties, monarch of many lands ; not Francis I., losing all but honour at Pavia, perhaps without honour to lose ; not Henry VIII., self-willed, sensuous, disowning popes and burning bishops, that he might marry as he willed! The age owed little to these men ; all they did was to do their best to mar it. Its makers were Luther, the man of quickened conscience, of strong faith and true heart, who first taught the Scriptures to speak German and German to become a tongue of the learned ; Zwingli, the heroic soldier-preacher, who loved his kind as he loved his reason, and believed in a God so good as to mean His heaven for man ; Calvin, the theocratic legislator, the man stern of spirit, resolute of will, as strong in practice as in intellect, building his City of God according to the severest principles of a theology so like ancient Stoicism, yet so infinitely more ; Tyndale, the man who loved the Gospel and made it live for the English people by clothing it in their English speech ; Knox, the preacher, loyal to his people, tender of heart, bold in word, creating at the same moment and by the one splendid act a nation, a Church, and a school system, best and broadest of his own day, and even of ours. These were the men who made the century, but who made the men? In whose name, in whose strength, by obedience to whose will, as they understood and believed it, did they live and act? Did not their inspiration come straight from Christ? Abolish these men, and the sixteenth century loses its significance ; abolish Christ, and you abolish the men. Yet what is true of it, is true of all the Christian centuries. Subtract the Christian personalities and the ideas that reigned in and lived through them, and you have but the struggle of brutal passions, of men savage through ambition and lust of power; subtract Christ, and you dry up the source of all Christian personalities and ideas, you leave man to go his old blind way, ungladdened by faith in heaven, uncheered by the ideal of a humanity to be made perfect through realizing the mind of its Maker.

Now, Fathers and Brethren, what bearing have truths and principles like these on ourselves and our Churches? We live to be vehicles of Christ's ideas, to persuade men so to believe them as to be made by them Christlike men. Our Churches ought to be societies so possessed and ruled by these ideas as to make them inform and penetrate through and through the immense society and people of England, and even the far immenser peoples of the world. To do this, we must preach Christ. Unless we preach Christ we cannot make men Christians. The call to the individual must come first, but the first must not here be the last; we must reach the lost, save the lost, but only that the kingdom may come, that the city, which has been so long a-building, may be built into harmony and holiness in the Lord. Let us make the men in our pulpits and the men in our pews embody, in the forms our age so deeply needs, the thoughts, the spirit, the love of Christ. And we are Free Churches of Christ, free that we may the better obey Him, follow the laws immanent in our very nature, fulfil the ends given in our being. Churches dependent on the State live by favour of the parties that rule it, do not sanctify the State, are rather made secular by it. They tend to become political rather than theological, reflecting the ideas current in the party they live by rather than the ideas that come by the inspiration of the living God. We stand fast in the liberty wherewith Christ made us free, determined to be in no way tempted or bound to maintain a political party because it undertakes to maintain the political privileges of a church. We need freedom in order to the highest spiritual service, that we may so embody the ideas, so incorporate the mind of Christ that He may take possession of the whole soul, heart and conscience of our race. We are free that we may freely serve our King, serve Him not simply in things political, or civil, or religious, but in all things absolutely, in our whole nature, with our whole spirit. So banded together in loyalest brotherhood, let us for the service of man and for the glory of God be supremely obedient to the Jesus Christ who is "the same yesterday, to-day, and for ever."

"' He saves the sheep, the goats He doth not save.'
So rang Tertullian's sentence, on the side
Of that unpitying Phrygian sect which cried:
'Him can no fount of fresh forgiveness lave,

Who sins, once washed by the baptismal wave.'—
So spake the fierce Tertullian. But she sigh'd,
The infant Church! of love she felt the tide
Stream on her from her Lord's yet recent grave.

And then she smiled; and in the Catacombs,
With eye suffused but heart inspiréd true,
On those walls subterranean, where she hid

Her head, 'mid ignominy, death, and tombs,
She her Good Shepherd's hasty image drew,—
And on His shoulders, not a lamb, a kid." [1]

[1] Matthew Arnold.

III.

THE RICHES OF CHRIST'S POVERTY.

> "*For ye know the grace of our Lord Jesus Christ, that, though He was rich, yet for your sakes He became poor, that ye through His poverty might be rich.*"—2 Cor. viii. 9.
>
> "*Unto me, who am less than the least of all saints, is this grace given, that I should preach among the Gentiles the unsearchable riches of Christ.*"—Eph. iii. 8.

THE truth that lies at the centre and constitutes the heart of the Christian faith is sacrifice. The highest in the universe stoops to be the humblest, the loved and accepted of Heaven appears as the despised and outcast of earth, and becomes obedient unto death, the death of the cross. Strip from the gospel the halo of our love, the reverence of the hoary centuries, the lustre of its splendid conquests, the graces, the virtues, the noble enthusiasms it has created in persons, the culture, the light, the "sweeter manners, purer laws," it has made for peoples, and what remains? The story of a lonely and homeless life lived long ago in obscure Judea, of a death upon the cross amid the hatred and mockery of earth, and apparent neglect of Heaven. Yet this history has been the creator of our mightiest and divinest religion, the religion that, majestic in its meekness, unsearchable in the wealth of its immense poverty, has stood through the Christian centuries the visible demonstration that the foolishness of God is wiser than men, the weakness of God stronger than man's utmost might.

There is nothing so familiar to us as the gospel of Christ; it is so common as to threaten to become commonplace. Men so know His words, the facts of His history, the issue of His life, that they can hardly be got to think of them; the speech has become so familiar that it has ceased to convey knowledge. It has, as it were, so worked itself into the very consciousness of the time that the time is almost unconscious of its meaning. Many feel that the newest truth is the truth most worth believing; the latest guess of the scientific or critical imagination comes with a surprise that creates enthusiasm, while ancient certainties plead in vain for recognition or even toleration. A truth that costs no thought wields no power. Religion has more to fear from unthinking acceptance than from hostile criticism. And where faith is too familiar to be thoughtful, it lives by help of the accidents rather than through possession of the essentials of the truth. There are men who believe more strongly in miracles than in God. Were there no miracles there would be for them no God; for them law exists only by virtue of its violations. But the great miracle is the absence of miracles; it is the universal order that most speaks to us of a universal will, so reasonable in its action as to be everywhere capable of rational interpretation. So we need to become less familiar with the accidents of our faith that we may the better comprehend its permanent facts, its fundamental and eternal truths. We need to see them out of the setting of custom and commonplace, standing out, as it were, sharp against the background of eternity. To changed minds, things have changed meanings. Day by day the Italian goatherd may drive his flocks across the old Campagna and rest under the shadow of some mighty aqueduct or on the base of some fallen column, without ever asking whence these came or what they signify; or the Roman monk may sing his matin or his vesper hymn within hearing of the ancient Forum or majestic Coliseum, and catch only the echoes of his own song, hear no voice speaking out of a vanished and glorious past. But let a man laden with the treasures of ancient culture cross the Campagna and stand among the ruins of the once Eternal City, and his imagination is thronged with the voices of long silent orators, the songs of long dead poets, visions of the greatest empire that ever aspired to control the destinies of men and nations. Day by day the Arab merchant or the Jewish trader may cross the brow of Olivet, see the sun gleam on the minarets of Jerusalem, and yet only ask, "What is new in the bazaars? or what goods for sale? what persons likely to buy?" But let a man fresh from the Christian West, nursed in its deepest faith, cross for the first time the same hill, and as the Holy City breaks upon his view, what thoughts, what visions possess him! "Is this the city loved of God, where David sang, where Isaiah preached, where Jehovah reigned? And Bethany, where art thou, the sweet place where my Master tasted one blest hour of human love ere He entered the valley of the shadow of death? And Gethsemane, may I visit thee and see where His sweat fell as great drops of blood to the ground?" The scene is to him transfigured, the land is made holy by the light under which it lies, the history it once beheld suffuses its face with imperishable glory. So the facts of our gospel must be ever anew illumined by the truths of our faith if they are to live in our hearts and reign over our spirits as the vehicles of the grace and symbols of the might of God.

The gospel of Christ not only is a history, it has a history, and its history is the grandest chapter in the life of man. Think what these verses suggest, especially as to what Paul had found in two cities, and what through his gospel he had attempted and achieved. Take Corinth, consider what it had been and what it was. Paul had been wandering in the Troad preaching Christ. In vision a man of Macedonia had appeared to him and cried, "Come over and help us!" He obeyed, the first apostle to reach Europe and claim it for Christ. But what found he? The men of Philippi "thrust him into the inner prison and made his feet fast in the stocks." He tried Thessalonica, but certain envious Jews and "lewd fellows of the baser sort" "set all the city in an uproar," and forced the brethren to send away Paul by night. He passed to Berea, found there men of a nobler order; but the hate of Thessalonica followed him, and once more compelled him to depart. He next sought Athens, and there, in the synagogue with the Jews and in the market-place with the Greeks, he reasoned daily; but though the city was on tiptoe to hear new things, it could not deem Paul's good news true news. The supercilious Greek, disdainful of the Jew, could only ask, "What doth this babbler say?" and when he heard what, either mock at the resurrection, or in polite but incredulous indifference make answer, "We will hear thee again of this matter." So, weary, disheartened, as far as the conduct of man could dishearten him, Paul passed from Attica into Achaia, and suddenly came in sight of Corinth lying white and beautiful under its radiant Greek sky. "Here," he may have thought, "I shall at last find audience fit; the ear Macedonia and Attica have refused, Achaia shall give." But what did he find? A city busy, commercial, luxurious, licentious, too utterly steeped in its love of lust and gain to care to expel him. Men of many nations met on its streets, mixed and trafficked in its marts. There was the swart Egyptian, with his chartered ships laden with the produce of his own rich land, anxious to hear where famine prevailed that he might sell in the dearest market the grain he had bought in the cheapest. There, too, was the Jew, already skilled in usury, cunningly making profit out of people's poverty, determined to live in spite of the Gentile he despised, to live at his expense, too, and, if need be, by his very sins. The Greek, of course, was there, supple, subtle, sinewy, proud of his illustrious ancestry, vain of their noble deeds, unashamed of his own ignoble state, unconscious of his own mean spirit, made the meaner by the splendid past he professed to understand and inherit and admire. And over all was the martial, mighty Roman, their common master, everywhere victorious, everywhere sovereign, looking on all peoples as existing mainly that they might be conquered and ruled of Rome.

And to these men, and such men as these, Paul came to preach his gospel, a salvation by grace that made all men stand equally without merit before a God who had no respect of persons. The Egyptian listened incredulous, contemptuous: this gospel was a new thing, a thing of yesterday; the peoples around him were but infants to him, he had a faith rich in mysteries and secret wisdoms, older than the oldest of them could dream of. The Jew heard, scornful, obdurate, angry that his Messiah should be identified with the crucified Jesus of Nazareth, angrier that the exalted truths and privileges of his race should be published to the hated Gentile. The Greek loathed the very idea of a God manifested in a Jew, incarnated in a man of sorrows, without visible glory in life or grandeur in death. "The cross" was enough for the Roman; He who had been doomed to a death no citizen of Rome could suffer could be no God or Saviour for him. And so Paul preached his gospel to men worse than deaf, to men whose ears were stopped by the thousand passions and prejudices of peoples old in selfishness, of a world possessed by sin. But as they were too careless to be intolerant, he preached on; the very permission to preach was to a man who had hitherto been denied it a Divine boon, rich with golden opportunities of success. He had zeal enough to supply a whole city with enthusiasm; faith strong and far-sighted enough to conquer an unbelief that was simply perverse and blind. So he preached till he prevailed, till the dark Egyptian became a child of the new light, till into the breast of the Hebrew the heart of soft innocence came, till the Greek embraced a nobler wisdom than his fathers had known, and the Roman became the more loyal to Cæsar that he was so loyal to Christ. And now a wonderful change was seen. The old antipathies of race and caste and speech vanished, and in their place a new sense of brotherhood came. The men who believed themselves to be sons of the one God, knew themselves to be brother-men. And the new consciousness was so large that it went far beyond Corinth, achieving strange things, things absolutely new, yet full of infinite promise to the history of man. News came from Jerusalem that poverty reigned there. The new sense of kin created the sense of new duties, the wealth of Corinth must help the poverty of Jerusalem. The family of God was a brotherhood of mutual help, and the saints of Judea realized how good it was to stand with the saints of Achaia in the one commonwealth of Israel. And Paul, as, thankful, he watched the wondrous change, traced all to its Divine and sufficient source: "Ye know the grace of our Lord Jesus Christ, that though He was rich, yet for your sakes He became poor, that ye through His poverty might be rich."

1. "*Ye know the grace of our Lord Jesus Christ.*" "Grace" is a beautiful word, expressive of a still more beautiful thing. It awakens our oldest and sweetest memories, stands at the heart of our most sacred associations. Men explain it by "favour," but the richest favour is poor grace. The Greek word which is in its root the cognate of the English term, was more suggestive to the Greek than even Grace can be to the English mind. It runs back into a root expressive of joy, to be glad or happy. Now the happy is ever the benevolent man, the miserable is the malicious. The happy must create happiness, the joy of beatitude is beneficence. The glad presence makes

gladness; to perceive it is to share it. But misery cannot bear joy; its one pleasure is to cause pain. The devil when most devilish is most pleased; the shadow lightens on his spirit as he sees it deepen on another's. But the being absolutely happy is absolutely good, rejoicing only in joy, bound by inmost necessities of nature to diffuse and enlarge it. Had God embanked, as it were, His nature in order that the fountains of beatitude within it might never overflow, then these fountains had dried up; joy, denied expression, would have refused to live. Creation rose in obedience to the Divine beatitude, was like the echo which answered the multitudinous laughter of the infinite joy. So to the Absolute Happiness the creation of happy beings was a necessity, and of this necessity the universe was begotten. But the blessed must not only be the beneficent; He must be the beautiful and the bountiful as well. These are branches of the same rich root. The Greeks had their graces, forms of ideal loveliness, shapes of such perfect beauty that to have beheld them was to possess a perennial joy. So the ever blessed is the ever beautiful God; His infinite joy works the wondrous glory that makes the vision of God the last beatitude of man. Inner happiness translated into outer form is absolute loveliness; beauty is the radiant garment by which the indwelling joy becomes visible to men. And the joy clothed in beauty is bountiful, its being is giving, to see it is to share it, to taste its infinite delight. It must give that it may live, and the more it gives the more it lives. As the inner sees the outer joy multiplied it grows fuller, deeper, higher. It cannot be happy in the face of suffering, can rejoice only in the presence of joy. So He whose nature is gracious could not allow misery to prevail where He had designed happiness to abide. The sin that made sorrow was a pain to the perfection of God, and the necessity, born of grace, that had made Him Creator now made Him Redeemer. In "the grace of our Lord Jesus Christ" we see the beatitude of God stooping to work out the salvation or last beatitude of man.

"The grace of our Lord Jesus Christ." "Unto me was this grace given." Note the distinction: in the one the grace was derivative, in the other original. In Christ it was immanent, existed by necessity of nature; in Paul it was implanted, existed as a gift of Christ; yet in both it was as to character the same—the joy that breaks into spontaneous beneficence, a happiness so driven to make happy as to endure any pain, any sacrifice that it may accomplish its end. This "grace" immanent made Christ the Redeemer; imparted, made Paul the apostle. He believed himself to be a creator of joy, a maker of happy men, of a happier world. When the belief was looked at through the man, it might seem paradoxical, even absurd. When the man is looked at through the belief, he lives before us transformed, glorified. No presence could appear less gracious, no man less an abode of the radiant joy that broke unbidden into deeds of gentleness and love. A distinguished French scholar, who was meant by nature to be a romancer, who has striven by laborious art to become an historian of the greatest events in religion, has, in order that he may the better depreciate Paul, described him as an "ugly little Jew," blear-eyed, diseased, a poor itinerant artisan, herding with his kind on the quays or in the slums of the greater Roman cities. Well, grant the description true, and what then? Does it not only the more victoriously prove his saying true, "unto me," a person so ungracious by nature and bearing, "has this grace been given"? The grace bestowed can alone explain the work performed. Imagine yourself a Roman provincial visiting, in the year of grace 60, the imperial city. You have seen its wonders, and have gone out the Appian Way to breathe a fresher air, to look at the monuments and think of the famed men whose ashes and whose memories are there preserved. You pass many travellers from the country or from over the sea moving Romewards. A group remarkable for its poverty catches your eye. The faces are neither Roman nor Greek, but unmistakeably Jewish. In the centre walks the poorest yet apparently most important Jew of all, a man short of stature, weak in bodily presence, with pained eyes and anxious face, ill-clad, strongly stamped by the marks of recent shipwreck and years of ungrudged yet unremunerative toil. Something in this group, so obscure and unknown, yet so absorbed and unconscious of its great surroundings, might have held you wondering, had not a murmur of delighted surprise come rippling along the Way and tempted you to look toward the city. Lo! a cloud of dust, and out of it emerging a chariot drawn by splendid horses; and as they approach the murmur becomes articulate—"'Tis Nero! the Emperor himself." You draw to the side and look with all your wits in your eyes as the chariot bearing the master of the world sweeps grandly past. You return to your provincial home, and in quiet hours say to your neighbours in the market-place or your family sitting round the hearth—"Think! how fortunate I was. I had gone out the Appian Way just to escape the noise and crowd of the city, and as in utter idleness I was watching a little Jew who, oblivious to the glory of the place, was speaking to obscure persons of his own race eagerly clustered round him, the Emperor suddenly appeared, driven in his chariot, and I saw him as plainly and as well as I now see you." And the tale seemed so wonderful that to all the village you were to your dying day known as the man who had seen Nero face to face.

So much for the hour and the year; but let a generation pass, and what then? That Nero, dead now, murdered in utter hate, is so abhorred, even as a memory, that men hardly dare believe in his death, dread that he may still be alive, his death but feigned that he may the better seize an unexpected moment to resume his cruel tyrannies; while that little Jew, now Paul the sainted, lives in letters that incarnate his invincible spirit, in churches that trace their being to his toil, and his name is, in all the cities that stand round the tideless Mediterranean, a name of light and joy. Pass from then till now, look over the intervening centuries, and what find you? That Nero an almost unknown name, known only to be despised; that Paul a foremost king of men, reigning by his imperishable words, clearest interpreter of the deepest mysteries of being, shaping noblest spirits to noblest uses, forming the men that lead the nations, making the minds that make the thought and faith and freedom of the world. So has God vindicated His own ways and the words of His apostle—" Unto me was this grace given."

2. "Ye know the grace of our Lord Jesus Christ,

that, though He was rich." Rich! The conventional idea of riches is pecuniary abundance, superfluity of goods possessible and heritable. The typical rich man is Dives, "clothed in purple and fine linen, and faring sumptuously every day." His riches are pre-eminently calculable, can be written down and reckoned up in black and on white. Riches of this order the average English mind instinctively understands and appreciates. There is nothing so wonderful to it, as property. To own it is to be a great man, and the more he owns the greater a man he is. The millionaire is our permanent social wonder, a man made admirable by his millions. And there is a point where material wealth is a thing of quite infinite significance, the point where it expresses immanent energies, is the outcome and product of a nature so rich that it must to fulfil itself burst into wealth. An empty nature feels no oppression in a vacant universe; a rich nature must strenuously labour to create a without that at once reflects and satisfies the within. And Paul conceives Christ as of a fulness so infinite that He could not but create, and of His fulness all creation had received. Of Him, and to Him, and through Him, were all things; in all His thought was manifested, His energies active; He was before all things, and in Him all stood together in divinest system for divinest ends. And to be so rich within and without was indeed to have infinite wealth. The universe intellect may for ever explore, but can never exhaust; to sense it is bounded, but to spirit it is boundless. Awe comes into the soul of man as he looks into the clear midnight heaven and watches its innumerable hosts, each a point of light to the eye, yet so speaking to the imagination as to bewilder it by visions of a starlit immensity, of a space mind cannot limit instinct with thought, throbbing with generative, progressive, mighty life. If you stood on what seems the remotest star in space, trembling like the veriest rushlight on the verge of outer darkness, you would find yourself in the heart of a mightier sun than our own, while all round new constellations would glow like the myriad eyes of God, looking through the very points that made space visible into the minds that made it living; and if there stood beside you a master spirit to teach the bewildered, his response to your cry—"Whose are these?"—would be: "The eternal Reason men call the Christ made and owns the worlds! So rich was His essential nature that He thought into being whatever is. The universe is His wealth, and its weal His joy."

But there is a higher idea of riches—the wealth that is well-being. The poverty of the friendless Master of the world is proverbial. Happiness refuses to be bought, even poor contentment spurns the bribe of the buyer. Imagine a witling, who had fallen heir to large possessions, going, in a moment of sated pleasure, round the Exchanges of Europe and asking, "Where do they sell happiness? I am without it, and want it, but can buy it; tell me where?" Before his question, men who believed in the might of money would for the instant feel feeble, and discover that there were capacities and needs in human nature that mocked the power of their golden god. But Christ was not doomed to the splendid misery of being alone in His ownership of the worlds, of having nothing but material, calculable wealth. He was rich in the honour God enjoys, in the worship of angel and spirit, in the happiness which is at once the essence and the manifestation of Divine perfection, in the affection given by the Eternal Father to the only begotten Son. Did you ever think what the mystery we call Trinity means? You speak perhaps of the time when God was alone, when, ere the worlds were, He dwelt solitary in His own eternity. But God was never alone, could never be alone. He is by His very nature not solitude but society. Were He solitude, He could not be the absolute perfection which is our only God. God is love, and love is social. You cannot have love without a subject loving and an object loved. The object is as necessary as the subject, Where there is no person to be loved, love is impossible. God is reason, and reason is social. Knowledge implies subject and object, the person that knows, the person known. Deny the distinction of knowing subject and known object, and the very possibility of knowledge is denied. But if God is essentially love and knowledge, He is essentially social; and if the time never was when these were no realities to Him, the time never was when His nature was without the loved person and the known object. When we speak of the person loved, we name Him Son; of the object known, we name Him Word. And who shall tell the Divine beatitude of the eternity when the Son lay in the bosom of the Father, and the arms of the Father held the person of the Son, and the tides of love flowed and ebbed with a rhythm that beat out as it were the music of the eternal joy? In that wealth of essential being Christ lived with the Father "before the foundation of the world," so "rich" that "in Him dwelt all the fulness of the Godhead bodily."

3. "*Though rich, yet He became poor.*" Poverty is

a very terrible thing; so terrible that nothing seems to deal so hardly with all our fairer and gentler humanities. Where the face is pinched with habitual want, the heart is seldom the home of scrupulous veracity or chivalrous honour. When the struggle for life grows deadliest even the sternest of the virtues begin to fail. There sit two men on a raft afloat on the mighty deep; it is all that remains of a once goodly ship, they all that survive of a once jovial and kindly crew. In the solitude of the ancient ocean, faced by grim starvation, what do they? Clasp each other in a last fraternal embrace, and die together in a love victorious over famine? No, not they; rather they sit and watch each other with hungry eyes, and each thinks what chances he may have in the struggle that is to determine which of the two shall give his life for the other. Nay, poverty is not kindly, famine does not come with grace in her hand and magnanimity in her heart; and natures that find it easy to be good with riches find it hard to be good with enforced poverty.

And Christ "though rich became poor." On a long distant winter eve when there was no room for Him in the lowliest inn, He stepped in divinest silence across the threshold of the world, and stood before it the Child of Mary, the Son of Joseph. The material conditions of His life were hard enough; poverty ruled His lot. The Holy Family of Rembrandt rather than of the Italian masters is the Holy Family of history. Wonder did not surround Him, adoration did not meet Him, reverence did not salute the Child in His mother's arms; rather the chamber where He was rocked to sleep was His father's workshop, the sounds amid which He waked were made by the carpenter's tools. Within and around His boyhood's home was hardness, industry alone held the wolf from the door. While the father worked, the mother toiled, baked the bread of the household, kept it clean, served it, made by prudent economy its scanty income suffice for its wants. And as it had been with the boy, so was it with the man. Nature did not minister to Him of her substance; He had to earn it by His daily toil. He knew the weariness of labour, the sweetness of rest. Even in the grandest moment of His work as a Teacher, poverty so held Him in its lean and iron hand that He could say: "The foxes have holes, and the birds of the air have nests, but the Son of man hath not where to lay His head." Yet this poverty did not impoverish His spirit; seemed rather only the more to enrich Him. He rises out of it the gracious Son of man, filling the atmosphere that floats over and enfolds humanity with the fragrance of His virtues. It is strange that He should be in His weakness so strong, in His poverty so rich. Men love power, rank, feel the very drapery it wears to be a thing most wonderful. Majesty may not be simple, must show its dignity by its pomp, prove its might by its magnificence. An Augustus Cæsar cannot suffer Rome to remain a city of republican brick, must leave it a capital of imperial marble. But here is the wonder of history—the mightiest Person it knows came of poverty, lived in poverty, and died forsaken and alone. Nay, so great is He that the regal state had lessened rather than enlarged the majesty of His person, the imperial purple had hidden the glory which the garments of His poverty reveal. Cæsar placed in the obscurity which beset the Christ had been abolished; the Christ placed amid the splendours of the Cæsars had derived thence no glory, nothing that could have added to His influence or His fame. Strength like His must have nothing between it and our humanity; must meet it face to face, in naked majesty, as it were, that it may the more perfectly subdue the evil and command the good.

The relation, as exhibited in history, of Christ to man and man to Christ is a most marvellous thing. He is all the mightier a reality to the spirit that He is so obscure and impoverished to the sense. The poverty is felt to be immensest wealth, laden with the riches of God. No man pities Him, all men admire Him, seek His help, desire His approval, covet His Spirit, and wish to imitate His character. Kings have bowed down before Him, and owned Him their King. The queenliest of women have done Him homage, and learned to live their noblest in the light of His presence. The largest intellects have humbled themselves at His feet, and learned through their knowledge of Him to speak of the highest mysteries as discovered and imperishable truths. The saintliest of men have by Him come to know their sin, and to see afar off a more perfect saintship towards which they would need an eternity to strive. The guiltiest men, held fast in the arms of the most utter vice, enfeebled by passion, made miserable by conscience, haunted by remorse, have turned to Him and cried: "O Christ! rich in Thy poverty, save us, make us holy and peaceful as Thou art, own sons of the Eternal Father;" and He has heard their prayer, sent them peace, and changed them from the guiltiest into holiest men. There is no wonder like this ; what the imagination could never have dreamed, history has shown as accomplished fact—the Christ so rich in His poverty as to be the wealth of the world.

4. And what has happened was what was intended, the actual result was the ideal end : " For your sakes He became poor, that ye through His poverty might be rich." Nothing could have seemed less calculated to enrich man than Christ's poverty ; nothing has ever or anywhere so mightily added to the mass of the world's weal. For affirming that it would do so, Paul was charged with foolishness ; in confessing that it has done so, we but acknowledge " the wisdom of God."

To see the relation of His poverty to our enrichment, we must see its relation to His own person and will and work. The outward poverty is but a symbol that enables us the better to apprehend the essential wealth. Look at the Sufferer in His last agony, regard it, and it alone, and what do you see ? A Person of perfect innocence, of silent meekness, too good for our evil time, hated by it, scorned for His weakness, chided for His gentleness, scourged to please the coarse humour of brutal soldiers, pitied by a judge who can find in Him no fault, but will not be at the trouble to save Him, dying amid the merciless mockery of jealous and offended priests ! Were this all, His history had only been pitiful, tragic, another added to the many tales of friendless virtue despised and trodden down by proud and victorious wrong. But it is not all ; it is only what is visible to sense ; behind lies what is revealed to spirit. " Though rich, yet for your sakes He became poor." The poverty meant sacrifice ; it was the symbol of a Divine renunciation. He had no need so to suffer; He did it spontaneously, out of love to man. The history of His coming takes us back into eternity, and up into the sublimest secrets of the Divine nature. The God of all grace is a God of a beatitude so perfect that it could not allow misery to live unrelieved. The God whose very being is the being of conscious love, could not so forget the creatures He had formed as to leave them to their sin. So to leave them had been to confess that their sin was mightier than His love, that evil could vanquish good, and the disobedience of man overcome the will and purpose of his Maker. He was too perfect a Being to permit the permanence of moral disorder and all its miseries, to allow His universe to become the home of His ruined ends. And so, to work out His great remedial purpose, to bring the wealth of the Divine nature into the poverty of the human, to create in the breast of man the filial heart that should lift him out of his sin into conscious sonship to God, Christ, "though rich, became poor." His coming made all the relations of man and God new. In and through Him men discovered the Fatherhood of God and the sonship of man; discovered what man was made to be, what he might yet be, what all Divine agencies were working to make him become. Jesus Christ created the very idea of the love that saves: "Herein is love, not that we loved God, but that He loved us, and sent His Son to be the propitiation for our sins."

I do not wish to be here tempted into a discussion on high doctrinal matters; yet there is one point I would note—the universal importance Paul ascribes to the humiliation and death of Christ. His appearance was no accident; it was purposed from eternity. The gospel was the revelation of a mystery which from the beginning had been hid in God. Now, to Paul a "mystery" was not mysterious, a high, incomprehensible speculation, but it was a spoken secret, as a secret unknown, indiscoverable till spoken, but once spoken intelligible enough to all who would listen. The mystery had been from eternity God's secret; it became through Christ man's possession. The secret had been the deepest purpose of Deity; in its interests, for its ends, He ruled, waiting only till the times were ripe that He might make it known. And so when Christ came it was as the manifested mystery of God. In Him all the Divine remedial forces are centred, through Him Providence works our redemption. He "died for all;" in Him all things in heaven and upon the earth are summed up, co-ordinated and combined into the head that unifies, rationalizes, perfects all. By the Church He founded there is "made known unto the principalities and powers in heavenly places the manifold wisdom of God."

And this Divine purpose is expressed in the phrase, "*for your sakes* He became poor, *that ye through His poverty might be rich.*" "Now that is absurd," the successful man may say; "His poverty in no way enriched me. I was the architect of my own fortune. All I have is the creation of my own industry." "Nay," adds the working man of secularist temper, "it is more than absurd, it is altogether untrue. I earn all I need by the cunning of my own deft fingers, the labour of my own hard hand." "What," argues the skilled economist, "could His poverty do for us? Poverty is simply a state of want, weakening the person who suffers it and the society he lives in.

Wealth is created by production, equalized by distribution." Well, now that we have heard what these wise people have to say, let us turn from what is individual and speculative to what is universal and historical; and in order that we may understand matters let us ask, What are riches? What is wealth? Wealth is the state of weal; weal is opposed to woe or ill, and as *ill-th*, were there such a term, would stand to ill, so *weal-th* stands to weal. The man who is not weal cannot have wealth; to be wealthy is simply to have utmost weal. As is wealth, so are riches; the one is but the means, the other the state it creates and secures. If you think money riches, the moneyed the wealthy man, be courageous enough to bring your thought to the test of reality, and then watch the result. Take from man conscience, virtue, truth, faith in God, love to man; leave him his power to make money, multiply it if you like a thousandfold. He can have no joy in persons, only in possessions. What hinders possession causes pain. The money that goes to make another's comfort works him grief, envy of the prosperous consumes him, jealousy of his rivals possesses him, his blind lust feeds his passions, and what he has not is a greater misery than what he has is a joy. Were Mammon the one god that ruled men, he would make them like beasts ravening for prey, meeting each other only to tear each other, maddened into fiercer savagery by the plunder which was expected to satisfy. Imagine a Mammon's paradise. Suddenly religion and all it represents perishes, and every man awakes to find himself a millionaire. With religion there vanishes the order and reign of righteousness, the infinite spiritual heaven that spans our lives and enlarges them with the immensest meanings, the immortality that cheers our manhood and illumines it with the glory to be revealed, all the beliefs and ideals that make man in the midst of his time the son and heir of eternity; with the absolute reign of Mammon there would come to a being who was but a mass of organized passions the means to gratify every desire, to indulge every lust, to live for the ends prescribed by the bad self in the supreme moment of apotheosis. All at once men cease to toil, the fisherman leaves his boat to rot upon the beach, the ploughman allows his plough to stand idle in the furrow, the miner forsakes the dismal mine to return to it no more, the workers pour out of the factory and the untended looms are abandoned to silence, and rust, pens lie unused on desks where busy clerks once sat, and shops are vacant of sellers as of buyers. And now amid this universal idleness, caused by indulgent Mammon, what of man? Void of Deity, possessed by greed, he lives envious, jealous, fierce, dissatisfied with what he has, covetous of what he has not, governed by no law but the law of his own bad will, deterred by no fear but the fear of his neighbour's greater strength. In a society so constituted every evil passion would rage, discord and wrong would reign, no life would be safe, no property secure, no home possible, no joy tasted, no weal realized. The supreme calamity would be its continuance; the supreme mercy its early and utter destruction.

You see, then, wealth is not a thing of material conditions simply; bills of exchange and minted gold do not constitute riches. Wealth and riches concern persons. What makes man attain the fullest and best being possible to him makes him wealthiest; where there is most weal there is most wealth. The means that create most well-being and well-doing are the best riches, most enrich humanity, individual and collective. If generous material conditions are to be good, the persons who produce and enlarge, distribute and enjoy them, must be made out of other than material forces, must be formed by spiritual agencies, be guided and ruled by spiritual laws. But this brings us to the cardinal question, Who has been the generator of our most regenerative spiritual forces? Who has been the mightiest creator of moral persons, of men who have lived for man? Who begat the enthusiasm of humanity, the ideal of a love that is happy only as it serves and saves? Can any one doubt or question the answer? The Christ who "for our sakes became poor." Great truths are great forces; the highest ideals are the mightiest factors of progress; and does not Christ stand alone as the Teacher, as the Maker of our humanest ideals? This old earth of ours has been girdled with a zone of light since He lived on it, has floated amid its sister spheres as one that feels its affinities with the Infinite. Our wasted humanity has burned with new passions, has tasted the exhilaration of new hopes, since He by wearing it created in its heart a new consciousness of dignity and worth. The Divine Fatherhood He revealed has made the awful problems of our whence and whither look at us with kindlier faces, has made order and beneficence begin to emerge from the confused relations of our present, and has risen on millions of benighted hearts like a spiritual sun creating an eternal summer, with its bright days, its short beautiful nights, its soft showers and glorious sunshine. The brotherhood of man He disclosed has abolished, or is abolishing, the old despotisms and enmities, the tyrannies of rank and power, and is slowing awaking the affections that shall link in subtle alliance the most distant and dissimilar and estranged families of earth. Maternity has become a higher and more sacred thing since Jesus called Mary mother; and since He loved and was loved of woman, womanhood, to a degree that had been unintelligible to the purest of the ancients, has been ennobled, honoured, loved with the chaste love that at once creates and graces the home. The watchwords of human freedom and progress, the ameliorative agencies that are in dark places doing battle with the causes and the issues of our human ills, the ideals that are evoking our best ambitions and working out our highest civilizations, are either directly of His creating or find in Him their ultimate occasion and source. And if such has been His action, has He not by His poverty made us rich, formed the elements, the organizing principles, that are building up the commonwealth of man?

But hitherto we have been discussing only one side of His enriching action—that which relates to the forms of our being, individual and collective, realized in time. Yet behind this there is a deeper and richer action still. His action has been regenerative of the spirit, creative, re-creative through and through. The man who is in Christ finds old things passed away, all things become new: God no terror, but a trusted Father; the future no horror of great darkness, but a loved home of light; man no enemy to be watched and spoiled, but a brother to be honoured and served. The salvation Christ brings is no fancy, but a glorious reality attested by the consciousness of all the Christian men who have lived or still live. It is a state in which man is rescued from sin, where its power over and in him is broken, where he lives at peace with God, justified before conscience and law, possessed of the virtues, adorned with the graces that make him a whole, which means a holy man. Men who know that state to be theirs stand above the limits of time, know themselves to be citizens of heaven, naturalized members of its commonwealth, heirs of God and joint heirs with Christ.

"The riches of Christ" in this sphere of action we may not attempt to describe; they are too "unsearchable." Yet there is one way in which we may as at a glance see and measure their extent and variety—as reflected in the consciousness of the saved, the hearts of His people. Think what He has been and is to those who have lived and yet live by faith in Him. Look at this moment over England, over the continents of the East and West, and what see you? Millions of men and women burdened with sin, laden with sorrow, troubled with the anxieties and weariness of inconspicuous and uneventful human life, possessed of the joys too common to be noted, the hopes too familiar to cheer, have met or are meeting to praise His name, to feel for an hour that shall sanctify days penetrated with a new sense of the mercy of God, lifted into fellowship with Him and into participation in His eternity. To-morrow, when the tide of busy life rolls high and strong through our streets, it may seem as if for the time His reign were over; but in lone garrets where weakness struggles with want, the knowledge of His presence is more than strength, in rooms made dark by the shadow of death, His face sheds light about the spirit, gives comfort and a courage that fears no evil. He is active every moment, and at the touch of His hand eyes red with weeping over sin or loss grow clear and calm, men tempted to evil turn to good, and those sick of the mean ambitions of the Exchange or the Senate or society are born into a nobler manhood by the faith of the Son of God. Turn now towards the past, and ask whether any consciousness has been so rich, and varied in its riches, as the consciousness of obligation to Christ. Here come toward us an army of great Thinkers, led by Paul the Apostle, bringing in their ranks fathers and schoolmen, reformers and statesmen, philosophers and divines, men who by arduous thought have builded systems, striven to interpret the universe, to spell out the mysteries of the Divine nature, to read the riddle of the human; and they come confessing that the spring of all their action, the one point that shed light into the darkness, order into the confusions of being, was the knowledge of Christ. There follow an immense host of Poets, headed by the great masters of the Christian epic: the sad and banished Florentine who set before us in measures of wondrous music the hell that was a pit of darkness and house of pain, and the heaven which was a mount of light and home of joy; and the still sadder Englishman, whose " soul was like a star and dwelt apart," whose voice had a sound as of the sea: and they bring with them out of many ages and lands and tongues the singers of sweet songs, giving words and wings to the faith and hope, the penitence and joy, the aspirations and the peace of the saved soul; and as the host advances it breaks into a hymn in praise of Him who woke their spirits to music by filling them with the harmonies of His own rich love. And who are these that stand beside the Poets? Painters, are they not? The men who made our modern art, and made it so full of light and tenderness and love, an interpretation of the grace of heaven as it strove to create the graces of earth. Builders, too, are there, men who so believed and loved that they made the very stone quick with their faith and affection; and there, too, are the Masters of music, men who heard harmonies human speech could not utter, and translated them into a language so woven of multitudinous sweet sounds that the many-voiced orchestra alone can express it. And what do all these say? To whom do they trace their inspiration? Whence have they their sublimest theme? Do they not, with the poets and thinkers, the saved and the saintly of all Christian ages and tongues, join with one accord to ascribe all unto Him who, "though rich, yet for our sakes became poor, that we through His poverty might be rich"?

PART FOURTH.

I. *THE QUEST OF THE CHIEF GOOD.*
II. *THE LOVE OF CHRIST.*
III. *THE CITY OF GOD.*

"*Sith God hath deified our nature, though not by turning it into Himself, yet by making it His own inseparable habitation, we cannot now conceive how God should, without man, either exercise Divine power, or receive the glory of Divine praise. For man is in both an associate of Deity.*"—Hooker: "Ecclesiastical Polity," Bk. v. § 54.

"*For life, with all it yields of joy and woe,
And hope and fear,—believe the aged friend,—
Is just our chance o' the prize of learning love,
How love might be, hath been indeed, and is;
And that we hold henceforth to the uttermost
Such prize despite the envy of the world,
And, having gained truth, keep truth; that is all.*"
    Robert Browning: "A Death in the Desert."

"*As he thereon stood gazing, he might see
The blessed Angels to and fro descend
From highest heven in gladsome companee,
And with great ioy into that citty wend,
As commonly as frend does with his frend.
Whereat he wondred much, and gan enquere,
What stately building durst so high extend
Her lofty towres unto the starry sphere,
And what unknowen nation there empeopled were.*

'*Faire knight*,' *quoth he*, '*Hierusalem that is,
The New Hierusalem, that God has built
For those to dwell in, that are chosen His,
His chosen people purg'd from sinful guilt
With pretious blood, which cruelly was spilt
On cursed tree, of that unspotted Lam,
That for the sinnes of al the world was kilt:
Now are they saints all in that citty sam,
More dear unto their God than younglings to their dam.*' "
    Spenser: "The Faerie Queen,"
      Bk. 1. Canto x., Verses 56–57.

I.

THE QUEST OF THE CHIEF GOOD.

> "*But seek ye first the kingdom of God and His righteousness; and all these things shall be added unto you.*"—Matt. vi. 33.

MAN is always in search of the chief good, the thing that will make him happiest. What this thing, or even what happiness is, he may be quite unable to tell; yet he knows that he was made to be happy and is not what he was made to be. Nature is wise, she determines our ends, though we may use means that baffle her and disappoint ourselves. Man was not made to be miserable; no man intends his own misery, yet every man often so acts as to cause it, not indeed of purpose even where most surely of will. Our very sins are attempts to be happy, efforts to reach nature's ends by ways she disowns and God condemns. Where God fixes the end, but man has to choose the way, it is certain that the way will be to all long and toilsome, to many a path of failure crowned with success, to others a path of promise terminating in disastrous failure. So, while all seek the good which God intended for all, many fail to find it, discovering, when too late, that the things they had expected to be sweetest turned out the most essentially bitter. Happiness, indeed, never comes to the man who consciously seeks it; it must come unsought if it is to come at all. The man who does a thing in order that he may be happy, is never made happy by the thing he does. The ethical theory which makes pleasure the chief end of action is only a doctrine as to the best methods of mitigating pain, may teach men how to act so as to be least miserable, cannot teach them how to act so as to be most happy. The supreme good is complex, is reached only where perfect virtue and perfect happiness are together realized; but the happiness must be the fruit of the virtue, cannot be its root. For the man who made his happiness the standard or end of all his actions would be the least happy of men, unable to attain what he wished because of the very desire to attain it. Joy must spring up unbidden, and, as it were, blossom unseen to be real. It comes not to the man who consciously lives to increase his own pleasure; it comes spontaneously to the man who follows virtue and loves God.

Now what I have just been trying to say was said more simply and beautifully by the older divines when they described holiness and happiness as not two things, but only different sides of the same thing. Yet a man was not to seek both in the same spirit and way. He was not to seek happiness that he might get holiness, or even holiness that he might get happiness, but he was to seek to be holy as God is holy, and then he should be happy as God is happy. But, then, this holiness after the Divine sort seems so ideal, so transcendental a thing, that to bid men, harassed with the hard and merciless necessities of life, seek it, is either to use an unmeaning form of speech or to indulge in cruel mockery. The world grows more and more; to men immersed in it, speech of high spiritual things seems less and less real, words that sound rather than sound words. They are coming to think that the struggle to satisfy the ceaseless hunger of the present is so severe as to forbid anything more in religion than a decent attendance to the respectabilities of conduct and worship. Those who best know the sublimer ideals of our faith may feel rebuked by them into silence when they have to speak of them to men who have no choice but to bear courageously the cares of the world. He but little knows business or politics, the task of the brain-worker or the handicraftsman, who thinks these cares friendly to the nobler life of the soul, or conquerable by the familiar platitudes that lower religion down to man rather than lift man up to religion. Mammon was in the olden time a kindly deity; it was competition in all arts and trades and markets, aided by the telegraph, the railway, and the steamship, that made him so stern as to fill the whole man and the whole life with his concerns. Yet even in the olden times "no man could serve both God and Mammon;" a divided service may be service of Mammon, cannot be service of God. To seek first what we shall eat, what we shall drink, and wherewithal we shall be clothed, is to sacrifice the God of eternity to the god of this world, is to lose the very essence and end of life in a vain pursuit of the means of living.

Now the words of Jesus in the section of His discourse from which we have quoted, though spoken to a stiller and simpler world than ours, are as appropriate, as full of spiritual counsel and healing to the care-laden and anxious men of our age as to those of

His. He sees that it is the possibilities more than the realities of life that weaken and sadden; it is the fear of to-morrow that most threatens faith in God. They say, "It is the pace that kills;" but it is not so much the pace as the fear that begets the pace, the terror lest the strength fail ere the goal be reached. And fear creates its own object; no terror paralyses like the terror for things unreal. He who stands with foot firm planted on the realities of God and eternity will feel no fear in the presence of any to-morrow or the evils it may bring.

The first thing to be done is to understand what Jesus means, a matter the more necessary that it is here so easy to misunderstand Him. In the text there is a command and a promise; the command is, "Seek ye first the kingdom of God and His righteousness;" the promise, "And all these things shall be added unto you." "These things" are the food and raiment, the necessities and the comforts of life, for which men so arduously toil and so anxiously care; they are to be the certain and inalienable portion of the man who seeks first "the kingdom of God and His righteousness." Now what does this mean? Does it mean, "attend to nothing but religion, pray, fast, wait on Providence, without work or will of your own, and Providence will see that you never want"? That would make Jesus teach the most idle and extravagant quietism, while He means to teach doctrine "profitable for life and godliness." "The kingdom of God" was to Him the reign of the Divine moral law. To seek it was to become in it a dutiful citizen, doing the will of God on earth as it was done in heaven. To "seek His righteousness" was to attempt to realize His ideal of obedience, to become perfect as God is perfect, to attain a life beautiful and dutiful to man because inspired by love to God. But, so understood, to seek the kingdom and righteousness of God is to seek to imitate Him, to be in our little world what He is in the infinite universe, the unwearied Worker, the sleepless Providence, the Source and Guardian of good, the Enemy and Judge of evil. To win the Divine holiness is to share in the Divine happiness; a life framed after the Divine idea participates in the Divine reality. If we live in harmony with the will that made and rules the world, the issue of our life must be good. Our part is, to be and do our best in the present; God's part is, to make our future correspond to the present out of which it grows. If he so lives, man may not fear to-morrow, for to-morrow is God's, and He will see that to the man who is dutiful it is as good as to-day. He who truly believes in Providence will live a provident man, dutiful in the passing hour, not bringing the cares of to-morrow into to-day, not leaving the cares of to-day as concerns for to-morrow, but enjoying his actual good untroubled by the fear of possible evil. To him whatever comes in the train of realized righteousness is good.

Christ, then, here gives us a Divine clue through our care to its cure. He bids us do as He did, begin with God, that we may be as He was, without care for the morrow. He tells us to seek what He sought, to fulfil all righteousness, and we shall find what He found, perfect happiness even in sorrow, though unto death, sweet peace amidst the suffering that teaches obedience. His cure for care is no vain remedy, His secret of happiness no Utopian dream. His own life was the splendid proof that His way was right, that His ideal could be realized. He knew no surface joys, none of the mere delight in living that gilds the soul with a radiant beauty like the sunlit face of the sea, none of the glad laughter that breaks spontaneous from the heart like music from the murmuring wave or rippling stream. The burden of a great mission lay upon His spirit, sorrow for the world's sin filled His heart. The knowledge that He had His " Father's business " to do, saddened the boy; the foresight of the cross He had to bear, awed the man. His life seemed all shadow, deep, sombre, without the sunshine that tells of the light above the cloud, that is all the sweeter from the contrast of the shade. Yet He had a joy too deep to be touched by the accidents of life, however tragic, too sacred and strong to be dependent on the pleasure or pain of a passing hour. Obedience was His happiness, which was only intensified by the struggle it cost to win it. His soul, open on all sides, through all its senses, to the Divine, was too full of God to be either ravished by the best or dismayed by the worst of man. To Him earth was apparelled in celestial beauty, because only the visible garment of celestial truth. The stars in their courses, the orient heavens, glorious alike in sunlight, moonlight, or starlight, meadow, hill and grove, every common stream and flower had to Him Divine meanings, and were sources of endless joy. The sermon on the lily shows how He could admire its pure and tender loveliness while He pitied the gaudy splendour of the king. His parables show how deeply He had communed with nature, how He had watched the sower casting his seed and the reaper plying his sickle, the growth of the mustard-tree and the culture of the vine and the fig, and He must have drawn from these their sweetest essence for His own spirit before distilling it into counsel and comfort for man's. His silent walks along the banks of the Jordan, on the hills round about Jerusalem, in the valleys that run out from Nazareth, must have been fruitful of the quiet joy that comes from "pious meditation fancy fed." He began with God, and so nature was but the mirror of His Father's mind. His battle was the hardest man ever fought, and so His need of God was the greatest man ever felt. And His faith was never less than His need. In the hands of the Father He lived, as in them He died, and every insult of man only made Him more conscious of their tender strength, every moment of sorrow only revealed their muffled gentleness. Because He sought the kingdom of God and His righteousness first, He found what made His lonesome life beautiful with Divine holiness and human trust.

Christ, then, is the most illustrious proof of His own principle. He here communicates the golden secret that made Him while the "Man of Sorrows," whose "visage was marred more than any man's," also the holy and peaceful Son of God, glorious as the King in His beauty come from the land that is very far off. What He experienced and exemplified, He commands us to practise and realize. The kingdom of God ought to be our first and chief quest, for in it every actual and possible good is to be found,—the obedience that ends in righteousness, the trust that can walk through sorrow into chastened and patient love, the hope that can sit peacefully in the darkest night and wait for the coming of the day. It may be worth while, then, to look at a few of the manifold applications of the principle, and it may help us to feel that we can pursue the path between the source and end of our being without allowing the troubles of life either to poison the one, or to destroy the other.

1. The first and chief quest of the individual man, as a being with work to do and manhood to realize, ought to be the kingdom of God. By seeking it first, the condition of the highest well-being is gained; by seeking it last, both it and the well-being will be lost.

Every man is born into the midst of conflicting tendencies. Evil and good wage within and without him their ceaseless struggle. He is at once battle-ground and warrior; they fight in him and for him, and he must so join in the conflict as to decide the issue. So accustomed are we to the strife that we regard a state of war as our state of nature, and we are too often contented to allow it to be so to the very end. But peace is of God, and man as His child and very image was meant to be the home of harmony and not of discord. The Divine in us struggles towards the Divine above and around us, seeks to fall in with the eternal purpose that gives unity and beauty to the creation. To be reconciled with God is to attain His righteousness; to fail of this is to be but a waif in the universe.

Man cannot escape the responsibility of choice; it faces him at every moment of his life, most of all in those beautiful and strenuous days when the bases of his manhood are being laid. Then it is that he ought to seek the kingdom that he may win the noblest manhood. How shall we make the need manifest?

Imagine a child born a man full-grown, as Adam was when fresh from the hand of God, like him standing innocent, wondering, wonderful in the face of creation. Yet all is not now as it was then; humanity is old if this man is young, and old humanity were a strange riddle to young manhood. Imagine then our man-child introduced into society, standing in the midst of it perplexed, puzzled. He asks many questions, but it is only to find his confusion worse confounded by the answers. How are men related to each other? What law governs their conduct and their affections? He enters a home and finds love reigning, the suffering of one the sorrow of all, the joy of each becoming a common happiness, soft speech made sweet by tender words, weariness chased from the face of the father by the gracious ways of the mother and the loving prattle of the child; and so by help of the home he seems to understand how love is of God, and how through love God forms the generations and rules the world. But next day he visits the Exchange, where speculation runs high and confidence and panic follow each other in swift succession through the busy and agitated groups. He meets the father of yesterday and hardly knows him, his face and speech are so changed; he hears him speak of losses that leave widows penniless and orphans without a home, of famine or pestilence abroad, of politics and labour at home, of the wars and diplomacies of nations, as matters of merest business, important only as they affect the rise or fall of stocks, the rate or payment of interest; and he begins to think that man is to man only a counter of exchange or instrument of production, to be valued by what he may buy, to be handled according to what he can produce. He then turns to inquire into the thoughts of men, what they believe, how they conceive themselves, their whence, their whither, by what law they seek to walk from first to last, from source to end. He listens to the speech which expresses the thoughts of the most thoughtful, and finds it altogether confused, bewildering, contradictory, a Babel of voices worse than inarticulate, where most clear least positive, speech designed rather to controvert and contradict their neighbours' faith than to confess their own. The confusion troubles him; but one thing awes him, the prevailing levity, the light-hearted and thoughtless way in which men speak, affirmatively or negatively, of the awful mysteries which surround their lives, those dark immensities amid which they float, those all-devouring eternities which beset them behind and before. But if thought be so confused, what of conduct? It only reflects and articulates the other, moral standards are as variable and varied as intellectual beliefs, within the gayest societies dark shadows flit, fine manners are made to clothe, though not to hide, the most brutal profligacy, and faces that ought to be young and bright with blooming manhood are old and blanched with crime. Our man-child, full of the wonder native to a new made soul, faces the problems so suddenly set before him, makes one intense effort to master them, but only to find his wonder die in despair. For high above all the others the personal problem rises, "How am I to order my life? Whither go, that I may realize my end?" With that dread problem in his brain he looks out into the life that seems but a struggle of clashing and conflicting whirlpools, each swirling round him with its strange bewildering spell and terrible suction. If he had as he stood there no sovereign principle, no strong hand by which to hold, no high end to which to look when dizzy from the confused whirl and noise, what could he do but, where the whirl was mightiest, eddy round and round, now drawn to the good, now sucked in by the evil, till when his brain was dizziest, he was carried round its sloping edge and vanished down its awful and insatiable throat. So the end of inexperienced, unguided, innocence has been too often the dark stained and remorseful guilt which had too much of " the conscience prick and the memory smart" to be able to "abide and grow fit for a better day."

But imagine our man-child entering the world through the kingdom of God. He gets there a sovereign principle, an affection that rules him, a law he feels bound to obey. He comes to know God and therefore to love Him, and that love can not only, like the spear of Ithuriel, compel the most carefully concealed evil to cast off its disguise, but can also steel the heart against its most fascinating witcheries, the will against its most potent seductions. He finds, too, faith in a Divine presence ever around him, ever helpful, a Father's heart that will grieve over every sin, a Father's hand that holds his spirit and guides him in all his ways. He sees, too, the eternal beauty of God's righteousness, the sweet peace, the perennial happiness it gives, and in the contrast sin loses its power to tempt because its ability to deceive. Thus panoplied our man-child goes forth, proof at once against the coarser forms of evil, to learn by experience to be proof against the finer. Obedience becomes the basis

of his manhood, love to God the rule of his life.
There is flexible but massive gentleness in him of the
Divine sort, gentleness that is soft to the guilty, but
only stern to guilt. He lives by love, and love that is
strong to hold evil out of himself, to cast it out of
others. And so the kingdom of God has secured to
him whatever was necessary to the highest manhood,
to make life in its progress a development of the
Divine idea, in its fruition a realization of the Divine
ideal. Nature, then, realizes its end, for man only
becomes man when he embodies or expresses God's
conception of manhood.

2. Citizenship in the kingdom of God is the
primary condition of all good to man in the home and
family. God "sets the solitary in families." He has
no better gift to man than a happy home, but that it
might do its beneficent and educative work the better,
He made it, while a source of happiness, a source
also of manifold anxieties. God were no Providence
without a universe; man were without humanity were
he without home. The universe in taxing the energies
manifests and ministers to the beatitude of God; the
home in developing the humanities contributes to the
perfection of man. But in doing this work it brings
varied temptations. The children that widen a man's
affections multiply his cares; what enlarges the heart
may overwork the intellect or overburden the strength.
Many a generous man has become covetous through
natural affection, many a noble nature has been narrowed
into parsimony by the thought, "want may assail those
I love." The fear of lean and merciless penury
invading his home when he was no longer there to
drive it back, has before now forced the man who

could cheerfully for himself have faced struggle and poverty, into hasty and not too scrupulous ways of getting rich. We all remember how one of the most honoured names in literature, one who has thrown the glamour of his genius over almost every mountain and loch and river in the land of his birth, brought, by his strong ambition to found a house, on his closing days the shadow and the burden under which they perished. "Lo, children are an heritage of the Lord," and happy is the man who remembers, "except the Lord build the house they labour in vain that build it."

For let us look at how citizenship in the kingdom affects the man who is a father. It may not make the best of both worlds for him, securing as at a stroke a fortune on earth and a crown in heaven, but it will do infinitely better, make the best possible out of himself. Without good men we can never have good homes, the parents' honour is its joy and strength. Virtue, chastity, truth, love, are the truest riches a family can possess. Prosperity based on these lives, does not wither before any breath of adversity, however bitter. The man is never bankrupt who keeps his honour, and without honour affection has no durable foundation, nor has either self-respect or the respect of others, especially those dearest to us. The man who grows mean or sins for his children loses pleasure in them, and they lose reverence of the deeper sort for him. If a man ever feels that he is less honourable with a home than he would have been without it, then he has begun to find it an inverted good, which means an actual evil, whose action on him will be altogether mischievous. But the man within the kingdom will never be lowered by his home; it will only help the enlargement of his spirit. The goodness which is of God is assimilative, it draws out and draws to it all that is noblest alike in the man and his home. They become more like and worthier of each other. It awakens what is best in him; he evokes the latent possibilities of good in it. The higher his character the stronger and less destructible his influence; the mightier his influence the more does the home become an organ for its exercise, a vehicle for its transmission. Modern science is coming round to the ancient faith, that a man may bless or ban the generations after him. There is nothing more real or potent than the transmission of hereditary qualities, the action of the dead ancestor in the living man. Piety does not perish with the pious, it lives after him, descends like an invisible and impalpable heirloom to his children and his children's children. Moral influence is indeed the one universal inheritance; no man can alienate it, no man destroy it. Now and then we become conscious of its reality; for the most part we receive without knowing what or how much we have heired. May I, on so high a matter, be allowed to speak of so small a thing as a personal experience? To my manhood there has become evident what was quite hidden from my youth: the most potent personal force in shaping my character and determining my work in life was that of a man I never saw, who died many years before I was born. But that man was familiar to me from childhood, his name was often on the lips of one who loved him as became a daughter; his history, his sayings, his aspirations and conduct, as recalled and repeated through the medium of a filial reverence as tender as it was true, fell like rays of living sunlight upon the sensitive spirit of the boy, touched and possessed the imagination of the youth, helped to form the thoughts and purposes of the man. Out of the past come the invisible but plastic hands that shape us for work in the present, for use in the future, making us vehicles of the influences and qualities we inherited that we may transmit, not as inherited but as modified and changed by our individual action. He who thus stands amid the generations of men can serve the order and ends of a beneficent Providence only as he "seeks first the kingdom of God and His righteousness."

But there is another aspect of the matter, and it must not be forgotten. The man who is a citizen in God's kingdom, believes in God, in the reality of His Providence, in the sufficiency of His wisdom and might. And Providence does not exist simply for the universe as a whole, or for individuals, it is exercised over families. Now the God of the fathers does not forget the sons; to the faithful household as to the faithful man "light ariseth in the darkness." Where this is a living belief, it brings comfort to those who live in families, who without concern for themselves suffer deep concern for their children. What we fear, are the possibilities rather than the actualities of life, what may be rather than what is. Now the Christian man can set over against his fear of the future his faith in God. And He who is sufficient for to-day will be sufficient for to-morrow, He who is trusted as able to do divinely well for the everlasting future may be trusted to do humanly well for the vanishing present. The father who believes that much as he loves his boys, God loves them still more, tender as he is to his girls, God is yet tenderer, can hardly think that either he or they will ever be comfortless. The belief will stimulate his forethought, neglect of those for whom God cares becoming to him sinful, but it will be without the old corrosive and distracting anxiety. The future is not in his hands alone, it is in God's as well, and he will work for his home with nobler energy when he feels himself "a worker together with God." Wife and children are never so creative of joy as when loved in God, believed to be conscious or unconscious objects of His care, subjects of His kingdom. Then the work of the present can be done untroubled by fear of the future. Its untoward possibilities can never outwit or master the calm but invincible Providence that guides our lives, teaches suffering to make us perfect, adversity to work out our good.

3. The truth stated in the text concerns man also as a social and political being. Citizenship in the kingdom of God best qualifies for true and efficient citizenship in the civil kingdom. These two do not exclude or oppose each other; nay, the kingdom of God includes whatever is true, righteous, humane, in the kingdom of man. The religion of a good man is not the antithesis of his politics, rather we may say, his politics are his religion applied to the conduct and the affairs of state. And the more religious the man the better the citizen. The highest duty man owes to society and the State is to be the best that is possible to him, for the nearer he comes to the best possible the more will he do the best he is capable of doing. "Ye are the salt of the earth," said Christ, conserving society; "Ye are the light of the world," making evident to the State the ways of righteousness and peace.

Exalted personal characters exalt whole peoples; the higher our character the higher our service to the cause of civil order and progress. But the highest is ever the hardest service. Any man can gravitate to the level of inconspicuous commonplace; only elect spirits can rise above it. And the kingdom of God makes its every citizen elect, a spirit gifted with Divine insight and purpose, conscious that the Eternal lives in every moment of his time, that the inspiration of the Almighty acts in every choice of his will. No duty that is proper to man will then be wittingly neglected. Justice will not rejoice over generosity, nor generosity over justice. The secular and the spiritual will not then be distinguished as two worlds with their respective laws and principles, under which the man may alternately live; but the two will be unified in the simple yet sublime unity of a character to which every secular act is spiritual, and every spiritual duty secular, because done in and for a living world.

But this highest and hardest service can yet be rendered by the lowliest; where the goodness born of God is, it is performed without effort or consciousness. Man has found out many inventions which have almost infinitely enriched the earth, increased its wealth, sent it through many channels to many lands and many men, lessening year by year the area of famine and pestilence, enlarging daily the reign of health and plenty. But we may say with reverence, though the things be incomparable, that a single character has achieved more of social good for man than all the inventions of men. The character of Christ has been the soul of all philanthropic action in the modern state, has been the dynamical force in all the beneficent agencies in our modern civilization. But every man who, seeking the Divine kingdom, labours to realize Christliness of character, does a similar work; by being a contribution to the forces active for God and goodness helps to lift man throughout the world. There is nothing that so makes vice impossible as the presence of virtue, nothing that makes freedom so natural and necessary as the liberty man realizes in Christ. He who best loves the ideals of the Eternal will do most to create their realization in time.

Christ then here teaches a truth of universal application, a truth the more universal that it is so individual. It applies to every man and to the whole man, and to all his duties and relations. By making the best of him it does the best for him, and so does enough. He can demand no more, no more can be demanded of him. To be righteous is to be right in all things—character, state, relations, to be lifted above doing wrong or being wronged, for nothing can be to us an ultimate injury which leaves us morally right. Society is to a man what the man is to society. We receive but what we give. If we are sources of evil, we cannot be recipients of good, and so long as He reigns who can make even the wrath of man to praise Him, and suffering become the minister of obedience, all the other forces in the universe will never be able to work us ill. Seek ye first then the kingdom of God and His righteousness, and in a grander sense than you dream of all things will be added unto you.

> "Then fearless walk we forth,
>   Yet full of trembling, messengers of God;
>   Our warrant sure but doubting of our worth,
>   By our own shame alike and glory aw'd."

II.

THE LOVE OF CHRIST.

"*Whom having not seen, ye love.*"—1 Pet. i. 8.

1. AFFECTIONS are evoked, not created, educed from within, not implanted from without. Conditions or occasions of action may be external, but the forces that act are internal; the objects men love may live without the spirit, but the love itself lives within. Every child born into the world is a centre of latent loves, and these but need appropriate objects and conditions of action to be drawn into exercise and nursed into strength. The child may grow into an unloving man, but he does it by repression of nature, not by expansion of soul. The quality of the object determines indeed the kind and quality of the affection. There cannot be a good and happy love of a bad being. Love of a bad person either debases the person loving, or becomes in him a pity, painful in proportion to his own goodness. Perfect love is perfect joy only where the loving and the loved are alike good, holy, and true. The one love that has had power to transform and command men, is the love of the Holiest and the Best, and the more man has loved Christ, the holier and the better has he become. Here it is that belief creates love, and the love rises into a joy that is unspeakable and full of glory.

Love again may be evoked or awakened in one of two ways—by instinct and nature, or by reason and spirit. The object that calls it from latent into actual and active being may appeal to our instincts or to our deeper and immortal qualities. Instinctive love may be spiritual—will be spiritual if it be pure. The affection parent has for child, or child for parent may be instinctive, but it may also be penetrated and glorified by the purest and holiest spirituality—will be so where it is most real. Yet it may, and often does remain merely instinctive, a thing of nature rather than of spirit. Animals in their own way love their offspring. The passionate devotion of the tiger to its cubs, or the bear to its whelps, is proverbial. Animals, too, in their own fashion, love their mates. The birds that pair, the lions that frequent the same den, are, after their kind, patterns of mutual affection. But in such cases the affection is a mere instinct, a blind impulse which asks no reason for its existence, and gives none; and when love in man is mere devotion to offspring as such, it is mere instinctive affection. If a man loves his son simply because the boy happens to be his, or a woman her daughter simply because the girl chances to be hers, and for no other and higher reason, the love is only blind impulse; it has no regard to actual or possible spiritual qualities, or any high moral end. The child is loved as the mortal child of a mortal man, not as the immortal son of the eternal God, with possibilities of the highest excellence latent in him. The nurture is according to instinct, not according to conscience; determined by momentary passion, or passing impulse, not by an enlightened moral sense. Chastisement is for what annoys rather than what is wrong; approval for what relieves or saves trouble rather than what is right. Instinctive love is thus, while blind to moral qualities and ends, alive to what is sensuous in conduct, rejoices in the wel*fare* rather than the well*being* of its object.

But love awakened through the reason and in the spirit is spiritual love. The qualities admired belong to the spirit, the eye that sees is the spirit's, and the admiration excited lives in the spirit. The physical eye can see the beauty of a flower, but the spiritual eye alone can see the loveliness, which is also the loveableness, of a fine character. Neither bodily sight nor social intercourse is necessary to spiritual vision. We can love the myriads of the great and good, whom with our mortal eyes we have never beheld. The knowledge, mediate or immediate, of heroic and noble qualities, awakens love to the person to whom they belong, and whether centuries or seas lies between us and that person, our love is none the less real. This affection, then, not springing from a natural relation, but from perceived moral qualities, will always be due to its object, the deserved and rightful tribute to its intrinsic worth, and as its object is spiritual, as its seat is in the spirit, so being spiritual, it will be immortal. The love that is derived from instinct with instinct will die, but the love awakened in the spirit will be as immortal as the spirit itself. Instinctive affection is blind and arbitrary, but spiritual is not. Many a man would perceive and despise in another boy the moral qualities he scarcely observes in his own son. As self-love is only blindness to the faults of self, so instinctive love is often only blindness to the faults of its object; but reason looks at the person as he is, considers his real and characteristic qualities, and then renders the affection they deserve. The first is due to a relation, natural or arbitrary, but the second to worth, personal, inherent, moral, real. Instinctive affection may be blind and impure, but spiritual must be altogether lovely and true.

Perhaps it may now be superfluous to remark, that the Christian's love to Christ must be of the latter kind, the spiritual. The eye that sees Jesus is the mind's, and the heart that loves Him is the mind's too. The sight is spiritual and the affection the same. The love may lack the passion and intensity of instinct, but it has the calmness and the power of spirit. The claims of Christ have not appealed to eye and ear, but to heart and mind. We love Him, not for His beautiful face, or fine voice, or winsome ways, but for His mercy and grace, the righteousness and truth that blend so perfectly in His character. We love Him, not so much for what He did, as for what He is. Gratitude for salvation may be the first, but is never the final form of Christian love. He who loves his deliverer simply as a deliverer loves for the lowest of all reasons, merely because he has been rescued. But he who loves his Saviour for what that Saviour is, loves Him for the highest of all reasons, because He is Supreme Love, perfect Grace and Truth. Jesus seems infinitely lovely and loveable to angels, though He never died for them, and the moment will come when the glorified saints will love Christ, not because He saved them, but because He is divinely gracious and good. The moral excellencies of Jesus, and these alone, can be inexhaustible sources of spiritual love.

The distinction made above may enable us to deal

with a too common difficulty. Many a devout soul has said :—" I cannot love my Saviour as I love my child. I do not, I cannot, love God more than I love my husband. There is an intensity and heartiness in my affection for my family and friends entirely wanting in my affection for Divine things. I need to be reconverted. I must be altogether wrong." But the error lies in confounding things that differ. Man's affection for man must be more or less instinctive. Man's love for Christ must be altogether spiritual. The instinctive must be intense, because passionate and confined; but the spiritual mild, because calm and expansive. The eagerness of the first, and the serenity of the second belong to their respective natures. The one derives its intensity from our physical constitution, but the other its calmness from our spiritual. Instinctive affection is born of flesh and blood, but spiritual of the will of God; and the nature of each corresponds to its parentage. Our love for Christ, then, while wanting the warmth of our love for man, has more depth and root in our being; while its form is less fervent, its essence is more real. The one seems to be, but the other in reality is, the greater. Indeed, it cannot be rightly compared to our love for the living. It resembles much more closely our love for the dead. Death at once sanctifies and spiritualizes our affection. The departed orb into clear and perfect stars in the heaven of memory, where the lurid fires of earth no longer burn, where only the light of immortal purity gleams, and the emotions they awaken are no more intense, instinctive, passionate, but gentle, spiritual, calm. Our love of the dead knows neither the pang of jealousy, nor the agony of suspicion, nor the fear of loss, but is serene and strong as death itself. The dead never die to us. They live in our hearts purified, beautified, exalted into minor deities whom we can reverence without idolatry. Ah! I once knew and loved a man—a right earnest, manful, chivalrous soul, who could, because his own spirit was attuned to divinest harmonies, strike the chords of the human spirit as David struck his harp; but he died, and no more on earth will his voice be heard, or his face be seen. Yet I know and love him still, not as of old with a very earthly love, but rather with a heavenly, a love clarified, etherealized, which jealousy cannot touch, nor suspicion disturb, nor envy trouble—the love felt by a man who lives on earth for a man who lives in heaven. And of this kind is our love of Christ; we love the Saviour as we love the dead, not as we love the living.

2. It is, then, no calamity or hardship to have an invisible Saviour. We can love Him the better that He is unseen. Sight assists the affection that is akin to instinct, but not that which lives in the spirit. That which the eye sees and the hand handles is commonplace and gross, loses in ethereality by what it gains in visibility. Were God localized, He would seem to our thought much less awful and majestic than when He is conceived as everywhere, like the air we breathe, the element in which all beings live. If there were only one spot on earth where God and my heart could stand face to face, God would seem to my heart much less Divine than He does now, when I can meet Him anywhere, speak to Him anywhere, just as my soul has need. So a Jesus visible to the eye, tangible to the touch, would be a Jesus too limited and gross to

be the object of a universal and spiritual affection—a Jesus known to the senses rather than to the soul. And so, while God gave us an historical Christ on whom our faith could rest, He made the history but a moment in the heart of His invisible and eternal being, that we might be compelled to love Him, if we loved Him at all, in spirit and in truth.

It is, perhaps, not too much to say that the disciples never loved Christ aright till He became invisible. Their love had much of the intensity and selfishness of passion, co-existed with much self-seeking and jealousy. Perhaps the lying upon the Master's breast at supper had something to do with John's love—perhaps, too, something with the apostasy of Judas; it may have caused in the others heartburning, and a little criticism of the ungenerous sort. There was certainly much of the instinctive in Mary's affection, and possibly it mingled in the love of the other women. But when Jesus ascended all this was changed. Their affections were enlarged and clarified. Jealousy perished for ever; love celestial and serene was born in their hearts, each man feeling that he who loved most was best.

Note, now, how this invisibility enables the mind to glorify, to idealize Jesus, as the object of its love. The senses are very prosaic and tyrannical. They see but a little way into a man, and retain only what of him is superficial and transient. The image of Christ that haunted the disciples would be very unequal, one of blended power and weakness, glory and shame. He would rise in their memories now as a weary man, sitting on Jacob's well, or asleep in the hinder part of the ship, and again as a mighty God, feeding the hungry multitude, or stilling the tempest. Now, He would be seen amid the glories of the transfiguration, or in the ascension stepping into His cloudy chariot, and anon, in the agonies of the garden, amid the mockeries of the judgment-hall, or the shame of the cross. And this changing, marred image of the Saviour would tyrannize over their hearts; would hinder their love from rising into the most perfect ideal form. But in our case there is no such hindrance. We enjoy the privilege of never having seen Jesus. Ours is the blessedness of those whose eyes have never beheld the marred visage, whose fingers have never felt the wounds. The memory of weakness, or shame, or death, never troubles our love. The Saviour we know is one whose griefs are past, whose glories have come, "whom having not seen we love."

Imagination should often come to the help of love. What is often pictured or imaged to the mind becomes to the mind more real. When the heart looks at its object through the imagination, that object becomes more defined and loveable. Think of the emigrant in an infant colony, suffering hardship, discomfort, isolation: does not the old home, when, in the quiet pensive hours, it creeps into the study of his imagination, glow in a soft, sweet light, a glory unknown to common day? Does not the loved, lost mother appear adorned with every grace, and the father apparelled in every virtue? Does not boyhood, too, gleam to the old man, when he recalls the meadows on which he played, the hills over which he roamed, the adventures in which he joined, with a light such as the sun never threw from its burning face? And since imagination can lend a brilliance of hue, a splendour of colour to the objects of time, calling forth deeper and tenderer love, why not to the Object at once of sacred memory and eternal hope—the invisible Saviour? Let us imagine Him as the centre of the moral universe, the object of celestial praise, the orb round which all the hosts of heaven cluster and circle and sing, and then think, "We too can love Jesus, our hearts have as good a right to love Him as the heart of the highest angel, or the oldest saint;" or let us imagine how many human beings have loved Him, and what that love has enabled them to do, how it has strengthened, almost transfigured, the martyr at the stake and the prisoner in his dungeon; how it has moved the tempted man to do right, the afflicted to bear suffering, the dying to die in peace, and then think, "We can feel the same love, and all that it has done for others it can do for us." Imagination thus picturing all the excellencies of Jesus, His character, achievements, and glory, will fill the mind with His image, bring Him nearer to the heart, and make Him a more real, loveable, Divine-human Person, round whom our affections can gather, He whom, not having seen, we yet love.

The love of the invisible Jesus may thus be developed in us like any other normal affection, and our growth in grace will be commensurate with this development. Here we may note God's wisdom and goodness in thus enlisting our natural capacities on the side of our own eternal interests. In his own wise way, old Archbishop Leighton saith, " Grace doth not pluck up by the roots, and wholly destroy the natural passions of the mind, because they are distempered by sin ; that were an extreme remedy, to cure by killing, and heal by cutting off. No, but it corrects the distemper in them; it dries not up this main stream of love, but purifies it from the mud it is full of in its wrong course, or calls it to its right channel, by which it may run into happiness, and empty itself into the ocean of goodness." It is little wonder that weak human love should grow to something excellent and sublime when its object is the invisible Christ.

3. But can we define this love? What are its constituent elements? Love, like light, seems simple, but is in truth compound. In a simple beam of white light there are varied colours. Pass the beam through a prism and it breaks into those bright and dark hues that blend so beautifully in the rainbow. The beam is one, yet several, each constituent colour being necessary to its very existence. The sombre softens and tones the light that it may not be a fierce glare, painful to the eye, withering to nature; the brilliant intensify and brighten the light that it may extinguish darkness, and be the glorious robe that envelops our earth, and makes it beautiful with the green of spring, or the glories of summer, or the mellow hues of autumn. So love has its essential elements, each complementary to the other, and all combining to give it real and ample being—goodwill, approbation, delight, desire, and trust. Where any of these is not, love cannot be. There must be goodwill, the desire to promote the happiness of the object loved. Hate strives to injure, love to benefit—the one bans, the other blesses. Hate is wretched when the person hated is happy, but love rejoices in its object's joy. It is like the sun shining upon the earth, and charming it into fertility and beauty, fruits and flowers. Then there must be approbation. Affection directed to one whose cha-

racter can only merit our disapproval may be mercy, or pity, or sympathy, or instinct, or fancy, but is not love. Approbation is simply moral admiration, and what we cannot admire our spirit cannot love. Then there is delight—delight in the society and favour of the person loved. Love and fear are incompatible. There is no love in fear, as there is no fear in love. Where the society of a person is not enjoyed, his favour not desired, his influence not welcomed, affection after a sort may be possible, but love is impossible. Another essential element is desire—the desire of possession. We long for what delights us. We desire what pleases. Love stretches out its hand to grasp its object, extends its arms to embrace. And finally, to crown and complete the emotion, there must be trust. Suspicion begets dislike—trust fosters love, where suspicion enters love departs; where trust dwells, there love soon enters to abide.

Now these elements are pre-eminently necessary in our love of Christ. Where they are not, it cannot be. He who loves Christ must have the goodwill to Him which seeks every opportunity to further His cause, extend His influence, and enlarge His kingdom; the approbation which admires His character as "the chief among ten thousand," and "the altogether lovely;" the delight that rejoices in the Lord always, and waiteth for Him "more than they that watch for the morning"; the desire that cries, "As the hart panteth after the waterbrooks, so pants my soul after Thee, O God"; the trust in His Word, in Himself, which says, "Though He slay me, yet will I trust in Him." Do all these elements live in our affection for Him? Alas! how often do we love, as we know, only in part.

What is called Christian love is, in many cases, a very shadowy, unsubstantial thing: gratitude to a deliverer, simply as such—not affection for one's truest, tenderest Friend. Christ is chosen often as the least of two evils; as, at least, better than the wrath and curse of God. The soul feels to Him as the traveller feels to the great rock in the weary land—not as the living child feels to its living mother, or as the living angel feels when entranced in the vision of God. The gallop over the plain, the saunter under the palm-trees, sweet dalliance in garden or grove, would be infinitely more delightful; but then the fierce wind, the blinding sand, the burning sun, are unendurable, and the shadow of the rock a kindly shelter; the best thing in the circumstances, not the best possible. Ah, my brother, Christ does not want you to love Him as you love a sheltering rock, but, as you love a MAN—a living soul like yourself. He wants you to love Him as your Chief Good, as the noblest Friend your heart can love, the grandest Being your spirit can know. O Thou Christ of the living God, teach us to love Thee, not simply as a short and easy method of deliverance, not as a convenient way of escaping the terrible pains of hell; but as our Brother, our Fellow, our Friend, our one Supreme Good, in whom alone everlasting happiness and peace can be found!

And now, consider what a privilege, what an honour thou hast in being permitted to love the invisible Jesus. Thou art more blessed than the disciples. They had the less blessing of loving One they had seen; thou hast the greater blessing of loving One thou hast not seen. Thy love to be Christian must be spiritual, through and through. Consider this strange fact: the

Gospels give no hint as to Christ's personal appearance, the colour of His eyes or hair, the cast of His features, the form of His head, the fashion of His body. Christ, as to physique, is to us an absolutely unknown being; but as to spirit, is the best known of all beings. While physical descriptions help us to understand other persons, they would mar our conception of Him. In ordinary cases a good portrait is better than a big biography. Sokrates would be to us much less real did we lack the picture of the squab, ill-shaped, pug-nosed, pugnacious little man—inquiring, questioning, punning, puzzling in the streets of Athens. How much better do we understand Dante, when we study his sad yet severe, worn yet ethereal face, with its keen, clear-cut features, yet look as of infinite remoteness from the world men most realize? or Luther, when we examine the lines of his heavy and broad, yet massive and mighty countenance, so full of laughter or tears, the loud indignation of the controversialist, and the inflexible resolution that could stand solitary against the world? or Oliver Cromwell, in whose large eyes, seamed brow, cheek furrowed and warty, and strong mouth, the mystic and soldier, the man of iron will and silent counsel, stands expressed? But so little has the outer man to do with Christ, so little is the face capable of expressing what was within, so impossible is it to human flesh or form to reveal the grace and truth that were in Him, that we should feel a description or a portrait an injury to our faith, a depravation to our spiritual ideal. There is, indeed, no one who has been so often painted, so idealized and served by human art. Everything that painting or sculpture can do to glorify its object has been done, that it may fitly express its conception of Christ. Men of highest spirit and purest devoutness, like Fra Bartolomeo, who painted out of truest piety; men whose art was religion, and whose works are joys for ever, like Raphael and Angelo, Titian and Rubens, have exhausted the resources of their genius and their art in giving form and colour to their ideal of Him who was at once "the Man of Sorrows" and the "altogether lovely" Son of Man. Go where we may in search of the noblest creations in art, His is the image that ever meets us, His the form in which the painter has striven to embody his sublimest dream. But whatever the æsthetic faculty may have felt in the presence of these creatures of the imagination, the spiritual has never been satisfied. From the purest and most perfect picture of the Christ, in infancy or manhood, in sorrow or in glory, it has turned away, pained, perhaps offended, saying, "My Master is lovelier and more Divine than these. Pencil cannot delineate His perfection; colour cannot express His beauty. The human form must be transfigured and transformed into the Divine ere it can tell the glory and the grace of the indwelling Christ." We would not then, O Christ, wish Thee to become visible—One we could see with our fleshly eyes, and handle with our fleshly hands. Remain Thou within the veil; there Thou art worthier to be loved; and while here we abide we shall enjoy the blessedness of those who, because they have not seen, have only the more believed and the better loved.

III.

THE CITY OF GOD.

"*Glorious things are spoken of thee, O city of God.*"
—Psalm lxxxvii. 3.

I.

1. AUGUSTINE, the greatest and the noblest of the Western Fathers, lived when the Empire of Rome was far gone in decay. The growth of luxury, the deterioration of morals, the decline of the old Roman virtues before an almost oriental licence, wasted her energies within, while the barbarian hosts assailed her in quick succession from without. Those inner and outer forces of decay were stronger than the strength of the Cæsars. Though the religion of Christ had poured new blood into the state, yet it could only prolong the days, could not restore the exhausted energies of the immense body politic. The Cross had indeed given the crown to Constantine, but it could not secure their authority and dominions to his successors. And so the Romans, enfeebled throughout, were forced to look on in almost utter helplessness while the barbarians spoiled their cities, made their most fertile plains desolate, seized and held their splendid colonies, ravished their hearths, and defiled their altars. Amid the universal misery and impotence, so sternly and terribly brought home to every mind by the storm and sack of the Eternal City herself, many a noble heart

recalled for comfort the ancient valour and fame, the days of Roman heroism, when the old gods reigned and made the state they loved victor and queen of the world. They thought of the strong patriotism that had driven the Tarquins forth and held the Tarquins out, of the spirit that could face unconquered the swift victories of Hannibal; of the Scipio who saved Rome by assailing her enemy in his home; of the Cato, so stern in spirit and mighty in arms, who had destroyed more towns than he had spent days in Spain, and then they said :—

"If we had the old faith we should have the old days. If Rome had her ancient gods she would regain her ancient majesty. This Christian faith has many mysteries; one God who is yet conceived to be Three, springs from a Man, yet speaks of Him as God. But these mysteries are small things, might be believed were it not that this new Faith has been so fatal to our city. Ever since the Cross floated from the Capitol disaster and defeat have come to Rome. We hate this new religion, not for its doctrines, but for its action on our state; its life has worked our death. We will not believe that what has caused so many calamities is Divine. Our divinities are those of our fathers, the men of our heroic and glorious past."

Augustine stood forward to defend the Faith so gravely assailed. His apology was twofold—concerned at once fact and idea. As to the matter of fact, Rome, he pleaded, was dying of her pagan vices. They had weakened her, stolen away her courage, dimmed her ancient honour, poisoned all the springs of liberty and action. But the new Faith had created new virtues, which were working like a healing and beneficent spirit in the heart of Society. When the barbarians besieged and sacked a city, what happened? The Church of Christ awed them and stayed the ruin. The pagans, selfish while rich, fled from danger, famine and pestilence; but the Christians remained, opened to the perishing their sanctuaries and their churches. And those they sheltered were saved alike from the sword and the lust of the barbarians. And so mighty for good was the new Faith, that it made weak woman strong, so pure that the rampant evil of the world could not defile her, so good that as matron, gentle yet deft of hand, or as maiden, soft of voice and swift of foot, she loved to feed the famishing and nurse the diseased. The Rome that had died of paganism Christ was doing His best to save.

But it was the matter of ideal principle that moved Augustine to grandest eloquence and argument. He said, in effect: "Ye were proud, O Romans, of your city. Ye called her eternal, imperial, divine. But her history has rebuked your pride and proved her deities false. There is another city, so glorious in ideal and achievement that yours may not be named beside her. Two cities began to be with man, founded by two loves. The one by the love of self, even to the despising of God; the other by the love of God, even to the despising of self. The first is the city of earth, whose grandest creation was Rome, which glories in self and seeks glory from men; but the second is the heavenly city, whose greatest glory is God, whose witness is conscience. In the one city its princes and people are ruled by the love of ruling; in the other city the princes and subjects serve one another in love. This city is coextensive with the good, comprehends all the saints of earth, has created all its virtues and graces, all its truth and righteousness and love. It is the true divine city, for it is built by the only true God; it is the alone eternal, for it shares the eternity of its Builder. The city of Rome ruled the bodies and died through the vices of its people; but this city rules the spirits and lives through the virtues of its citizens, the saints of God." And so he answered the lament of the Romans by setting over against their ideal of the state a state which incorporated an infinitely loftier ideal, stretching not from Romulus till then, but from creation to eternity, and the words which began his splendid apology were but a paraphrase of these: "Glorious things are spoken of thee, O city of God!"

2. Abraham lived in an age very unlike Augustine's. The world was yet young, the mighty empires were still in the distant future, though the foundations of the earliest were being laid. From his home in Ur of the Chaldees he could see the builders at work, the men of Babylon and Nineveh. But he saw that they were building their cities on idolatry, and he knew that a multitude of gods meant a divided sovereignty, man the master of the gods rather than God the master of man. He knew, too, that to abide in his ancestral home would be to be absorbed into its idolatries; but to his open spirit the Divine voice came calling him to go forth and build a city on a simpler and purer faith, to become the father of a people who should be the people of God. So in his early manhood, with all its boundless promise unrealized, he and his beautiful Sarah turned their backs on the valley which the rivers of Paradise watered, and on the mighty builders who were at work on the foundations of empires vaster

than they dreamed of; and, hand in hand, they moved westward in search of the land God was to give that they might found a people and a city for Him. They wandered long, saw the wealth of Egypt, fed their flocks on the broad plains of Mamre, looked wistfully on the fertile fields and valleys of Canaan, felt age and feebleness steal on apace, and yet no land or child was theirs. And when at length the promised son came, the gentle Isaac, they loved him with so large a love that the old man feared lest he were dearer to them than even their God. But the sacrifice which at once took and restored the son assured the father, and he waited in eager hope the word that was yet to be fulfilled. But he waited in vain, no land, no field even, became his, and when the beautiful Sarah of his youth, the lovelier, for the more loved, Sarah of his age, died at his side, the old man, bearing the common human sorrow that does not grow lighter for all the centuries of our collective experience and life, had to stand up before the sons of Heth and say :[1] " I am a stranger and a sojourner with you : give me a possession of a burying place with you, that I may bury my dead out of my sight." Yet his faith did not fail; he did not think that God had made a promise to the ear only to break it to the hope. He thought rather, " The word of God is larger and diviner than I had believed; the city is to be His, not mine, built in man's time, but for His own eternity. The cities of earth, they perish, but the city of God remaineth." And so from his disappointment a sublimer hope was born, and " he looked for the city which hath the foundations, whose Builder and Maker is God."[2]

[1] Gen. xxiii. 4.   [2] Heb. xi. 10.

3. John lived in an age unlike Augustine's, still more unlike Abraham's. The men of Egypt and Mesopotamia, Persia and Greece, had successively made their endeavours at empire, had each seemed for a few centuries to succeed, but only the more disastrously to fail. The multitude of deities could not keep their cities, the watchmen waked in vain. But an immenser, mightier state filled their vacant places. Rome from her hills beside the Tiber ruled the world. She seemed at the moment to merit her proud name of "the Eternal." The change Cæsar had worked in the empire was thought to have its type in the change Augustus had worked in the city. He found it brick, he left it marble, all graceful, strong, durable. Who could resist her will? Did not all peoples bow down before her? Feeblest of all the hostile forces, if hostile this could be called, was the society of men who were known as Christians. The empire had but to say, "Let them perish," and its will would be done. And so who cared,—who, indeed, was there to care, but a community so poor as to awaken concern in no one?—when John was banished from the Church and city he loved to a solitude he hated? In Patmos, as the image of his scattered flock rose before him, the sunny Ægean, with all its laughter and music, could not woo him to happy thoughts; but visions at once darker and brighter came both to awe and to cheer his spirit. He saw Rome seated on her seven hills, drunk with the blood of saints, drawing upon herself the judgment of Heaven; but as he turned from the wicked present to the righteous future, from Cæsar to God, a grander image met his sight. He saw, as only the seer can see, what centuries were to be needed to

make visible, "the Holy City," the substitute and supplanter of Rome, "New Jerusalem coming down from God out of heaven, made ready as a bride adorned for her husband."[1]

II.

In these so dissimilar and distant men a similar faith stands expressed. There is a city of God invisible, spiritual, which knows no place or time, which embodies God's ideal of society, the ordered and obedient life of man.

1. As so understood and interpreted, they supply the point of view from which the city is to be here regarded. It does not mean to us either a material heaven or a visible church. There are men who feel as if heaven could have no being unless placed in a city which stands square and strong to every wind that blows, whose walls are of precious stones, whose streets are of fine gold, paced perpetually by pilgrims who sing and carry palms, while in the midst, visible to all, is the throne of God and the Lamb. And there are men who think that the city of God must be a kind of political corporation, an articulated and organized system, which can boast a continuous life, an immense body of tradition, and can speak with the authority which belongs to its inherited experience, its collective wisdom, and its supernatural gifts and powers. But these ideas are alike sensuous, stand on the same level as regards spiritual culture and significance. A heaven which were but a city of marble palaces and streets resonant with song, would grow so wearisome to spirits that loved contemplation, or to

[1] Rev. xxi. 2.

spirits devoted to beneficent service, that they would soon become unable to distinguish its pleasures from pains,—might even come to think annihilation better than such bliss. And were the city of God identical with any church, or even with all the churches, then so much of human craft and error would enter into it,— so many things not noble or gentle would have been done in its name, it would so often have condemned as false what God has proved most surely true, that it would have to descend from its ideal perfection and stand among the imperfect and not rarely unjust states or societies of men. But the city of God may not be so construed; it is spiritual throughout. He is a spirit, and it is to be realized in and through the spirits He has formed. But it is on this account only the more real. The region of the spirit is the region of the eternal, therefore of the sublimest realities. In this region the city of God has its seat, that it may the more absolutely mould man in the days of his mortal being into the very image and form of his immortality.

What is a city? As men now understand it, it is but a place where men have most congregated and built to themselves houses and workshops; where the exchange and the cathedral stand together, the one for admiration, the other for business; where warerooms run into long unlovely streets; where narrow and unfragrant closes are crowded with the poor, and spacious yet hard and monotonous squares are occupied by the rich. But city was not always so conceived. The Latin *civitas*, the Greek πόλις, had nobler meanings. Their cardinal and honourable sense was not the place, but the living community,—the men of kindred blood and spirit, who claimed the same parentage, heired the same past, lived under the same laws, possessed the same privileges, liberties, and rights, followed the same customs, observed the same worship, believed the same religion. They were terms that expressed all that was ideal in the state and fatherland,— all in them that appealed to the heart and conscience, evoked patriotism, and made freedom better and dearer than life. Over the men of Thermopylæ the words were written,

> "To those of Lacedæmon, stranger, tell,
> That as their laws commanded, here we fell."

They fell not for the Spartan earth, but for the ideals embodied in the community and its liberties, for Sparta as she lived to faith and love. A Greek tragic poet speaks of his fatherland as his mother, nurse, sister, the anchor and home of his soul. It made his manhood, and he loved it for what it made. So these words πόλις and *civitas* were to the Greek and Roman respectively the parents of the terms that expressed their noblest ideas as, to the collective and corporate life of their peoples, the qualities which gave them distinction, made them freeborn and privileged men. Outside the πόλις men were but slaves or barbarians; within the *civitas* men were civilized, lived ordered, kindly, courtly lives.

And the city we here speak of bears this high ideal sense, only enlarged, exalted, and transfigured by the relation in which it stands to God. It is the society He has created, the community of men who know that they are His sons, regenerated and inspired by His truth, possessed of His spirit, obedient to His will, working for His ends. What the Jew meant by the kingdom, the Greek meant by the city of God; but they viewed the truth they so expressed under different aspects and from different standpoints. The kingdom accentuated the idea of the reign of God realized in the righteousness or obedience of man; but the city accentuated the idea of the Divine law or will realized in his free and ordered and richly beautiful social life. Spirits were needful to the realization of this ideal, but still more the creative and constitutive truths which made the spirits and organized the society. It was too immense to be limited to earth: the sainted dead and the saintly living were alike citizens. It was too imperishable to be bounded by time; the possibilities of obedience were inexhaustible. The realization of the ideal—though not the ideal itself, *that* was as eternal as God—had its beginning in time, but it would proceed throughout eternity. The more perfect a spirit becomes the greater its conformity to the Divine will. But above the highest degree reached, higher degrees rise in endless progression. The city of God is the society of godlike spirits with all their godlike capabilities and affinities in exercise and development, moving, as it were, out of their imperfection as creatures to the perfection loved and desired of the Creator.

2. The city of God, then, is an eternal, unrealized, yet realizable ideal,—an ideal that is to be for ever in the process of realization. This everlasting process is its very glory and last excellence, the secret of its endless attraction, the spell that awakens the activities that constitute heaven. God's is the only absolute perfection; man's is relative, contained in the high destiny which bids him ever struggle towards the Infinite

which he yet can never reach. There is no perfection so incomplete as the one which admits of no increase; *that* is the imperfection of death, not of life. God thinks too highly of man to be ever satisfied with what he is. The best possible for one moment is only the condition of a better possible for the next. But it is not enough that the city be a progressive ideal; it must possess the means and agencies necessary to the realization. And these exist. The eternal truths as to God and His Christ, the Divine energies and influences active in man, working in and through the churches, the benevolent and beneficent forces which act in society, in politics, in commerce, in art, in civilization as a whole, are of the city and work for it. Without these it could never be. They are the builders of the city, the agencies God uses to prepare and lay the living stones of the temple He designed, and inhabits and glorifies. By His truth He makes true men, conformed to the image of His Son. By His Spirit which dwelleth in them He brings them into a unity which expresses and exercises their life divine. Through the truths of God the ideals of God are realized, and the eternal way which leadeth to perfection opened to the energies, endeavours, and hopes of man.

Now, it is at this point that we see the relation of all our past discussions to the idea and ideal of the city of God. They have been concerned with the truths that make it at once possible and real,—that are, as it were, the factors of its reality, the conditions and agencies that work its realization. The eternal God builds the city, creation happens that He may build it. Man was made to be a citizen, and all his religions witness to his yearning after his end, his passion for the fulfilment of his being. God calls, disciplines, and guides Israel, that He may the better bring to man the truths that at once create and qualify for citizenship. Jesus Christ comes as the Way to the city, the Truth from God which gives the Life of God, so creating the new or filial humanity, whose units are as He is, sons of God. To this end Christ was born and died and rose; to this end He reigns as King, He saves as Priest, He speaks as Prophet the things of God to men. Creation stands rooted in Him, and He completes it. Redemption, though later in history, was not later in the Divine purposes. God being God, the home of all rectitude, truth and graciousness, would never have made a world He did not mean to redeem; and Jesus Christ, the chief Corner-Stone of the city designed from eternity, its creative and normative personality, appeared in the fulness of time to bring in the everlasting righteousness. Through Him man becomes a "fellow-citizen with the saints," reaches and realizes his chief good, finds the way to that complete harmony with the Eternal Will which is purest beatitude and highest perfection.

III.

But these discussions must have a practical end. What function has the faith in the eternal city, with the hopes it creates, to fulfil in the common and often commonplace life of man? It were too large a matter to attempt to look at and answer this question on all its sides. The action of the ideal in humanity has been most beneficent; it is at this moment a centre of mighty moral energies. What forbids hope paralyses effort. Men speak of the strength of despair, but despair has no strength; it is only impassioned weakness struggling with a might that mocks it. There is strength in hope, and the energy of the present works for good when it believes in a better and happier future. But to believe in a better future a man must believe in God. The energies of the universe must work for righteousness if righteousness is ever to prevail. And so the Pessimism that denies the beneficence of Deity, and the Pantheism that can allow Him no power of moral initiative, are unable to create the hopes that call into action those moral and ameliorative energies that are the great progressive forces in history. From this point of view we can certainly say that man's belief in the city of God, with all it involves, has created ideals, awakened enthusiasms, inspired hopes, developed energies and agencies that have lessened the miseries, increased the happiness, enlarged the liberties, augmented the righteousness and quickened the progress of mankind. But these are matters we may not touch; our concern must be with the worth of the ideal to the individual man, its action and function in our every-day and commonplace lives.

1. The belief in the city creates hopes that exalt, ennoble, and transform our ordinary lives. These are in good sooth tame and mean enough. Angels have always been rare guests, more through man's fault than their own. To see God face to face is the joy of eternity. The most that time knows is the season of quiet communion which rises now and then like a beautiful sunlit island out of the troubled ocean of life. All men feel more or less the monotony, the satiety, the sickness born of the weary labour with which we toil

over the immeasurable levels of commonplace. Work in these days becomes ever more strenuous, approaches nearer and nearer to drudgery, and drudgery more than anything not immoral bemeans man, takes out of him all incipient nobleness. The man who works in a dismal mine, or digs in a ditch, or drives a laden cart, with eating and sleeping or drunken play as the only relieving conditions of his life, does not rise very far above the level of the toiling animal. The man who stands behind the counter retailing day by day slander or sentiment as the humour of the customer may demand, speaking truth or untruth, with small conscience of the distinction between, as the interest of the seller may require, may well feel now and then as if in his calling as he lives it there was little to exalt or honour his manhood. The woman whose spirit is burdened with a multitude of minutest cares, distracted besides by the need of solving the rather intractable problem, how to reconcile an increasing expenditure with a stationary or diminishing income; or her still unhappier sister whose soul kindles to nothing higher than the now vacant, now spiteful, gossip of society,— must surely in their serener or better moments come to know how little the water drawn from the common springs of life can satisfy or cheer. Our age boasts its men of action and invention, praises them according to the amount of work they can do and their skill in doing it; but physical endurance and mechanical ingenuity are poor characteristics for man, especially in presence of the forces that work in nature or the instincts that act in the brute. We hear now and then the quantity and quality of a man's brains determined by his ability to make money—brains good at that, good for anything; poor at that, good for nothing—but if the power to accumulate and distribute constitutes man's best title to manhood, what do the arts, the sciences, the literatures and religions that have enriched the world signify and mean? Reduce man to the categories of the political economist, make him a mere producer, distributor, and consumer, and where is his manhood? If man could be defined as a creature who makes, sells, carries, eats, would he be man—made of God for God—any more?

Man, then, needs more than this prosaic and narrow life, with its material comforts, its toils that harden, its rewards that punish the spirit, its worship of secular success and unpitying blame of secular failure. He needs the hope of a nobler future, the vision of the city of God. Without this vision, earth, even where most full of material wealth, can be but a galley and the man a galley slave, or, with its hard limitations, its rules that cramp most where they most exercise, like a menagerie with its herd of bond animals, shadows of the free born, soured by the well-fed bondage that frets though it may not break the spirit. Man the worker is changed by the hope of a diviner hereafter into man the immortal; by it man the artificer becomes a spirit conscious of a Divine descent and destiny. When out of the future the light of the eternal city gleams it glorifies the meanest moments of the present. The dignity it brings to man affects all he touches, dignifies through him toil, the commonest everyday mechanical labour. The citizen of heaven feels no work drudgery, for he can never be a drudge; in the hour of humblest endeavour he stands in the midst of the immensities, in the centre of the eternities which God inhabits.

Dusty and wayworn, he may have long, bare, burning roads to travel, but he will find here and there hills he can ascend, whence he can see the light of the Celestial City afar, hear its angel-music, feel its fragrant and grateful breezes on his heated brow. He may with little strength of arm or skill of weapon have to fight a hard battle for life ; but if the nights he spends in the tented field be nights of Bethel-visions, when, with sense asleep and imagination awake, earth and heaven melt into the common home of God and man, then the rest that comes will be rest that brings a nobler and more regal manhood to the life of the morrow. The royalties of earth grow dim in the light of immortality, but its obscurities grow lustrous. It is a splendid hope that quenches fictitious dignity, but touches with radiant glory the common nature of man.

Can anything speak to the imagination of man so mightily as this hope ? Is it not immense enough to change the most prosaic and dull of wit into a being of spirit all compact ? And is not a hope endowed with such potencies a truly divine hope ? In it God speaks that He may enlarge our time with His eternity, our earth with His immensity. The stream that flows from the distant Mexican Gulf through the broad bosom of the Atlantic, brings in its genial warmth health to these shores, and so the river that makes glad the city of our God sends the kindliest and healthfulest currents through and across the troubled ocean of life. Abraham must have felt life in his tent and on the desert tedious and tame enough. The fierce glare of the Eastern sun striking day by day on the hot yellow sand, the monotony of the same voices ever heard and the same faces ever seen, the disputes, small, spiteful, retaliatory, of Sarah and Hagar, must have vexed the patient and manful soul of the old Patriarch to utter weariness; but these things ceased to embitter, became bearable and then blessed, when the old man's imagination was filled by the vision of the city which had "foundations, whose Builder and Maker is God." Moses, too, knew the tedium of forty years' wanderings in the wilderness, the vexation of leading querulous and ignorant and obstinate men; but their discontent ceased to annoy and worry passed into quiet when he stood on Pisgah and saw the goodly land beyond Jordan, sleeping in the glorious sunshine of the East. John, too, shut up in Patmos, separated by the mocking sea from the flock he loved, must have known heart-ache and loneliness; but his heart ceased to ache, and hope rose and rebuked despondency, when he saw the New Jerusalem descend out of heaven from God, adorned like a bride for her husband. So the voices that speak of the city ought to be to the tired or discouraged spirit like the songs of angels in Paradise. I know and love a city on whose streets as boy and youth and man I have stood while the tide of life swept past like the rush of a vast river, which quenched all thoughts save the thought of its mighty waves, a multitude of atoms which no atom could stay. But just outside the city lies an ancient hill, and, passing from the streets, I have climbed its grand and storied sides to find that the higher I rose man became less, Nature became more, until on the proud summit, with the city beneath, the sea and far-spreading landscapes around, I felt as if the distant life were but a noisy moment in the being of the Eternal, which in the calm, blue, boundless, majestic heaven seemed to hold me in its everlasting arms. So let there rise straight from the heart of our crowded and toilsome lives mounts of vision which the spirit can ascend, and where the imagination can be free to hear "the glorious things spoken of thee, O city of God."

2. These high hopes look for realization to the city of God; it is the sphere of their fulfilment. City is the synonyme for Society in its richest and most varied forms; there the privileges, rights, liberties, and honours of citizenship are combined with the grandest opportunities of mutual service, the ministries of love and devotion, the fellowship of living minds. In the first aspect the city is the realm of law and order, where man, knowing and obeying the will of God, lives to realize the ideals of His eternity; in the second aspect the city is the arena where spirits know and serve each other, where the joy of each contributes to the common beatitude, and the beatitude of the whole to the perfection of each. Without the city the highest qualities of the man lie unexercised, held in the iron hands of the death that is the more awful for having never known life. The city of man is a hot-bed where virtues and vices are alike reared, though its fruitfulness is often like the abundance of the grave-yard, fed by the corruption that lies rank beneath. In it the scoundrel can ply his scoundrelism in secret, the villain can mask while he indulges his villainy; the pride that is only inflation, the pretence that has no bottom, the wealth that is a sham and a cheat, walk abroad, undiscovered and unashamed. But while the city of man can nourish the most vicious vices, it can also evoke and foster the highest and most self-forgetful virtues. The honesty

that is at once just and honourable, the courage that is brave to do right and endure wrong, the goodness that delights not to be ministered unto but to minister, the charity that does not weary in well doing, that thinketh no evil, that beareth all things and hopeth all things,— indeed every virtue that can ennoble, every grace that can adorn man, may find room for growth and exercise in the city. Isolation engenders the selfishness which is spiritual death; life dutifully lived in society calls the better qualities of the man into activity and strength.

The city of God, then, as the realm of love and obedience, ministry and fellowship, is the sphere for the development and realization of all the Divine ideals in man, individual and collective. It is a society of spirits on their way through obedience and service to perfection. All spirits are akin; we are human not by virtue of our bodies, but by virtue of our souls, and man stands related to man through all time and over all the world as brother to brother because all have been made in the same image and bear the same nature. And the city of God but means that the ideal of each man and of all his relationships is being realized. Variety is not thus destroyed, but rather created. In this city there will be father and mother, sister and brother spirits, spirits married in the wedlock of mutual affinities, and spirits whose paths shall lie as far apart as the poles of God's intellectual universe. But variety only deepens joy and enlarges duty. Uniformity is the death of happiness. Men must differ if they are to rejoice in each other, to serve and be served. If the life of John was love, heaven must be to him an enlarged home of the heart. That were no heaven to

Paul where he was forbidden to speculate, to reason, and to teach. Abraham, as he gathers his children into his bosom, must have in a growing degree the father's joy. Every spirit that enters the city must be to the ancient citizens, the spirits of just men made perfect, a new object of love, a new call to new duty, a new source of pleasure. The elders of immortality must have strange things to tell its young men, and the young men may in their innocent ignorance have much to teach the elders. Human nature does not lose in interest by age, rather gains in it, becomes a storehouse of wisdom and wonders to the fresher mind. Imagine immortality realized under the conditions of time, a man as old as the race, yet retaining, as immortals must, unexhausted and exuberant, the energies and hopes of youth. He had met the fallen pair as—

> "They, hand in hand, with wandering steps and slow,
> Through Eden took their solitary way;"

had looked with Noah from the ark; had talked with Abraham after God had met him; had seen Moses as he came down from the Mount, and rejoiced with the multitude which accompanied David when he entered Jerusalem; he had visited the empires of Egypt and Assyria, and watched the meeting of their mighty hosts; had listened to the discourses of Plato, and followed the conquests of Alexander; had beheld the rise of Rome, and had been in Judea when the Christ was crucified; and had step by step, alongside the march of events between then and now, walked as counsellor and companion with the great men and thinkers of the Christian centuries. Now, would not this man,—an eager spirit all the time, open-eyed, hungry for knowledge, communicative, acquisitive, ever learning by experience how better to learn, to teach, to live,—be a mightier contribution to the knowledge of the world, a louder call to its wonder, than the vastest library it can boast? And in the city of God are there not innumerable spirits of even immenser experience, riper wisdom, more varied capabilities and knowledge? And why do these live except to communicate, to teach, to help to lift the ideal and achievements of the city, to raise its standard of obedience and beatitude? Immortality is not idleness; it must know progressive obedience to be happy, increasing activity that it may have growing beatitude.

3. The city, in order to fulfil the hopes of its citizens, must have throughout two qualities, it must be of God and eternal as God. These two are one. What is of God, spirit as He is, must partake of His eternity. Yet the two are distinct. To be of God is the source and spring of the city's perfection; to be eternal, the condition of its realization. The ideal is God's, the perfect mirror of His perfect mind, but it can be translated into reality only through obedience. And an obedience which answers to the idea in the Eternal Mind must be eternal. The relation of the city to God has its counterpart in man's relation to Him. The city is a city of sons, the will of the Sovereign expresses the love of the Father, the obedience of the citizen is the realized affection of the child. This affinity to God is the secret of our immortality; it is ours because we are akin to Him, of His kind. Give to a godlike spirit an immortality with God, and what height may it not win? What ministry of light, what

service of love and beneficence may it not perform? As hope looks down into a future rich in such infinite possibilities, man is now awed and humbled, now uplifted and ennobled, and whether he be the one or the other, he alike feels as if his time were eternity, and work among men service of God.

"Thus saith Jehovah, The heavens are My throne, and the earth is My footstool: what manner of house would ye build for Me? and what manner of place for My rest? For all these things did My hand make, and all these things came into being, saith Jehovah: but this is the man upon whom I look, even he who is afflicted and of a contrite spirit, and trembleth at My word."[1]

"He shall feed His flock like a shepherd: He shall gather the lambs with His arm, and carry them in His bosom, and shall gently lead those that are with young."[2]

"Ye are come unto Mount Zion, and unto the city of the living God, the heavenly Jerusalem, and to innumerable hosts of angels, to the general assembly and church of the firstborn, who are enrolled in heaven, and to God the Judge of all, and to the spirits of just men made perfect, and to Jesus the Mediator of a new covenant, and to the blood of sprinkling, that speaketh better than that of Abel."[3]

"And thus, Glaucon, the tale has been saved and has not perished, and may be our salvation if we are obedient to the word spoken; and we shall pass safely over the river of Forgetfulness, and our soul will not be defiled. Wherefore my counsel is, that we hold fast to the heavenly way, and follow after justice and virtue always, considering that the soul is immortal and able to endure every sort of good and every sort of evil. Thus shall we live dear to one another and to the gods, both while remaining here and when, like conquerors in the games who go round to gather gifts, we receive our reward, and it shall be well with us both in this life and in the pilgrimage of a thousand years which we have been reciting."[4]

---

[1] Isa. lxvi. 1-2.   [2] xl. 11.   [3] Heb. xii. 22-24.
[4] Plato: Repub. Bk. x. 11, 621. (Jowett's translation.)

"But I need, now as then,
    Thee, God, who mouldest men;
And since, not even while the whirl was worst,
    Did I,—to the wheel of life,
    With shapes and colours rife,
Bound dizzily,—mistake my end, to slake Thy thirst;

    So, take and use Thy work:
    Amend what flaws may lurk,
What strain o' the stuff, what warpings past the aim!
    My times be in Thy hand!
    Perfect the cup as planned!
Let age approve of youth, and death complete the same!"[1]

"Come, O Thou that hast the seven stars in Thy right hand, appoint Thy chosen priests according to their orders and courses of old, to minister before Thee, and duly to press and pour out the consecrated oil into Thy holy and ever-burning lamps. Thou hast sent out the spirit of prayer upon Thy servants over all the land to this effect, and stirred up their vows as the sound of many waters about Thy throne. Every one can say, that now certainly Thou hast visited this land, and hast not forgotten the utmost corners of the earth, in a time when men had thought that Thou wast gone up from us to the farthest end of the heavens, and hadst left to do marvellously among the sons of these last ages. O perfect and accomplish Thy glorious acts! for men may leave their works unfinished, but Thou art a God, Thy nature is perfection. When Thou hast settled peace in the Church, and righteous judgment in the kingdom, then shall all Thy saints address their voices of joy and triumph to Thee. In that day it shall no more be said, as in scorn, This or that was never held so till this present age, when men have better learnt that the times and seasons pass along under Thy feet to go and come at Thy bidding: and as Thou didst dignify our fathers' days with many revelations above all the foregoing ages since Thou tookest the flesh; so Thou canst vouchsafe to us, though unworthy, as large a portion of Thy Spirit as Thou pleasest, for who shall prejudice Thy all-governing will? seeing the power of Thy grace is not passed away with the primitive times, as fond and faithless men imagine, but Thy kingdom is now at hand, and Thou standing at the door. Come forth out of Thy royal chambers, O Prince of all the kings

---

[1] Browning: "Rabbi Ben Ezra." Poetical Works, vi. 109.

of the earth! put on the visible robes of Thy imperial majesty, take up that unlimited sceptre which Thy Almighty Father hath bequeathed Thee; for now the voice of Thy bride calls Thee, and all creatures sigh to be renewed."[1]

[1] Milton: "Animadversions upon the Remonstrant's Defence," Sec. iv.

www.ingramcontent.com/pod-product-compliance
Lightning Source LLC
Chambersburg PA
CBHW030402230426
43664CB00007BB/715